Crash Course
in
Creativity

A Creative Writing Curriculum

Sarah Hawkes Valente

www.whatislovely.com

©2017

WIL Publications

Contents

Unit I: Poetry

Unit II: Drama

Unit III: Creative Nonfiction

Unit IV: Fiction

Introduction

"Without words, without writing and without books there would be no history, there could be no concept of humanity." – Hermann Hesse made that statement in the early 1900s, but how much truer his sentiments should ring for believers in the wondrous God of Scripture. Our God is a best-selling author! He wrote the first hardback book on tablets of stone, He chose *written* words as His primary means of communication, and it is through His Word that we meet with Him daily. It is through Scripture that we learn who we are, and it is through Scripture that we see where we're going.

If you do not think of yourself as a writer, perhaps an extra-curricular writing course may not seem like a wise use of your time, but I direct your attention once again to the Scriptures. The men God asked to write down His words were shepherds and fishermen; they were not authors. It is not necessary that a believer be a writer, but it *is* important that he learn how to write and that he be willing to write if called to do so. As believers, we don't write simply to tell our own stories; we write to tell His story as well.

The electronic age has birthed a generation of writers. Email, texting, instant messaging, blogging, self-publishing—through Facebook posts alone, an average student can reach a global audience within less than a matter of seconds. As our verbal communication lessens and typed communication increases, it should follow that instruction in the art of writing is valued more and more. However, a quick sampling of the internet, as well as modern magazines and newspapers, will reveal the opposite truth. As the written word becomes a commonplace thing, in a world where an increasing number of individuals share in the blessing of freely voiced opinions, our words have become less comprehensible, and our subject matter has waxed far less profound.

For the believer in the God of Scripture, this backwards direction should not be deemed acceptable. Good grammar and correct spelling are essential, critical thinking is crucial, a broad vocabulary is fundamental. In order to tie these worthy elements in a package that people will read, creativity is required. All of these things are important because we are called to do *all* things to the glory of God.

In Mark 16:15, Jesus tells the eleven to "Go into all the world and preach the gospel to all creation." Here we are, in an age where the evangelist may travel to the farthest reaches of the earth without even leaving his home. Whether hiking through the jungles of South America or office-bound in a big-city, we should be prepared to give an account for the hope that is in us. If that account is written, it should be well-written. If it's worth writing, it's worth writing well.

The following four units and exercises are designed to instruct and challenge the Bible-believing high school student. The grading scales intended for each exercise are included in the back of the book.

"And whatsoever ye do in word or deed, do all in the name of the Lord Jesus, giving thanks to God and the Father by him." Colossians 3:17

—Sarah Hawkes Valente

Unit I: Poetry

Section A: What is Poetry?

Just as a painter holds a palette of color and with it reveals his own mind, so the poet holds close to his heart a palette of many words. Every word he or she has ever heard or read— illustrative words, lively words, common words, rare words, foreign words, eloquent words, *lugubrious* words—these are the poet's paint. It is with these words the poet carefully crafts his art, and it is through his art the poet teaches the world around him; he shares with the waiting world the invaluable mind of a poet.

We begin this course with poetry, but not because poetry is the easiest of all literary genres to understand; in fact, it is arguably one of the most difficult. Poetry, however, does not have to be considered *great* in order to draw greatness from the heart of the poet—or from the heart of the reader.

The dos and don'ts of poetry teach numerous skills and devices that are essential to all forms of literature, so it is only right that we start as poets. Poetry teaches us to think; poetry demands that we think. Poetry, or the writing of it, is about learning to perceive the world around us and then putting those perceptions into intimate and meaningful words.

In his preface to *Leaves of Grass,* Walt Whitman [1819-1892] states:

> The known universe has one complete lover, and that is the greatest poet. He consumes an eternal passion... All expected from heaven or from the highest he is rapport with in the sight of the daybreak, or a scene of the winter woods, or the presence of children playing, or with his arm round the neck of a man or woman... Nothing can jar him: suffering and darkness cannot—death and fear cannot. To him complaint and jealousy and envy are corpses buried and rotten in the earth— he saw them buried. The sea is not surer of the shore, or the shore of the sea, than he is of the fruition of his love, and of all perfection and beauty. The fruition of beauty is no chance of hit or miss—it is inevitable as life—it is exact and plumb as gravitation.

Where prose is expanded and conversational like a talk one has with a long-winded friend, poetry is condensed—thoughts squished and squeezed together until only the essential elements remain. The pain is more severe, the pleasure is more intense, and the lesson is often far more memorable in poetry. To truly explain and examine the thoughts within a poem, we, as the reader, expand it back to that plainer prose the poet worked so hard to avoid in the first place; but what makes a poem a poem is compression of the thoughts, feelings, sights, and sounds the poet is attempting to paint.

Although the honest heart of a poet is what we read when we read their words, the severe abridging of many words down to a chosen few creates a comfortable vagueness and a place of safety for the poet. *What does the poet mean?* We can never be completely sure of the full meaning the poet intended. This is why we *read* prose, but we study and analyze poetry. The same poem can be read and interpreted in a variety of ways—especially if the poet was intentionally vague.

Without effort, and without exposing in the least how it is done, the greatest poet brings the spirit of any or all events and passions and scenes and persons, some more and some less, to bear on your individual character, as you hear or read. To do this well is to compete with the laws that pursue and follow time. What is the purpose must surely be there, and the clue of it must be there; and the faintest indication is the indication of the best, and then becomes the clearest indication. Past and present and future are not disjoined, but joined. The greatest poet forms the consistence of what is to be from what has been and is. He drags the dead out of their coffins, and stands them again on their feet: he says to the past, Rise and walk before me that I may realize you. He learns the lesson—he places himself where the future becomes present.

Walt Whitman, preface to *Leaves of Grass*

To create this seemingly insignificant splotch of words representing pages upon pages of the poet's internal thoughts, varying literary devices are used like brushes putting word-paint to paper-canvas. We'll discuss many of these in the following sections and units.

Section B: Writing and Reading Poetry

1. Poetic Feet

One of the more crucial elements in poetry is the rhythm or the beat. In poetry, the beat in which we read is referred to as a metrical foot—and these feet do walk us through the poem just as the name would suggest. The most commonly used foot in poetry is referred to as an *iamb*. This might sound complicated, but we use iambs every day. Any two syllables with the accent/stress on the *second* syllable is called an iamb. In most two-syllable words or phrases, the stress of one syllable over the other is a very subtle thing. When saying, "the door," the word "door" receives the stress. However, this does not mean that we whisper *"the"* and yell "door". The difference between a stressed and an unstressed syllable must be carefully discerned.

For example:

- The boat (da-DUM)
- A jug (da-DUM)
- Remote (depending on dialect)
- A piece (da-DUM)
- Invite (da-DUM)
- And you (da-DUM)
- Aboard (da-DUM)
- The cough (da-DUM)

A well-known line by Robert Frost, "I **hold**/ with **those**/ who **fa**/vor **fire**," has four iambic feet. Can you hear the accented/stressed second syllables? Now practice writing a few iambs of your own:

- _____

- _____

- _____

Other two-syllable feet are the ***trochee***, the ***spondee***, and the ***pyrrhic.*** The opposite of the iamb is the ***trochee***. A trochee is a two-syllable foot with the accent on the *first* syllable.

For example:

- Dinner (DUM-da)

- Double (DUM-da)

- Acorn (DUM-da)

- College (DUM-da)

- Burning (DUM-da)

- Thoughtful (DUM-da)

- Planet (DUM-da)

Can you hear the accents on these first syllables? They are all trochaic feet. Now practice writing a few trochees of your own:

- _____

- _____

- _____

The **spondee** consists of two equally stressed syllables.

- Heartbreak (DUM-DUM)
- Shortcake (DUM-DUM)
- Childhood (DUM-DUM)
- Bathrobe (DUM-DUM)
- Black hole (DUM-DUM)
- Love-song (DUM-DUM)

Practice writing a few spondees:

- _____

- _____

- _____

The **pyrrhic** consists of two equally _unstressed_ syllables.

- In the (da-da)
- On a (da-da)
- Is to (da-da)

Practice writing a few pyrrhic feet:

- _____

- _____

- _____

Triplet is the term used to categorize all three-syllable feet. Types of triplet feet are the **dactyl** and the **anapest.** The **dactyl** consists of three syllables, one stressed followed by two unstressed.

- Carefully (DUM-da-da)
- Thoughtfully (DUM-da-da)
- Changeable (DUM-da-da)
- Merrily (DUM-da-da)
- Bitterly (DUM-da-da)
- Horrible (DUM-da-da)

Practice writing a few dactyls:

- _____

- _____

- _____

The **anapest**, also consisting of three syllables, is two unstressed followed by a stressed.

- Understand (da-da-DUM)
- Interrupt (da-da-DUM)
- Comprehend (da-da-DUM)
- Lend a hand (da-da-DUM)

- Walk a mile (da-da-DUM)

- In the blink/of an eye (da-da-DUM/da-da-DUM)

Practice writing a few anapests:

- _____

- _____

- _____

Words or phrases that would normally be read as iambs, trochees, spondees, dactyls, etc. can be slightly manipulated in order to serve the needs of the poet; three-syllable words can be squeezed into two—and two-syllable into one. A common example of this is the word heaven, written as *heav'n* in many old hymns, pronounced in one syllable. Despite exceptions, observing the natural poetic beat of words and phrases will aid in reading and writing poetry.

2. Meter

While the poetic foot reveals the accented and unaccented syllables, the **meter** dictates the number of feet-per-line. In the case of **pentameter**, there are five feet-per-line. The line we examined previously, "I **hold**/ with **those**/ who **fa**/vor **fire**," is written in **iambic tetrameter** (four two-syllable feet-per-line).

Types of line length are:

- One foot: **Monometer**
- Two feet: **Dimeter**
- Three feet: **Trimeter**
- Four feet: **Tetrameter**
- Five feet: **Pentameter**
- Six feet: **Hexameter**
- Seven feet: **Heptameter**
- Eight feet: **Octameter**

Practice writing a line in iambic trimeter (three two-syllable feet):

Example: I want/ to go/ to bed.

Practice writing a line in iambic tetrameter (four two-syllable feet):

Example: The wai/ting was/ the har/dest part.

Practice writing a line in iambic pentameter (five two-syllable feet):

Example: We go/toward/ where we/ are told/ to go.

_____

Let's examine the full text of the poem, "Fire and Ice," by Robert Frost:

Some say / the world / will end / in fire,	Some say the world will end in fire,
Some say / in ice.	Some say in ice.
From what / I've tas / ted of / desire	From what I've tasted of desire
I hold / with those / who fav /or fire.	I hold with those who favor fire.
But if / it had / to per / ish twice,	But if it had to perish twice,
I think / I know / enough / of hate	I think I know enough of hate
To say / that for / destruct / tion ice	To say that for destruction ice
Is al / so great	Is also great
And would / suffice.	And would suffice.

What is the more commonly used foot in the syllables, "Some say"? Is it, "SOME-say" (trochaic), "some-SAY" (iambic), or "SOME-SAY" (spondaic)? The line, "Some say in ice" reads as a trochaic foot followed immediately by an iambic foot: SOME-say / in-ICE. It's a quirky line. In fact, the first two lines of this poem keep the reader on his toes. It is not until the third line that we settle comfortably into clear *iambic tetrameter.* The last lines of this poem are actually one line of iambic tetrameter that is split into two for the sake of rhyme and drama.

Why does Frost choose to break from iambic tetrameter at the beginning and end of his poem? What effect does this produce?

Imagine driving down a long stretch of highway. The rhythm of the road is the same for miles. Now imagine the road as a long stretch of iambic pentameter (five iambic feet-per-line):

Da-DUM, da-DUM, da-DUM, da-DUM, da-DUM,

Da-DUM, da-DUM, da-DUM, da-DUM, da-DUM.

Da-DUM, da-DUM, da-DUM, da-DUM, da-DUM,

Da-DUM, da-DUM, da-DUM, da-DUM, da-DUM.

How long would that beat hold your interest before your mind began to daydream? Probably not very long. When a poet switches feet, for a moment or for a full line, this wakes the reader and reengages him in the poem in the way a sudden change in highway, a slow in traffic, or the quick THUD-ump, THUD-ump, THUD-ump, THUD-ump of railroad tracks jars the driver back to the road.

3. Free Verse vs Blank Verse

Robert Frost [1874-1963] was well-known as a masterful metricist. In fact, Frost once said, "I would sooner write free verse as play tennis with the net down." A good study of iambic meter is hardly complete without a careful look at Frost's poetry, as he claimed: "There are only two meters: strict and loose iambic." What did Frost mean by this statement? And why was Frost so against writing in free verse? To answer this, we must first look at the difference between *free verse* and *blank verse* poetry. We'll discuss *rhymed verse* poetry a little later on.

Free Verse

Free verse is, as the name suggests, poetry that is free from "limitations". In other words, everything we've learned so far in this unit can be both used and disregarded by the author of free verse poetry. Free verse is void of regular meter or rhythm; and though it may rhyme, it does not rhyme in accordance with fixed rhyme schemes. The poet may shape his words and rhythms as he or she desires. Emily Dickinson and Ezra Pound were both masters of free verse poetry.

As you can see from Emily Dickinson's "May-Flower," free verse poetry is not *void* of rhythm, it is simply without a set rhythmic pattern. In "May-Flower*,*" Dickinson begins with two broken, single syllables and then climbs up toward an iamb and a pyrrhic. The second line begins with a pyrrhic followed by a trochee and a single syllable.

> Pink, small, and punctual,
> Aromatic, low,
> Covert in April,
> Candid in May,
>
> Dear to the moss,
> Known by the knoll,
> Next to the robin
> In every human soul.
>
> Bold little beauty,
> Bedecked with thee,
> Nature forswears
> Antiquity.

The third line, "**Co**vert/ in **A**/pril," is written as trochee/iamb/single syllable. What feet do you see in the remaining lines?

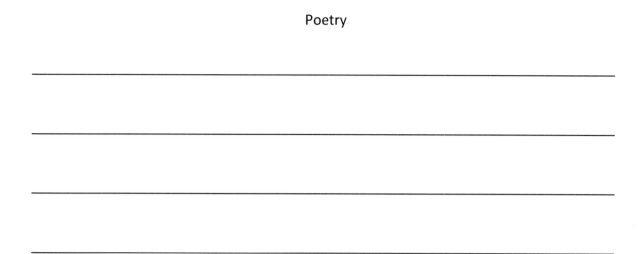

"A Few Don'ts by an Imagiste" [1913] is Ezra Pound's advice to beginning poets. In the article, Pound has the following to say about structure and meter:

> Don't chop your stuff into separate iambs. Don't make each line stop dead at the end, and then begin every next line with a heave. Let the beginning of the next line catch the rise of the rhythm wave, unless you want a definite longish pause. In short, behave as a musician, a good musician, when dealing with that phase of your art which has exact parallels in music. The same laws govern, and you are bound by no others. Naturally, your rhythmic structure should not destroy the shape of your words, or their natural sound, or their meaning.

A look at Ezra Pound's "Camaraderie" reveals how artfully he applied his own advice. The phrases "Summoneth to spring," "Wandereth across mine eyes," and "Halloweth the air awhile" all dance beyond the boundaries of a single line. The result is, as Pound's counsel suggests it will be, musical.

Camaraderie

Sometimes I feel thy cheek against my face

Close-pressing, soft as is the South's first breath

That all the subtle earth-things summoneth

To spring in wood-land and in meadow space.

Yea sometimes in a bustling man-filled place

Me seemeth some-wise thy hair wandereth

Across mine eyes, as mist that halloweth

The air awhile and giveth all things grace.

Or on still evenings when the rain falls close

There comes a tremor in the drops, and fast

My pulses run, knowing thy thought hath passed

That beareth thee as doth the wind a rose.

Blank Verse

Blank verse poetry does not need to rhyme or to have a set number of lines. It does, however, follow a conventional meter throughout. The most commonly used meter in blank verse poetry is iambic pentameter, though blank verse may be written in trochaic, anapestic, or dactylic meters as well.

Again, let's look to that great metricist, Frost, who wrote much of his own poetry in blank verse iambic pentameter. What do you notice about the following poem?

Mending Wall

Something there is that doesn't love a wall,

That sends the frozen-ground-swell under it,

And spills the upper boulders in the sun;

And makes gaps even two can pass abreast.

The work of hunters is another thing:

I have come after them and made repair

Where they have left not one stone on a stone,

But they would have the rabbit out of hiding,

To please the yelping dogs. The gaps I mean,

No one has seen them made or heard them made,

But at spring mending-time we find them there.

I let my neighbour know beyond the hill;

And on a day we meet to walk the line

And set the wall between us once again.

We keep the wall between us as we go.

To each the boulders that have fallen to each.

And some are loaves and some so nearly balls

We have to use a spell to make them balance:

"Stay where you are until our backs are turned!"

We wear our fingers rough with handling them.

Oh, just another kind of out-door game,

One on a side. It comes to little more:

There where it is we do not need the wall:

He is all pine and I am apple orchard.

My apple trees will never get across

And eat the cones under his pines, I tell him.

He only says, "Good fences make good neighbours."

Spring is the mischief in me, and I wonder

If I could put a notion in his head:

"Why do they make good neighbours? Isn't it

Where there are cows? But here there are no cows.

Before I built a wall I'd ask to know

What I was walling in or walling out,

And to whom I was like to give offence.

Something there is that doesn't love a wall,

That wants it down." I could say "Elves" to him,

But it's not elves exactly, and I'd rather

He said it for himself. I see him there

Bringing a stone grasped firmly by the top

In each hand, like an old-stone savage armed.

He moves in darkness as it seems to me,

Not of woods only and the shade of trees.

He will not go behind his father's saying,

And he likes having thought of it so well

He says again, "Good fences make good neighbours."

Frost's "Mending Wall" does not follow a proper rhyme scheme. It is an excellent example of blank verse, however, because of the consistent meter. Each line contains ten syllables, and it is written in the iambic pentameter pattern of five iambic feet-per-line. Only the first foot of the first line is trochaic. Do you see the difference between free verse and blank verse poetry? Blank verse must follow a conventional meter, while free verse is not bound by convention.

Poet and playwright, T.S. Eliot [1888-1965], once wrote:

The most interesting verse which has yet been written in our language has been done either by taking a very simple form, like the iambic pentameter, and constantly withdrawing from it, or taking no form at all, and constantly approximating to a very simple one. It is this contrast between fixity and flux, this unperceived evasion of monotony, which is the very life of verse.

Should the first type mentioned in Eliot's statement, "taking a very simple form, like the iambic pentameter, and constantly withdrawing from it," be classified as free verse? Or was Frost correct in referring to this type of writing as "loose iambic"? Before moving on to discuss rhyme scheme, let's examine the meter in Frost's "After Apple-Picking".

After Apple-Picking

My long two-pointed ladder's sticking through a tree

Toward heaven still,

And there's a barrel that I didn't fill

Beside it, and there may be two or three

Apples I didn't pick upon some bough.

But I am done with apple-picking now.

Essence of winter sleep is on the night,

The scent of apples: I am drowsing off.

I cannot rub the strangeness from my sight

I got from looking through a pane of glass

I skimmed this morning from the drinking trough

And held against the world of hoary grass.

It melted, and I let it fall and break.

But I was well

Upon my way to sleep before it fell,

And I could tell

What form my dreaming was about to take.

Magnified apples appear and disappear,

Stem end and blossom end,

And every fleck of russet showing clear.

My instep arch not only keeps the ache,

It keeps the pressure of a ladder-round.

I feel the ladder sway as the boughs bend.

And I keep hearing from the cellar bin

The rumbling sound

Of load on load of apples coming in.

For I have had too much

Of apple-picking: I am overtired

Of the great harvest I myself desired.

There were ten thousand thousand fruit to touch,

Cherish in hand, lift down, and not let fall.

For all

That struck the earth,

No matter if not bruised or spiked with stubble,

Went surely to the cider-apple heap

As of no worth.

One can see what will trouble

This sleep of mine, whatever sleep it is.

Were he not gone,

The woodchuck could say whether it's like his

Long sleep, as I describe its coming on,

Or just some human sleep.

The vast majority of feet in "After Apple-Picking" are iambic. Though Frost does, as Eliot recommends, withdraw from the iambic form on a regular basis. In this way, Frost allows "After Apple-Picking" to reflect normal patterns of speech in a way that would not be possible in strict iambic pentameter.

Let's examine Frost's use of varying feet: The first three lines are all written in iambic form. However, the meter of the first three lines is: hexameter, dimeter, pentameter. In line four we find our first break from strict rhythm:

Be-SIDE/it-and/THERE-MAY/be-TWO/or-THREE

Iambic/pyrrhic/spondaic/iambic/iambic

At the end of line four, and the beginning of line five, we also see a bit of Ezra Pound's advice being put into practice. "There may be two or three apples," is split before /A-pples/ (trochaic) to allow for the rhyme Frost wanted to emphasize at the end of line four. At the beginning of line eighteen, what do you see?

Magnified/apples/appear/and dis/appear

Is the first foot meant to be manipulated and read as a trochaic foot, or is it a triplet foot (a dactyl)?

/MAGN-fied/ or /MAG-ni-fied/

Upon first glance, how would you classify Frost's "After Apple-Picking"? Is it a free verse poem (the kind Frost said he refused to write)? Or is this simply "loose iambic"— withdrawing from and returning to iambic form for the sake of breathing life into the poem?

4. Rhymed Verse

Types of Rhyme

In order for two words to rhyme, there must be a similarity or identity of sounds between them. When the similarity is found in the stressed syllables of the words, this produces a firmer sounds that is referred to as a masculine rhyme. When the similarity is found in the unstressed syllables, the rhyme has a daintier affect and is referred to as a feminine rhyme.

Masculine (the rhyme falls in the stressed syllable):

He took an apple in his **hand**,

And he place it on the **stand**.

The children will a**stound**

With their ability to re**bound**.

Feminine (the rhyme falls in the unstressed syllable):

The boys and girls will go on swing*ing*

All through the winter's snow*ing*.

He put a yellow app*le*

On the teacher's tab*le*.

Perfect Rhyme:

A perfect rhyme, also called an exact, full, or true rhyme, happens when the sounds of and following the final stressed vowel are identical. In the word "bridal," the long /i/ is in the stressed syllable. To perfectly rhyme the word "bridal," we must find a word with the long /i/ sound followed by /dl/. The words "idle" and "tidal" both work as perfect rhymes. Other examples of perfect rhyme are: sight and light, right and might, close and dose, sun and fun, believe and conceive, ink and pink, skylight and highlight, cat and hat, egg and beg, stew and true, soap and cope... While a perfect rhyme can be great, there is no need to sacrifice meaning and impact just to squeeze in that *perfectly* rhyming word. Forms of general and imperfect rhyme are:

Alliteration:

Alliteration is the repetition of the first letter, or letter sound, in two or more words in a line or sentence. An example of alliteration is: Susie sells seashells by the seashore.

A less obvious example is: Turn toward me and tilt your ear.

Write a short line of alliteration:

_____

_____

Assonant rhyme:

Assonance is a similarity in the sound of two words' vowels. Examples of assonance are: lake and fate, call and fought, fight and bike, main and late, lit and hip...

Write a few word pairs that are examples of assonance:

_____

Consonant rhyme:

Consonance is a similarity in the sound of two words' consonants. Consonance can be difficult to spot, as it may be the ending consonants, the beginning consonants, or the interior consonants that are repeated. Examples of consonance are: bell and ball, blank and think, meter and miter, chuckle/fickle/kick, strong and swing, dump and camp, litter and batter, mile and mine…

Write a few word pairs that are examples of consonance:

_____

Eye rhyme:

An eye rhyme is a rhyme that appears in the spelled words but not in the pronunciation of those words. Examples of eye rhyme are: move and love, cough and bough, slough and rough, food and good, death and wreath.

Write a few word pairs that are examples of eye rhyme:

_____

Identical rhyme:

An identical rhyme is a word used to rhyme with itself—sometimes referring to a different meaning of the same word. An example of identical rhyme is:

She lay in the sun 'til her skin was dark.

Then she sat in pain and cried for days

Wishing the sun would be blotted dark.

Write a two to four line poem that shows an example of identical rhyme:

_____

_____

Light rhyme:

Light rhyme is the rhyming of syllables where one is stressed and the other is not. This type of rhyme is also referred to as a wrenched rhyme. Examples of light rhyme are: frog and dialog, caring and wing, lady and bee, truer and her, mat and combat…

Write a few word pairs that are examples of light rhyme:

_____

_____

Near rhyme:

A near rhyme happens when there is a rhyming of the final consonants, but not of the vowels or the initial consonants. Examples of near rhyme are: bent and rant, thick and quack, quick and back, gust and jest…

Write a few word pairs that are examples of near rhyme:

_____

_____

Oblique:

An oblique is the rhyming of words with *similar* sounding endings. Examples of oblique are: lap and shape, fiend and mean, tools and gruel, find and line, gun and thumb…

Write a few word pairs that are oblique:

_____

_____

Rich rhyme:

The use of words that are pronounced the same but have different meanings—homonyms—is called a rich rhyme. Examples of rich rhyme are: raise and raze, pair and pear, flower and flour, break and brake, vary and very, lessen and lesson.

Write a few word pairs that are homonyms/rich rhyme:

_____

_____

Scarce rhyme:

The term "scarce rhyme" applies to words that either cannot be rhymed perfectly or are difficult to rhyme. Examples of scarce rhyme are: cleansed, midst, gulf, false, wasp, angel, olive…

Write a few words that are hard to rhyme:

_____

_____

Semirhyme:

In a semirhyme, one word has an extra syllable after the rhyme. Examples of semirhyme are: mend and ending, rye and buyer, run and cunning, lick and fickle, clue and stewing...

Write a few word pairs that are examples of semirhyme:

_____

_____

Syllabic:

A rhyming of the last syllable is called a syllabic rhyme. A syllabic rhyme is also called a tail or end rhyme. Examples of syllabic rhyme are: wonder and finder, finding and wondering, prettiest and quietest...

Write a few word pairs that are examples of syllabic rhyme:

_____

_____

Rhyme Position

End rhyme is the most common rhyme position. You can see examples of end rhyme under the masculine and feminine rhyme definitions; the rhyme happens at the end of the line.

Internal rhyme occurs within a single line of poetry. For example:

I like to **hop** and never **stop**.

A famous example of internal rhyme is from Edgar Allan Poe's "The Raven":

While I nodded nearly **napping**, suddenly there came a **tapping**,

Beginning rhyme occurs at the beginning of a line. For example:

Strong were the winds

Long they howled

Crying o'er the rivers

Drying the dew

Rhyme Scheme

For an easy look at rhyme scheme, let's read through "Twinkle, Twinkle, Little Star," written by Jane Taylor in 1806.

Twinkle, twinkle, little star,	A
How I wonder what you are.	A
Up above the world so high,	B
Like a diamond in the sky.	B
Twinkle, twinkle, little star,	A
How I wonder what you are!	A
When the blazing sun is gone,	C
When he nothing shines upon,	C
Then you show your little light,	D
Twinkle, twinkle, all the night.	D
Twinkle, twinkle, little star,	A
How I wonder what you are!	A

Looking at the more common end rhyme position, we see the words: star, are, high, sky, star, and are. Then the words: gone, upon, light, night, star, and are.

The first line ends in the word "star". The first line receives the letter-label "A" because it is the first line. Now we'll look for a word that rhymes with "star". Luckily, we find it right away at the end of the second line. Because "are" rhymes with "star," the second line also receives the letter-label "A". The third line ends with "high," and the fourth line with "sky". These words don't rhyme with the lines labeled "A," so they receive the letter "B". Now we see the rhyme scheme: AABB. The fifth line rhymes with the lines labeled "A". The sixth line does as well. Therefore, both of these lines also receive the letter "A". The rhyme scheme for the first half of the poem is: AABBAA.

Each time we find a new word to rhyme, we label that line with a new letter of the alphabet. "Gone" and "upon" are a new rhyme in the poem, so they both receive the letter "C". In the same way, "light" and "night" receive the letter "D". The rhyme scheme in the second part is now: CCDD. Last we find a repeat in the final two lines: the words "star" and "are". Going back to the beginning, we notice that this rhyme received the letter "A". So, the rhyme scheme for this second half is: CCDDAA.

Did you notice a rhyme scheme when reading Frost's "After Apple-Picking"? Cover the right-hand column with a piece of paper, and see how you do!

My long two-pointed ladder's sticking through a tree	A
Toward heaven still,	B
And there's a barrel that I didn't fill	B
Beside it, and there may be two or three	A
Apples I didn't pick upon some bough.	C
But I am done with apple-picking now.	C
Essence of winter sleep is on the night,	D
The scent of apples: I am drowsing off.	E
I cannot rub the strangeness from my sight	D
I got from looking through a pane of glass	F
I skimmed this morning from the drinking trough	E
And held against the world of hoary grass.	F
It melted, and I let it fall and break.	G
But I was well	H

Upon my way to sleep before it fell,	H
And I could tell	H
What form my dreaming was about to take.	G
Magnified apples appear and disappear,	I
Stem end and blossom end,	J
And every fleck of russet showing clear.	I
My instep arch not only keeps the ache,	G
It keeps the pressure of a ladder-round.	K
I feel the ladder sway as the boughs bend.	J
And I keep hearing from the cellar bin	L
The rumbling sound	K
Of load on load of apples coming in.	L
For I have had too much	M
Of apple-picking: I am overtired	N
Of the great harvest I myself desired.	N
There were ten thousand thousand fruit to touch,	M
Cherish in hand, lift down, and not let fall.	O
For all	O
That struck the earth,	P
No matter if not bruised or spiked with stubble,	Q
Went surely to the cider-apple heap	R
As of no worth.	P
One can see what will trouble	Q
This sleep of mine, whatever sleep it is.	S
Were he not gone,	T
The woodchuck could say whether it's like his	S
Long sleep, as I describe its coming on,	T
Or just some human sleep.	R

5. Stanza

Just as other forms of literature are divided into paragraphs, poetry is divided into sections based on form and thought. The divisions in poetry are referred to as "stanzas".

Couplet (two-line stanza)

A couplet consists of two rhyming lines sharing roughly the same meter. Here are two couplets from Alfred Lord Tennyson's "In the Valley of Cauteretz" (page 57):

> All along the valley, stream that flashest white,
>
> Deepening thy voice with the deepening of the night,

> All along the valley, where thy waters flow,
>
> I walked with one I loved two and thirty years ago.

Tercet (three-line stanza)

A tercet is three lines with the same rhyme scheme (a a a) or a rhyme pattern (a b a). Here is an example of a tercet from Percy Shelley's "Ode to the West Wind" (page 58):

> O wild West Wind, thou breath of Autumn's being,
>
> Thou, from whose unseen presence the leaves dead
>
> Are driven, like ghosts from an enchanter fleeing,

Quatrain (four-line stanza)

A quatrain is a four-line stanza. It may be found in any of the following rhyme schemes: (a a a a), (a a b b), (a b a b), (a b c b), (a b c a) or (a b a c). Here is an example of a quatrain from Emily Dickinson's "I Had No Time to Hate" (page 55):

I had no time to hate, because

The grave would hinder me,

And life was not so ample I

Could finish enmity.

Quintet (five-line stanza)

A quintet is any five-line stanza. It is often found written as a cinquain (which we will discuss later on). Here is an example of a quintet from Henry Wadsworth Longfellow's "The Rainy Day" (page 64):

The day is cold, and dark, and dreary;

It rains, and the wind is never weary;

The vine still clings to the moldering wall,

But at every gust the dead leaves fall,

And the day is dark and dreary.

Sestet (six-line stanza)

Here is an example of a sestet from William Butler Yeasts, "The Wild Swans at Coole" (page 69):

The trees are in their autumn beauty,

The woodland paths are dry,

Under the October twilight the water

Mirrors a still sky;

Upon the brimming water among the stones

Are nine-and-fifty swans.

Septet (seven-line stanza)

Here is an example of a septet from George Herbert's "The Flower" (page 50):

> How fresh, oh Lord, how sweet and clean
>
> Are thy returns! even as the flowers in spring;
>
> To which, besides their own demean,
>
> The late-past frosts tributes of pleasure bring.
>
> Grief melts away
>
> Like snow in May,
>
> As if there were no such cold thing.

Octave (eight-line stanza)

Here is an example of an octave from Percy Shelley's "The Indian Serenade" (page 56):

> I arise from dreams of thee
>
> In the first sweet sleep of night,
>
> When the winds are breathing low,
>
> And the stars are shining bright
>
> I arise from dreams of thee,
>
> And a spirit in my feet
>
> Hath led me—who knows how?
>
> To thy chamber window, Sweet!

6. Other Types of Poetry

There are too many types of poetry to cover them all within this brief unit. The following are some popular forms:

Ballad:

A ballad is a narrative poem. The most popular ballads tell a story from folk-lore or legend. The stanzas within a ballad are typically two or four lines, and there may be repeated lines called a "refrain". A ballad should be moving and memorable—typically suitable for singing. Most ballads are written in alternating lines of iambic tetrameter and iambic trimeter with end rhymes in the second and fourth lines; this is referred to as "ballad meter". For an example of a ballad, see "The Unquiet Grave" in Section C of this unit (page 68).

Cinquain:

A cinquain is a short, five-line poem that was invented by Imagist poet, Adelaide Crapsey. A cinquain in usually unrhymed, and in its traditional form it is twenty-two syllables long. The first line consists of two syllables, the second of four, the third of six, the fourth of eight, and the last of two. For an example of a cinquain, see "Amaze" in Section C of this unit (page 49).

Clerihew:

A clerihew is a short and funny poem consisting of two couplets in the rhyme scheme: aa bb. This humorous poem was invented by Edmund Clerihew Bentley when he was only sixteen years old. A clerihew is about a person or character, and the subject's name is included in the first line. The second line ends with something that rhymes with the name of the person. The third and fourth lines go on to reveal something about the subject.

Sir Humphrey Davy

Abominated gravy.

He lived in the odium

Of having discovered sodium.

For other examples of clerihew, see "John Bunyan" and "Sir Walter Raleigh" in Section C of this unit (page 49).

Haiku:

A hokku or haiku is a little poem that has been written by Japanese poets for hundreds of years. The haiku comes from a poetry form called a **tanka**. A tanka is a five-line poem written by two people as a game—the first player writing the first three lines, and the second player ending the tanka with two lines. Over time, the first three lines became a popular form on their own, and these three short lines of poetry are called a haiku.

English syllables do not have a perfect equivalent in Japanese, but we can write English imitations of haiku by sticking with a three-line, five-seven-five syllable structure.

Haiku is about the here and now; it is usually written in the present tense, and it most commonly focuses on something from nature—like a microscope, haiku shows the importance of something small.

A starting point for beginning haiku poets is:

setting (5 syllables)

subject/action (7 syllables)

subject/action (5 syllables)

Example:

The leaves are falling.

Crunching, crunching, my feet go

Trampling o'er the leaves.

For other examples of haiku, see poems by "Yayu" and "Reikan" in Section C (page 54).

Limerick:

Invented in Limerick, Ireland a limerick is a rhymed poem that is either funny or nonsensical. Limericks have a set rhyme scheme of: a a b b a. The syllable structure of a limerick is nine-nine-six-six-nine. For examples of limerick poetry, see poems "1" and "10" from *The Book of Nonsense* by Edward Lear (Section C, page 58).

Sonnet:

A Sonnet is a fourteen-line poem written in iambic pentameter. Traditional sonnets adhere to one of the following rhyme schemes:

1. abab cdcd efef gg
2. abba cddc effe gg
3. abba abba cdcd cd

A Shakespearean (English) sonnet is written in three quatrains and a couplet: abab cdcd efef gg. For examples of sonnets, see William Shakespeare's "CXVI" and "CXXIII" in Section C (page 66).

Triolet:

A Triolet is an eight-line poem that follows a specific rhyme scheme and structure. In a triolet, the fourth and seventh lines are repeats of the first line. The eighth line is a repeat of the second line. The rhyme scheme is: a b a a a b a b. For an example of a triolet, see Thomas Hardy's "How Great My Grief" in Section C (page 55).

7. Literary Devices

In "A Few Don'ts by an Imagiste," Pound instructs:

> Don't be descriptive; remember that the painter can describe a landscape much better than you can, and that he has to know a deal more about it. When Shakespeare talks of the 'Dawn in russet mantle clad' he presents something which the painter does not present. There is in this line of his nothing that one can call description; he presents.

What do you think of the idea that a writer has the ability, even the responsibility, to present an aspect of a subject that would not be possible for a painter to convey? This is easier said than done. As we near the end of the instruction portion for this unit, we'll review a few literary devices that make Pound's goal more attainable:

Adynaton and Hyperbole:

Adynaton is a kind of _hyperbole_ (exaggeration for the sake of emphasis). However, adynaton is an extreme form of hyperbole. When the exaggeration exceeds what is possible in reality, the result is called adynaton. Both adynaton and hyperbole can be used to describe what is going on in a character's heart and mind in a way that would not be visible to an outside observer.

Statement A: He shoveled the snow on the mile-long driveway.

Statement B: Mary spotted the spider, and she leaped to the roof.

The average driveway is not a mile long. However, it is not completely out of the realm of possibility that one might have a mile-long driveway. This makes statement "A," when made about the average-sized driveway, a case of hyperbole. While shoveling the snow, the man *felt* as if his driveway was a mile long.

Mankind, average or not, does not have the ability to leap directly from the ground to the roof. Therefore statement "B" is not possible in reality and is an example of adynaton. The exaggeration serves to explain to the reader just how severe Mary's fear of spiders actually is.

Another use of hyperbole extending to adynaton is: "By my God I can leap over a wall." (Psalm 18:29)

Antistrophe/Epistrophe/Anaphora:

Antistrophe is a Greek word meaning, "turning back". Epistrophe is a Greek word meaning, "turning upon." Both of these devices involve repetition of the same word(s) at *the end* of consecutive phrases, sentences, and paragraphs. Anaphora is the deliberate repetition of the *beginning* of a sentence.

An example of antistrophe from the Bible is: "When I was a child, I spake as a child, I understood as a child, I thought as a child; but when I became a man, I put away childish things..."

An example of anaphora can be found in Psalm 103, "Bless the Lord" (page 63).

Apostrophe:

In a literary apostrophe, the writer might use the exclamation "O" to indicate that he is addressing a thing, person, or idea with whom he is not in direct conversation. There is an implied distance from present reality in an apostrophic statement.

For example: "Where, O death, is your victory? Where, O death, is your sting." (1 Cor. 15:55)

Caricature:

Not unlike a caricature drawing one might find for sale at a state fair, a literary caricature is a comical exaggeration of the subject's natural features.

Example:

As she cracked the door to retrieve the morning paper, she squinted her tiny eyes away from the sun that seemed to blind her…then she scurried back inside. I laughed at the image of a terrified mole that the sight of her brought to mind.

Imagery:

Imagery is the use of vividly descriptive words to do far more than simply *describe.* Imagery appeals to our physical senses. The phrase, "Where the ocean kissed the southern shore" paints a far more vivid picture than simply, "where the tide rolled in". Imagery paints a picture, evokes a smell, produces a sound, etc. for the experience of the reader. A writer could state, "The wet dog walked in from the rain. It smelled horrible." Or the writer could use imagery and metaphor to play upon the senses of his readers and actually cause them to smell the dog:

An open dumpster on four legs dripped in through the front door. It resembled a dog, but it smelled otherworldly and impossibly foul. A film of humid filth clung to everything in the room. The onlookers heaved a collective, inverted gasp, and everyone refused to breathe until the mutt had passed on toward the kitchen.

In Isaiah chapter 30, The Bible provides us with powerful, image invoking words:

See, the Name of the Lord comes from afar, with burning anger and dense clouds of smoke; his lips are full of wrath, and his tongue is a consuming fire. His breath is like a rushing torrent, rising up to the neck. He shakes the nations in the sieve of destruction...

Metaphor/Simile:

A *metaphor* is an implicit comparing of two things that are completely different yet share some characteristic(s) worthy of comparison. If we say, "She is a delicate rose," we do not mean that she has ceased to be human. We simply mean that she is delicate, feminine, and lovely—comparable to a rose.

If we were to say, "She is *like* a delicate rose," or "She's *as* delicate as a rose," the words "like" and "as" would make the comparison direct instead of implied. This form of comparison is referred to as *simile*. Consider the simile in "They are like trees planted by streams of water" (Psalm 1:3) versus the metaphors in "The Lord is my shepherd" (Psalm 23:1), and "You are the salt of the earth" (Matt. 5:13).

You'll find an example of *simile* in Edgar Allan Poe's "To Helen" (page 54).

Onomatopoeia:

An onomatopoeia is a word that sounds like the thing it is describing. It adds interest by acting as both description and sound-effect. Examples of onomatopoeia are: crash, gong, gush, gurgle, whisper...etc.

Personification:

Personification happens when a non-human thing is given human attributes. The animal, idea, or object is written about in such a way that we think of it as having human thoughts and feelings. A beautiful example is found in Psalm 98:9, "Let the hills sing together for joy". In Section C, Walt Whitman gives us another example of personification in his poem, "Old Ireland" (page 62).

Section C: Poetry

Amaze

Adelaide Crapsey [1878 – 1914]

I know

Not these my hands

And yet I think there was

A woman like me once had hands

Like these.

Clerifew

Edmund Clerihew Bentley [1875-1956]

SIR WALTER RALEIGH

Sir Walter Raleigh
Bickered down the valley.
But he could do better than the rill,
For he could bicker up-hill.

JOHN BUNYAN

I do not extenuate Bunyan's
Intemperate use of onions,
But if I knew a wicked ogress
I would lend her "The Pilgrim's Progress."

The Flower

George Herbert [1593 – 1633]

How fresh, oh Lord, how sweet and clean

Are thy returns! even as the flowers in spring;

To which, besides their own demean,

The late-past frosts tributes of pleasure bring.

Grief melts away

Like snow in May,

As if there were no such cold thing.

Who would have thought my shriveled heart

Could have recovered greenness? It was gone

Quite underground; as flowers depart

To see their mother-root, when they have blown,

Where they together

All the hard weather,

Dead to the world, keep house unknown.

These are thy wonders, Lord of power,

Killing and quickening, bringing down to hell

And up to heaven in an hour;

Making a chiming of a passing-bell.

We say amiss

This or that is:

Thy word is all, if we could spell.

Oh that I once past changing were,

Fast in thy Paradise, where no flower can wither!

Many a spring I shoot up fair,

Offering at heaven, growing and groaning thither;

Nor doth my flower

Want a spring shower,

My sins and I joining together.

But while I grow in a straight line,

Still upwards bent, as if heaven were mine own,

Thy anger comes, and I decline:

What frost to that? what pole is not the zone

Where all things burn,

When thou dost turn,

And the least frown of thine is shown?

And now in age I bud again,

After so many deaths I live and write;

I once more smell the dew and rain,

And relish versing. Oh, my only light,

It cannot be

That I am he

On whom thy tempests fell all night.

These are thy wonders, Lord of love,

To make us see we are but flowers that glide;

Which when we once can find and prove,

Thou hast a garden for us where to bide;

Who would be more,

Swelling through store,

Forfeit their Paradise by their pride.

God's-Acre

Henry Wadsworth Longfellow [1807 – 1882]

I like that ancient Saxon phrase which calls

The burial-ground God's-Acre! It is just;

It consecrates each grave within its walls,

And breathes a benison o'er the sleeping dust.

God's Acre! Yes, that blessed name imparts

Comfort to those who in the grave have sown

The seed that they had garnered in their hearts,

Their bread of life, alas! no more their own.

Into its furrows shall we all be cast,

In the sure faith that we shall rise again

At the great harvest, when the archangel's blast

Shall winnow, like a fan, the chaff and grain.

Then shall the good stand in immortal bloom,

In the fair gardens of that second birth;

And each bright blossom mingle its perfume

With that of flowers which never bloomed on earth.

With thy rude ploughshare, Death, turn up the sod,

And spread the furrow for the seed we sow;

This is the field and Acre of our God,

This is the place where human harvests grow!

The Grass

Emily Elizabeth Dickinson [1830 – 1886]

The grass so little has to do, —

A sphere of simple green,

With only butterflies to brood,

And bees to entertain,

And stir all day to pretty tunes

The breezes fetch along,

And hold the sunshine in its lap

And bow to everything;

And thread the dews all night, like pearls,

And make itself so fine, —

A duchess were too common

For such a noticing.

And even when it dies, to pass

In odors so divine,

As lowly spices gone to sleep,

Or amulets of pine.

And then to dwell in sovereign barns,

And dream the days away, —

The grass so little has to do,

I wish I were the hay!

Haiku

Yayu

You stupid scarecrow
Under your very stick-feet
Birds are stealing beans!

Reikan

Describe plum-blossoms
Better than my verses ... White
Wordless butterflies

To Helen

Edgar Allan Poe [1809 – 1849]

Helen, thy beauty is to me

Like those Nicean barks of yore,

That gently, o'er a perfumed sea,

The weary, way-worn wanderer bore

To his own native shore.

On desperate seas long wont to roam,

Thy hyacinth hair, thy classic face,

Thy Naiad airs have brought me home

To the glory that was Greece.

And the grandeur that was Rome.

Lo! in yon brilliant window-niche

How statue-like I see thee stand!

The agate lamp within thy hand,

Ah! Psyche from the regions which

Are Holy Land!

How Great My Grief

Thomas Hardy [1840 – 1928]

How great my grief, my joys how few,

Since first it was my fate to know thee!

- Have the slow years not brought to view

How great my grief, my joys how few,

Nor memory shaped old times anew,

Nor loving-kindness helped to show thee

How great my grief, my joys how few,

Since first it was my fate to know thee?

I Had No Time to Hate, Because

Emily Elizabeth Dickinson [1830 – 1886]

I had no time to hate, because

The grave would hinder me,

And life was not so ample I

Could finish enmity.

Nor had I time to love; but since

Some industry must be,

The little toil of love, I thought,

Was large enough for me.

The Indian Serenade

Percy Shelley [1792-1822]

I arise from dreams of thee

In the first sweet sleep of night,

When the winds are breathing low,

And the stars are shining bright

I arise from dreams of thee,

And a spirit in my feet

Hath led me—who knows how?

To thy chamber window, Sweet!

The wandering airs they faint

On the dark, the silent stream—

The champak odors fail

Like sweet thoughts in a dream;

The nightingale's complaint,

It dies upon her heart;

As I must on thine,

Oh, beloved as thou art!

O lift me from the grass!

Die! I faint! I fail!

Let thy love in kisses rain

On my lips and eyelids pale.

My cheek is cold and white, alas!

My heart beats loud and fast;—

Oh! press it to thine own again,

Where it will break at last.

In the Valley of Cauteretz

Alfred Tennyson [1809 – 1892]

All along the valley, stream that flashest white,

Deepening thy voice with the deepening of the night,

All along the valley, where thy waters flow,

I walked with one I loved two and thirty years ago.

All along the valley while I walked to-day,

The two and thirty years were a mist that rolls away;

For all along the valley, down thy rocky bed,

Thy living voice to me was as the voice of the dead,

And all along the valley, by rock and cave and tree,

The voice of the dead was a living voice to me.

Limericks

Book of Nonsense

Edward Lear [1812 – 1888]

1.

There was an Old Man with a beard,

Who said, "It is just as I feared!--

Two Owls and a Hen,

Four Larks and a Wren,

Have all built their nests in my beard!"

10.

There was an Old Man in a tree,

Who was horribly bored by a Bee;

When they said, "Does it buzz?"

He replied, "Yes, it does!

"It's a regular brute of a Bee!"

Ode to the West Wind

Percy Shelley [1792-1822]

I

O wild West Wind, thou breath of Autumn's being,

Thou, from whose unseen presence the leaves dead

Are driven, like ghosts from an enchanter fleeing,

Yellow, and black, and pale, and hectic red,

Pestilence-stricken multitudes: O thou,

Who chariotest to their dark wintry bed

The wingéd seeds, where they lie cold and low,

Each like a corpse within its grave, until

Thine azure sister of the Spring shall blow

Her clarion o'er the dreaming earth, and fill

(Driving sweet buds like flocks to feed in air)

With living hues and odours plain and hill:

Wild Spirit, which art moving everywhere;

Destroyer and preserver; hear, oh, hear!

II

Thou on whose stream, 'mid the steep sky's commotion,

Loose clouds like earth's decaying leaves are shed,

Shook from the tangled boughs of Heaven and Ocean,

Angels of rain and lightning: there are spread

On the blue surface of thine aery surge,

Like the bright hair uplifted from the head

Of some fierce Maenad, even from the dim verge

Of the horizon to the zenith's height,

The locks of the approaching storm. Thou dirge

Of the dying year, to which this closing night

Will be the dome of a vast sepulchre,

Vaulted with all thy congregated might

Of vapors, from whose solid atmosphere

Black rain, and fire, and hail will burst: oh, hear!

III

Thou who didst waken from his summer dreams

The blue Mediterranean, where he lay,

Lulled by the coil of his crystalline streams,

Beside a pumice isle in Baiae's bay,

And saw in sleep old palaces and towers

Quivering within the wave's intenser day,

All overgrown with azure moss and flowers

So sweet, the sense faints picturing them! Thou

For whose path the Atlantic's level powers

Cleave themselves into chasms, while far below

The sea-blooms and the oozy woods which wear

The sapless foliage of the ocean, know

Thy voice, and suddenly grow gray with fear,

And tremble and despoil themselves: oh, hear!

IV

If I were a dead leaf thou mightest bear;

If I were a swift cloud to fly with thee;

A wave to pant beneath thy power, and share

The impulse of thy strength, only less free

Than thou, O uncontrollable! If even

I were as in my boyhood, and could be

The comrade of thy wanderings over Heaven,

As then, when to outstrip thy skiey speed

Scarce seemed a vision; I would ne'er have striven

As thus with thee in prayer in my sore need.

Oh, lift me as a wave, a leaf, a cloud!

I fall upon the thorns of life! I bleed!

A heavy weight of hours has chained and bowed

One too like thee: tameless, and swift, and proud.

V

Make me thy lyre, even as the forest is:

What if my leaves are falling like its own!

The tumult of thy mighty harmonies

Will take from both a deep, autumnal tone,

Sweet though in sadness. Be thou, Spirit fierce,

My spirit! Be thou me, impetuous one!

Drive my dead thoughts over the universe

Like withered leaves to quicken a new birth!

And, by the incantation of this verse,

Scatter, as from an unextinguished hearth

Ashes and sparks, my words among mankind!

Be through my lips to unawakened earth

The trumpet of a prophecy! O Wind,

If Winter comes, can Spring be far behind?

Old Ireland

Walt Whitman [1819 — 1892]

Far hence, amid an isle of wondrous beauty,

Crouching over a grave, an ancient sorrowful mother,

Once a queen—now lean and tattered, seated on the ground,

Her old white hair drooping disheveled round her shoulders;

At her feet fallen an unused royal harp,

Long silent—she too long silent—mourning her shrouded hope and heir;

Of all the earth her heart most full of sorrow, because most full of love.

Yet a word, ancient mother;

You need crouch there no longer on the cold ground, with forehead between your knees;

O you need not sit there, veiled in your old white hair, so disheveled;

For know you, the one you mourn is not in that grave;

It was an illusion—the heir, the son you love, was not really dead;

The Lord is not dead—he is risen again, young and strong, in another country;

Even while you wept there by your fallen harp, by the grave,

What you wept for was translated, passed from the grave,

The winds favoured, and the sea sailed it,

And now, with rosy and new blood,

Moves to-day in a new country.

Psalm 103

King James Version

Bless the Lord, O my soul: and all that is within me, bless his holy name.

Bless the Lord, O my soul, and forget not all his benefits:

Who forgiveth all thine iniquities; who healeth all thy diseases;

Who redeemeth thy life from destruction; who crowneth thee with lovingkindness and tender mercies;

Who satisfieth thy mouth with good things; so that thy youth is renewed like the eagle's.

The Lord executeth righteousness and judgment for all that are oppressed.

He made known his ways unto Moses, his acts unto the children of Israel.

The Lord is merciful and gracious, slow to anger, and plenteous in mercy.

He will not always chide: neither will he keep his anger for ever.

He hath not dealt with us after our sins; nor rewarded us according to our iniquities.

For as the heaven is high above the earth, so great is his mercy toward them that fear him.

As far as the east is from the west, so far hath he removed our transgressions from us.

Like as a father pitieth his children, so the Lord pitieth them that fear him.

For he knoweth our frame; he remembereth that we are dust.

As for man, his days are as grass: as a flower of the field, so he flourisheth.

For the wind passeth over it, and it is gone; and the place thereof shall know it no more.

But the mercy of the Lord is from everlasting to everlasting upon them that fear him, and his righteousness unto children's children;

To such as keep his covenant, and to those that remember his commandments to do them.

The Lord hath prepared his throne in the heavens; and his kingdom ruleth over all.

Bless the Lord, ye his angels, that excel in strength, that do his commandments, hearkening unto the voice of his word.

Bless ye the Lord, all ye his hosts; ye ministers of his, that do his pleasure.

Bless the Lord, all his works in all places of his dominion: bless the Lord, O my soul.

The Rainy Day

Henry Wadsworth Longfellow [1807 – 1882]

The day is cold, and dark, and dreary;

It rains, and the wind is never weary;

The vine still clings to the moldering wall,

But at every gust the dead leaves fall,

And the day is dark and dreary.

My life is cold, and dark, and dreary;

It rains, and the wind is never weary;

My thoughts still cling to the moldering Past,

But the hopes of youth fall thick in the blast,

And the days are dark and dreary.

Be still, sad heart! and cease repining;

Behind the clouds is the sun still shining;

Thy fate is the common fate of all,

Into each life some rain must fall,

Some days must be dark and dreary.

The Road Not Taken

Robert Frost [1874-1963]

Two roads diverged in a yellow wood,

And sorry I could not travel both

And be one traveler, long I stood

And looked down one as far as I could

To where it bent in the undergrowth;

Then took the other, as just as fair,

And having perhaps the better claim,

Because it was grassy and wanted wear;

Though as for that the passing there

Had worn them really about the same,

And both that morning equally lay

In leaves no step had trodden black.

Oh, I kept the first for another day!

Yet knowing how way leads on to way,

I doubted if I should ever come back.

I shall be telling this with a sigh

Somewhere ages and ages hence:

Two roads diverged in a wood, and I—

I took the one less traveled by,

And that has made all the difference.

Sad Is Our Youth, for It Is Ever Going

Aubrey Thomas De Vere [1814 – 1902]

Sad is our youth, for it is ever going,

Crumbling away beneath our very feet;

Sad is our life, for onward it is flowing

In current unperceived, because so fleet;

Sad are our hopes, for they were sweet in sowing, —

But tares, self-sown, have overtopped the wheat;

Sad are our joys, for they were sweet in blowing,

And still, O, still their dying breath is sweet;

And sweet is youth, although it hath bereft us

Of that which made our childhood sweeter still;

And sweet is middle life, for it hath left us

A nearer good to cure an older ill;

And sweet are all things, when we learn to prize them,

Not for their sake, but His who grants them or denies them!

Shakespearean Sonnets

Sonnet CXVI

William Shakespeare [1564 – 1616]

Let me not to the marriage of true minds

Admit impediments. Love is not love

Which alters when it alteration finds,

Or bends with the remover to remove:

O, no! it is an ever-fixed mark,

That looks on tempests and is never shaken;

It is the star to every wandering bark,

Whose worth's unknown, although his height be taken.

Love's not Time's fool, though rosy lips and cheeks

Within his bending sickle's compass come;

Love alters not with his brief hours and weeks,

But bears it out even to the edge of doom.

    If this be error and upon me prov'd,

    I never writ, nor no man ever lov'd.

Sonnet CXXIII

William Shakespeare

No, Time, thou shalt not boast that I do change:

Thy pyramids built up with newer might

To me are nothing novel, nothing strange;

They are but dressings of a former sight.

Our dates are brief, and therefore we admire

What thou dost foist upon us that is old;

And rather make them born to our desire

Than think that we before have heard them told.

Thy registers and thee I both defy,

Not wondering at the present nor the past,

For thy records and what we see doth lie,

Made more or less by thy continual haste.

This I do vow and this shall ever be;

I will be true despite thy scythe and thee.

The Unquiet Grave

Anonymous

I

'The wind doth blow today, my love,

And a few small drops of rain;

I never had but one true-love;

In cold grave she was lain.

II

'I'll do as much for my true-love

As any young man may;

I'll sit and mourn all at her grave

For a twelvemonth and a day.'

III

The twelvemonth and a day being up,

The dead began to speak:

'Oh who sits weeping on my grave,

And will not let me sleep?'—

IV

''Tis I, my love, sits on your grave,

And will not let you sleep;

For I crave one kiss of your clay-cold lips,

And that is all I seek.'—

V

'You crave one kiss of my clay-cold lips;

But my breath smells earthy strong;

If you have one kiss of my clay-cold lips,

Your time will not be long.

VI

''Tis down in yonder garden green,

Love, where we used to walk,

The finest flower that ere was seen

Is wither'd to a stalk.

VII

'The stalk is wither'd dry, my love,

So will our hearts decay;

So make yourself content, my love,

Till God calls you away.'

The Wild Swans at Coole

W. B. Yeats [1865 – 1939]

The trees are in their autumn beauty,

The woodland paths are dry,

Under the October twilight the water

Mirrors a still sky;

Upon the brimming water among the stones

Are nine-and-fifty swans.

The nineteenth autumn has come upon me

Since I first made my count;

I saw, before I had well finished,

All suddenly mount

And scatter wheeling in great broken rings

Upon their clamorous wings.

I have looked upon those brilliant creatures,

And now my heart is sore.

All's changed since I, hearing at twilight,

The first time on this shore,

The bell-beat of their wings above my head,

Trod with a lighter tread.

Unwearied still, lover by lover,

They paddle in the cold

Companionable streams or climb the air;

Their hearts have not grown old;

Passion or conquest, wander where they will,

attend upon them still.

But now they drift on the still water,

Mysterious, beautiful;

Among what rushes will they build,

By what lake's edge or pool

Delight men's eyes when I awake some day

To find they have flown away?

Young Night Thought

Robert Louis Stevenson [1850 – 1894]

All night long and every night,

When my mamma puts out the light

I see the people marching by,

As plain as day, before my eye.

Armies and emperors and kings,

All carrying different kinds of things,

And marching in so grand a way,

You never saw the like by day.

So fine a show was never seen

At the great circus on the green;

For every kind beast and man

Is marching in that caravan.

At first they move a little slow,

But still the faster on they go,

And still beside them close I keep

Until we reach the Town of Sleep.

Section D: Exercises in Poetry

CREATIVITY EXERCISE: Fifteen minute free-write. Set a timer for fifteen minutes; then go and take a seat. Pick up a pen, and write about something, anything, until the timer chimes. Don't stop. Begin with the writing prompt, and if you get stumped, rhyme the last word you've written. One of these rhymed words should soon spark your interest. Have fun! (C3 Scale)

Prompt: Life is such a funny thing, the snow in March hides the flowers of spring…

Exercise 1: Go outside and observe your surroundings; take your time. Write two haiku about what you see. Use onomatopoeia. (C1 Scale)

Exercise 2: Choose one poem from Section C. Analyze the meter and rhyme scheme of the poem, and write a ½ page essay on its structure. (C2 Scale)

Exercise 3: Choose one poem from Section C. Write a ½ - 1 page essay explaining the setting, subject, and meaning. (C2 Scale)

Exercise 4: Write a limerick about something funny that has happened to you. (C1 Scale)

Exercise 5: Write a clerihew about someone you know (or a famous person). (C1 Scale)

Exercise 6: Write one free verse poem about a special memory. Use antistrophe or anaphora in your writing. (C1 Scale)

Exercise 7: Write one blank verse poem about your favorite season. Make use of metaphor or simile and imagery! Mark the feet and stressed syllables. (C1 Scale)

Exercise 8: Poets' Choice! Write one poem in the style of your choosing. Use personification in your writing. (C1 Scale)

Unit II: Drama

Section A: What is Drama?

In literature, **drama** refers to text that is meant to be performed rather than read—a piece of literature intended to stir people in mass rather than one person alone in his reading room. The two main types of drama are comedy (which ends in happiness) and tragedy (which ends in sadness), although a story might have elements of both. While stage directions are included—"enter from stage left," "a look of surprise crosses her face," "he reaches longingly toward her," "they sneak through the front door and shut it quietly behind them,"—the bulk of words in most dramatic writing is actual monologue from and dialog between the characters. Screenwriting (for film) and playwriting (for the stage) require very different approaches. We'll focus on those areas in which the requirements of screenwriting and playwriting are the same: plot, characterization, and dialog. Because learning to write true-to-life dialog is essential, not only for plays and scripts, but for short stories and novels as well, we'll spend some time examining the principles behind putting words into characters' mouths—or more correctly: first creating characters and then allowing them to speak.

People, in all their shades and distinctions, are what fill life with drama; they make life interesting. But what lies beneath an individual's public life tells the story we can't always see. It's *people*, portrayed in naked and humbled truth, that make for good dramatic writing. A talented playwright possesses the power to see through human skin to the frailty, insecurity, evil, and desire that lie below. According to George Bernard Shaw [1856-1950]:

> The great dramatist has something better to do than to amuse either himself or his audience. He has to interpret life. This sounds a mere pious phrase of literary criticism; but a moment's consideration will discover its meaning and its

exactitude. Life as it appears to us in our daily experience is an unintelligible chaos of happenings. You pass [Shakespeare's] Othello in the bazaar in Aleppo, Iago on the jetty in Cyprus, and Desdemona in the nave of St. Mark's in Venice without the slightest clue to their relations to one another. The man you see stepping into a chemist's shop to buy the means of committing murder or suicide, may, for all you know, want nothing but a liver pill or a toothbrush...To attempt to understand life from merely looking on at it as it happens in the streets is as hopeless as trying to understand public questions by studying snapshots of public demonstrations...Life as it occurs is senseless: a policeman may watch it and work in it for thirty years in the streets and courts of Paris without learning as much of it or from it as a child or a nun may learn from a single play by [the playwright] Brieux. For it is the business of Brieux to pick out the significant incidents from the chaos of daily happenings and arrange them so that their relation to one another becomes significant, thus changing us from bewildered spectators of a monstrous confusion to men intelligently conscious of the world and its destinies.

George Bernard Shaw, "How to Write a Popular Play [1909]"

How does a playwright accomplish his mission? How does he select a seemingly insignificant card from the deck of life and display it to his audience as something that has meaning and value? Many playwrights and critics, including Shaw, have formulated their own advice for accomplishing just that. In the next section, we'll examine counsel from some of them and read a few well-written play acts. First, we'll review the literary devices that are essential to dramatic writing.

Section B: Writing and Reading Drama

1. Literary Devices

Anti-Hero/Hero:

The protagonist, or the central character in a story, is typically brave, strong, charming, etc. He or she is often written as a **hero**. When the central character is deeply flawed, hopelessly human, and possesses characteristics opposite of those belonging to a typical "hero," he or she may be classified as an **anti-hero**. Consider the biblical characters of Jonah and Sampson. Ultimately, their actions lead to victory, but their many character flaws are apparent.

Antagonist:

An antagonist is a character, or group of characters, that opposes the protagonist (central character). This force which fights against the hero/anti-hero may be a physical antagonist, it may be a spiritual antagonist, or it may be an inner conflict that arises in the mind of the protagonist. In the life-story of Jonah, the conflict arises internally—Jonah is his own antagonist. In the life-story of Sampson, though most anti-heroes come equipped with an internal antagonist, the most easily recognized antagonists are Delilah and the Philistines.

Characterization:

Characterization is the manner in which the author highlights and explains the personality and background of his character(s). Typically the character is introduced, then behaviors of the character are shown or referenced. Lastly, the audience/reader is made aware of the thought-process of the character. Characterization is also established by the way those around the character respond to his/her behavior.

Climax:

The climax is that high-point in a story where the conflict or emotional tension is at its highest. This climax of emotion, also called a crisis, is the moment of decision/turning point in the plot. The author has carefully built to this crucial point, and now the rising action turns to a falling action as the conclusion is found in either happiness or tragedy.

Conflict:

Conflict is the literary term used to describe a struggle between two forces. This struggle usually involves the protagonist and a physical antagonist, though the struggle may happen within the protagonist (in his inner dialog). Internal conflict happens when a character is torn between two opposing emotions or desires: one positive or righteous and the other negative or self-serving. External conflict happens when a character finds himself in a struggle against a physical enemy or enemies.

Foreshadowing:

Foreshadowing is a literary device in which the writer hints to future events in the story. Foreshadowing is most often used in the opening chapters or lines. The writer may choose to use dialog between characters to reveal important facts and foreshadow upcoming happenings. Even the most seemingly insignificant detail, behavior, or statement may be used to slyly foreshadow the future. Additionally, the title of the book, play, or chapter may hint at the story's direction.

Juxtaposition:

Juxtaposition is a literary device in which two or more things are placed in close proximity to one another for the purpose of comparison or contrast. It is often easier to understand something's goodness, evil, etc. by comparing it to something else. A writer may choose to highlight a character's goodness by placing him in the company of objectionable or immoral people. In the same way, a character who is predominantly good may appear more flawed when juxtaposed with saintly characters.

2. Plot

The sequence of events that make up the primary storyline in a novel, play, short story, etc. is called the plot. A plot should contain five key elements:

- ***Introduction***: The characters are introduced and relevant information is revealed; the foundation for the crisis is established.
- ***Rising action***: This is the series of events that inevitably leads to the conflict or crisis.
- ***Climax***: Once the crisis/conflict is full-blown, we reach the highest point of tension before the crisis/conflict is resolved.
- ***Falling action***: The crisis/conflict is resolved and tension is relieved.
- ***Conclusion***: The story ends in either happiness or tragedy.

No matter how carefully knit the plot, and whether or not there are lesser knots (sub-plots) to be untangled, there should always be one moment of supreme entanglement. It is in this climactic point that all the story's threads become knotted within each other. The bulk of the story is written to explain exactly how this predicament has come to be. The rising action is sometimes referred to as the tying of the knot. With the exception of a detective tale in which the majority of the story is spent untying the tangled knot, the first three-quarters or so of a typical story is spent on the knotting of threads. In essence, a plot is simply a tangling (rising action) followed by an untangling (falling action). In most plots, but not always, the events that lead toward that moment of utmost disorder are at least somewhat more intriguing than the events involved in picking apart the threads. It is for this reason that the climax is usually placed at least three-quarters of the way through the story. While this might be the simplest format, the positioning of the climax is entirely at the discretion of the writer.

Now we know the elements of a plot, but knowing the elements of a plot do not necessarily make it easier to compose a captivating plot. Where does a playwright begin? Does he start by creating his characters? Is the climactic scene, or the opening scene, or the concluding scene the best place to start when writing?

When you have a character or several characters you haven't a play. You may keep these in your mind and nurse them till they combine in a piece of action; but you haven't got your play till you have theme, characters, and action all fused. The process with me is as purely automatic and spontaneous as dreaming; in fact it is really dreaming while you are awake.

Henry Arthur Jones [1851 – 1929]

In 1912, William Archer wrote *Play-Making: A Manual of Craftsmanship*. In his book, the Scottish born writer and critic tells a story about a problem he claims is common to playwrights. He states that in the first moments of writing, or perhaps before he has even planned on writing, the author is struck by a particularly wonderful idea. He sees a situation in his mind, and he knows it will entrance the audience. Around this scene, he begins to write a play. The first act goes smoothly—he knows he is headed toward that fabulous situation that is sure to wow his audience. As he approaches the third act, however, he realizes that he is stuck. After weeks and weeks of trying to make the play work, he realizes that the problem is in that one *perfect* scene. When he finally musters the courage to delete it, the rest of the play is written without a hitch. This is solid advice, as Archer encourages young writers to both to begin writing without fear, and to avoid becoming attached to any particular scene, line, or character.

The problem with becoming overly attached to one particular scene is summed up in a succinct piece of advice from Alexandre Dumas [1802 – 1870]. Dumas reminds us, "...a [scene] is not an idea. An idea, has a beginning, a middle and an end: an exposition, a development, a conclusion. Anyone can relate a dramatic [scene]: the art lies in preparing it, getting it accepted, rendering it possible, especially in untying the knot."

How does a playwright begin to write in confidence that the play will end well? Many playwrights have insisted that the last act should be written first. This advice was especially well-received in the days when high-impact, cymbal gonging, last-word endings were not only the norm but were regarded as the most important element of a play. In the early twentieth century, Archer insisted:

> Nowadays, we are more willing to accept a quiet, even an indecisive, ending. Nevertheless it is and must ever be true that, at a very early period in the scheming of his play, the playwright ought to assure himself that his theme is capable of a satisfactory ending. Of course this phrase does not imply a 'happy ending,' but one which satisfies the author as being artistic, effective, inevitable (in the case of a serious play), or, in one word, 'right.'

In other words, the ending doesn't need to be particularly eventful, but it does need to be "good". It may not be necessary to actually compose the last act, first, and in doing so the playwright may prevent his drama from evolving past his initial idea; but having an ending in mind, as he begins to write, is an important step toward a satisfactory conclusion.

An obviously makeshift ending can never be desirable, either from the ideal or from the practical point of view. Many excellent plays have been wrecked on this rock. The very frequent complaint that "the last act is weak" is not always or necessarily a just reproach; but it is so when the author has clearly been at a loss for an ending, and has simply huddled his play up in a conventional and perfunctory fashion. [The playwright] should, at an early point, see clearly the end for which he is making, and be sure that it is an end which he actively desires, not merely one which satisfies convention, or which 'will have to do.'

William Archer, *Play-making: A Manual of Craftsmanship*

According to English novelist and playwright, John Galsworthy [1867–1933], a plot is only as good as the headstrongness of its characters. If the characters' convictions and personalities are the driving force behind the plot, it has a good shot at being good. If the characters are ordered to fit into roles that were prewritten for them, they will never truly breathe and live, and the play will most likely die with them. Because a deep and purposeful understanding of one's characters is essential to the plot and the dialog, we will discuss the art of sketching characters in the next sub-section.

A human being is the best plot there is; it may be impossible to see why he is a good plot, because the idea within which he was brought forth cannot be fully grasped; but it is plain that he is a good plot. He is organic. And so it must be with a good play. Reason alone produces no good plots...A bad plot, on the other hand, is simply a row of stakes, with a character impaled on each -- characters who would have liked to live, but came to untimely grief; who started bravely, but fell on these stakes placed beforehand in a row, and were transfixed one by one, while their ghosts stride on, squeaking and gibbering, through the play. Whether these stakes are made of facts or of ideas, according to the nature of the

> dramatist who planted them, their effect on the unfortunate characters is the same; the creatures were begotten to be staked, and staked they are!
>
> John Galsworthy, *Some Platitudes Concerning Drama*

3. Character Sketches

> The story which is independent of character--which can be carried through by a given number of ready-made puppets--is essentially a trivial thing. Unless, at an early stage of the organizing process, character begins to take the upper hand--unless the playwright finds himself thinking, "Oh, yes, George is just the man to do this," or, "That is quite foreign to Jane's temperament"--he may be pretty sure that it is a piece of mechanism he is putting together, not a drama with flesh and blood in it. The difference between a live play and a dead one is that in the former the characters control the plot, while in the latter the plot controls the characters.
>
> William Archer, *Play-making: A Manual of Craftsmanship*

In a 1903 publication of *The Art of Writing and Speaking the English Language*, American writer, Sherwin Cody [1868-1959], discusses "The Use of Models in Writing Fiction". Mr. Cody equates the process of creating characters based on real-life people with a painter's use of live models. While it takes little skill to "put your friends into the story," characters based purely in imagination are typically unrealistic and flat. The solution, Cody suggests, is to use one's friends, enemies, and acquaintances as *models* for characters, and from those models to depart consciously and purposefully to create characters that are unique.

...during a lifetime one accumulates a large number of models simply by habitually observing everything that comes in one's way. When the writer takes up {the} pen to produce a story, he searches through his mental collection for a suitable model. Sometimes it is necessary to use several models in drawing the same character, one for this characteristic, and another for that. But in writing the novelist should have his eye on his model just as steadily and persistently as the painter, for so alone can he catch the spirit and inner truth of nature; and art...The ideal character must be made the interpretation of the real one, not a photographic copy, not idealization or glorification or caricature, unless the idealization or glorification or caricature has a definite value in the interpretation.

Sherwin Cody, *The Art of Writing and Speaking the English Language*

In order to successfully represent a character through his dialog, the author should know his characters as well as he knows his best friend. To ensure that the character is speaking as he has been designed to live, and not carelessly to suit the plot, a character sketch is helpful.

A character sketch should include as much detail as possible. When an author/playwright reaches the point in writing when he wonders, "Would so and so say that?" it will be helpful to return, again and again, to a consistent and thorough sketch of his characters. It is important to know the details about a characters' physical appearance, but we know some of those things about the strangers we pass on the street. When sketching characters, the author should note personality, history, and internal dialog as well.

The following is a sample outline of a thorough character sketch:

Character's Name, Age

I. Physical Description

    A. Hair

        1. color

        2. style

        3. What is the first thing one might notice?

    B. Eyes

        1. color

        2. Does he/she wear glasses? All the time or just for reading?

        3. What is the first thing one might notice?

    C. Height/Weight

        1. height

        2. weight

        3. body type

        4. Does the character appear thinner or heavier than he/she is? How does he/she carry his/her weight?

    D. Style

        1. daily clothing style

        2. favorite outfit

        3. jewelry

    E. Speech

        1. accent

2. grammar

3. favorite words or phrases

    a.

    b.

    c.

F. Walk

1. speed of walk

2. type of walk

3. Describe your character walking down a crowded sidewalk.

4. Describe your character walking alone through the woods in the afternoon.

II. Personality

A. Mannerisms

1. How does he/she sit when absolutely alone?

2. How does he/she sit when in front of people?

3. Does/how does the character fidget when waiting?

4. Does/how does the character fidget when nervous?

B. Bad Habits

1.

2.

C. Strengths

1.

    2.

    3.

  D. Weaknesses

    1.

    2.

    3.

  E. Likes

    1.

    2.

  F. Dislikes/Pet Peeves

    1.

    2.

  G. Hobbies

    1.

    2.

    3.

  H. Conviction/Conflicts

    1. Inner Conflicts

    2. External Conflicts

III. Family History

  A. Parents

    1.

2.

B. Siblings

    1. siblings important to the plot

    2. siblings not important to the plot

C. Extended Family

    1. Is the character close to his/her extended family?

    2. Describe an interaction between the character and his/her extended

family.

IV. Past

A. Childhood

    1. key event

    2. key event

    3. How does the character describe his childhood/relationship with parents?

B. Teen Years/Young Adulthood

    1. key event

    2. key event

    3. key event

    4. key event

C. Education/Job History

    1. grade school

    2. junior high

    3. high school

4. college

5. first job

6. second job

7. third job

8. career

9. interesting work experiences

D. Immediate Past

1. What was the character doing/where was the character living immediately before the start of the play/story?

4. Characterization

After a character has been created in the mind of the writer, it is up to the writer to decide how to communicate that character to his audience or to his readers.

1. *Directly, through third-part exposition*:

The simplest form of character introduction is done by third-party exposition. In this method, a narrator or fellow character will directly, usually toward the beginning of a play or book, tell about the character in question. This method is useful for relaying a great deal of important information in a short period of time. However, the information presented is abstract in that it has not been witnessed by the reader/audience. It does not allow the reader/audience to truly know the character; it simply allows them to know *about* the character. This method is useful for playwrights, as the playwright must communicate through his characters.

In *The Vicar of Wakefield*, Oliver Goldsmith, in the voice of the Vicar, tells the reader of his wife, Mrs. Primrose. He does not introduce the reader to her; he simply tells about her.

> "I was ever of opinion, that the honest man who married and brought up a large family, did more service than he who continued single, and only talked of population. From this motive, I had scarce taken orders a year before I began to think seriously of matrimony, and chose my wife as she did her wedding-gown, not for a fine glossy surface, but such qualities as would wear well. To do her justice, she was a good-natured notable woman; and as for breeding, there were few country ladies who could show more. She could read any English book without much spelling; but for pickling, preserving, and cookery, none could excel her. She prided herself also upon being an excellent contriver in housekeeping; though I could never find that we grew richer with all her contrivances."

2. *Directly, by Description*:

A novelist has a unique advantage in that he is able to describe a character in great detail. Oftentimes a playwright must rely on the effectiveness of his actors (and the perceptiveness of his audience) to communicate what a novelist can say directly. For example, a playwright might write a scene in which Mrs. Stevenson sits alone in a room before her husband comes in to join her. His audience will gaze upon Mrs. Stevenson and form many and possibly varying opinions about her, whereas the novelist may stand his readers before her and tell them exactly what he wishes them to see. He hasn't merely described her; he has introduced his readers to her.

For example:

> There was one hour of daylight left in the day, and Mrs. Stevenson sat where Mrs. Stevenson always sat at that time. She sat sewing tiny stitches in the torn seams of her

husband's clothes. Her legs stretched in front of her on the sofa, and her left foot sat perched upon her right. She hummed softly. Her top foot bounced gently with the rhythm of her tune. Her black, knee-high stockings could use the care she showed to her husband's clothes, but her face was freshly washed, and her hair was piled upon the crown of her head and carefully twisted and pinned. When Mr. Stevenson entered the room, he smiled, as he always did, at the sweet smell of her perfume.

3. *Directly, by Psychological Analysis*:

The novelist may also provide the reader with occasional glimpses into a character's thoughts and emotions. This can be important, because it helps the reader to understand the character and his motivation. Because the real-life observer cannot see into the mental processes of his friends and acquaintances, however, the illusion of reality is briefly shattered when an author takes this route. Because of this, it is better to weave these insights into the story. A playwright should ponder how to communicate these same thoughts through the careful movement of his characters.

She held her hand out of sight. Beneath a knit shawl that swallowed her whole, she looked more like a girl than a middle-aged woman. The shawl hung down from the top of her head, and the bulk of it curled like a cat in her lap. Under the folds her left hand hid fidgeting as she pushed her wedding ring with her thumb and it orbited 'round and 'round her finger. Her right hand moved freely and greeted the passersby. She smiled, because she always smiled when she didn't know what to do. When the wind picked up she'd use her right hand to pinch the shawl tightly beneath her chin. It was cold out, and she was glad. It made her hiding acceptable. If she could have made a child's fort from that shawl and crawled unnoticed inside, she would have. If the train didn't arrive soon, or if her husband wasn't on it, she might resort to that plan.

4. *Directly, by Reports from Other Characters*:

It is more natural and believable, in most cases, to hear others tell about a person than to hear someone tell about themselves. Even more believable is when the character in question comes up in conversation between other characters. An added bonus to this approach is that the characters who are speaking are also characterized through their speech.

For example, in chapter thirty-three of Jane Austen's *Emma*, Mrs. Elton prattles on:

> "Jane Fairfax is absolutely charming, Miss Woodhouse. I quite rave about Jane Fairfax—a sweet, interesting creature. So mild and lady-like—and with such talents! I assure you I think she has very extraordinary talents. I do not scruple to say that she plays extremely well. I know enough of music to speak decidedly on that point. Oh! She is absolutely charming! You will laugh at my warmth—but upon my word, I talk of nothing but Jane Fairfax."

Through her breathless chatter we learn as much, or more, of Mrs. Elton as we do of Jane Fairfax.

5. *Indirectly, by Speech*:

Another form of characterization, available both to playwrights and to novelists, is dialect. Few traits cause human beings to jump to a quicker assumption of character than the way a person speaks. After only the first few lines of *A March Wind* (page 166), the reader will have already begun to formulate fixed ideas about Melia and Enoch:

> MELIA: *[To Enoch.]* What's the matter with [the clock]?

ENOCH: Dunno yet. She's balky.

MELIA: When it give up strikin' I lost all patience. Let's cart it off into the attic an' buy us one o' them little nickel ones.

ENOCH: Oh, I guess we'll give her a chance. *[Lifts it down carefully.]* Should you jest as soon I'd bring in that old shoemaker's bench out o' the shed? It's low, an' I could reach my tools off'n the floor.

MELIA: Law, yes. It's a good day to clutter up. There won't be nobody in.

6. *Indirectly, by Action:*

No telling can equal showing. Just as in real life, actions speak louder than words. For example, we could have heard, first-hand or second-hand, about the way Jimmy found the four kittens, but witnessing the event gives us unique knowledge and perspective about Jimmy as a person:

His breath froze quietly in the air before he'd stepped one foot out of the house. Once outside, the cold took his breath altogether. He couldn't remember a morning this bitter, not this early in winter. He walked as quickly as he could to the corner. If he didn't catch the bus, he'd have to walk another mile. He could hear the familiar squeaking as his school bus rounded the corner, but then another sound slowed his steps. It wasn't a cry for help, but it was an unnatural sound. Jimmy bent his ear toward it and followed it into the bushes. There huddled four half-frozen kittens under the stiff body of their mother. He scooped them up one by one and lowered them down between his undershirt and his warm body. "Well, I guess I'll be late," he told them.

7. Indirectly, by Effect on Other Characters:

Another sure way of communicating the personality of a character is through the way other characters respond to them. For example, in *Her Tongue* (page 103) we know that Patty is very long-winded and that she hasn't much to say, but the grating nature of her personality is made abundantly clear as her suitor rapidly becomes disenchanted.

In this case, the playwright illustrates his disenchantment through careful stage direction:

> [During the following scene he gradually gets into window--she gradually follows him up, gets on the right side of table, which is on casters; she unconsciously pushes it toward the window until she has hemmed him in the lower bay of the window, with the table diagonally across from middle of window to the corner of the bay, so that he cannot escape. This is done very gradually and quite unconsciously.]

8. Indirectly, by Environment:

Another way to cause a reader/audience to make instant judgments about a character is to carefully depict their environment:

> The dirt floor made the room feel dusty, but there wasn't any dust on the small table and chairs that stood in the middle of the room, and there was not a crumb on the floor. There were never any crumbs; every last crumb was eaten. Light filled the front room from its two south-facing windows, and a fire crackled in the stove. It was a warm house, plain and simple, he was sure its owners must be warm as well.

5. Dialog

The literary definition of dialog is the exact words the characters speak, but dialog in a story is not the same as dialog in a play. In a novel or short story, the dialog is the description of a conversation as well as portions of direct quotations. It is rarely a full and exact report of what is said on each side, because dialog is not the novelist's only means of communication. For example, in addition to writing dialog where Greg and Michelle discuss their favorite memories, a novelist can also speak of Greg and Michelle in the third person: "Greg could see that it was getting late; he wondered if Michelle had noticed. The night had been an unexpected gift, and he didn't want it to end…"

Playwrights, on the other hand, must communicate solely through the words their characters say and the way their characters move. Each line of opening dialog should reveal the characters' relationship to the plot and increase tension as the story moves toward the climax. Likewise, each line of closing dialog should accurately and realistically bring the crisis to a believable close. Although the use of a narrator is optional, narration diminishes the feeling of intimacy between the characters on stage.

Playwrights must be precise in their characters' speech. Because pauses and silences in dialog can often tell the audience as much as the dialog itself, playwrights must be careful to note every sigh and stillness.

When writing dialog, it is important to remember that a person's speech is born out of many factors: their thoughts, desires, relationships, upbringing, education, location, etc. This is where a character sketch will prove invaluable. The language used by people in a specific location is referred to as "dialect". The dialect of US Northerners is different than US Southerners; this involves not only colloquialisms, but also grammar and the pronunciation of words. To communicate pronunciation, the playwright will often spell words in the way his or her characters speak them—instead of how they are spelled. The language in *A March Wind* is an excellent display of dialect. The players are characterized brilliantly. We know exactly how each character sounds; and because of this, we are able to picture their appearance down to their clothing and their surroundings.

Alice Brown is so well-acquainted with her characters that each word from their mouths is consistent in communicating who they are. This is the secret behind good dialog.

> The reason good dialogue is seldom found in plays is merely that it is hard to write, for it requires not only a knowledge of what interests or excites, but such a feeling for character as brings misery to the dramatist's heart when his creations speak as they should not speak -- ashes to his mouth when they say things for the sake of saying them -- disgust when they are 'smart.'
>
> John Galsworthy, *Some Platitudes Concerning Drama*

A carefully crafted character will not misspeak. First, he is created; then what he should say is apparent to the playwright. A clever line is worthless if it would not be spoken by the character presented to the audience. The key to dialog does not lie in the writing of dialog but in fully knowing one's characters. As Henrik Ibsen once said, "Before I write down one word, I have to have the character in my mind through and through. I must penetrate into the last wrinkle of his soul."

6. The Principles of Playmaking

Brander Matthews [1852 –1929] was a full-time professor of dramatic literature at Columbia University. Through the late 19th and early 20th centuries, Matthews was considered to be a leading authority on drama. In his 1919 book, "The Principles of Playmaking," Matthews references four supposed rules of dramatic writing; he then discusses those rules in relation to well-written, and not-so-well-written, plays. The principles he mentions are: "Never keep a secret from the audience!" "Never try to fool the audience!" "Begin in the thick of the action, and quit when you are through!" and "Show everything that is important to the plot!" A fifth principle, cited in William Archer's *Play-making: A Manual of Craftsmanship* (which he dedicated to his close friend, Brander Matthews), can be added to this list: "No obstacle, no drama." The first and the second are closely related, and the fourth seems to speak for itself; we'll focus on the first, third, and fifth.

Never Keep a Secret from Your Audience!

The idea that by *surprising* an audience one might diminish the impact of drama seems completely backwards at first. Though it's not a hard and fast rule, and there are many occasions to break it, this prohibition against secret-keeping should be carefully considered when deciding which conversations and situations the audience should be allowed to witness. Which method will successfully attached the viewers to the protagonist? Which method, telling-all or keeping quiet, will push the audience to the edge of their seats?

As a warning *against* secret-keeping, Matthews retold a story that was shared with him by a friend. One evening Bronson Howard went to the theater to see *Henry Dunbar*, a play based on a novel of the same name. In the play, the protagonist is the daughter of an unfortunate man. She is told that Henry Dunbar has wronged her father and trapped him in a life of crime. Her father writes her to tell her that he is planning to find Henry Dunbar and settle the score between them. After the letter, the daughter doesn't hear from her father again, and she begins to worry about him. Deciding that he must have kidnapped her father, the daughter begins to search high and low for Henry Dunbar. On several occasions, she almost catches up with him, but somehow he evades her. In the end of the play, the daughter finally does find Mr. Dunbar; but as she approaches, she sees that the man living his life as Henry Dunbar is her own father. She realizes that her father has killed Henry Dunbar and assumed his identity.

Of course, as Bronson Howard told Matthews, the audience was shocked to learn the truth. They were shocked at the exact moment that the protagonist was shocked. Therein lies the problem. According to Matthews retelling of Bronson's "boring evening at the theater," the shock was cheap and to no real effect. Had the audience known what the daughter would find when she met Mr. Dunbar, they would have held their breath every time she came close to meeting him. As it was, the only emotion produced by the play's climax was short-lived and easily forgotten.

Matthews goes on to quote the eighteenth century German playwright, Gotthold Lessing, who once explained:

> Our surprise is greater if we do not know [a fact before the character] knows it. But what a poor amusement is this surprise! And why need the poet surprise us? He may surprise his characters as much as he likes; and we shall derive our pleasure therefrom, even if we have long foreseen what befalls them so unexpectedly. Nay, our sympathy will be the more vivid and the more vigorous, the longer and more certainly we have foreseen it...Let the characters knot the complication without knowing it; let it be impenetrable for them; let it bring them without their foreknowledge nearer and nearer to the untying. If the characters feel emotion, the spectators will yield to the same feelings.

"If the characters feel emotion, the spectators will yield to the same feelings." This sums up the basis for the anti-secret keeping rule—as well as the reasons for breaking it. If what is kept secret from the characters is not secret from the audience, the audience will wait in expectation of the characters' inevitable reaction. The spectators will sit breathless, heartbroken, amused...waiting for the hero to realize that missing piece of information which the audience already possesses. In what scenario might a playwright *withhold* information from the audience and still produce that same breathless anticipation?

Example:

Imagine a newlywed husband and wife. The husband's first wife died just a few short weeks before the newlywed couple met. The couple is extremely happy, and the husband is doting. The new wife has no reason to doubt the character of her husband until his first wife's brother accuses him of murder. There is no real evidence accusing the husband of murdering his first wife; still, doubt has been planted in the mind of his newlywed bride.

What would be the more effective approach for maintaining the audience's interest and holding them in suspense: keeping or revealing the husband's guilt or innocence? If the husband is innocent, it would create a great deal more suspicion to keep that fact from the audience and allow them to suffer along with the young wife. This would work well whether the play was written as a comedy or a tragedy. If the husband is guilty, however, that is another story. If the playwright hides his guilt, the audience will be shocked and horrified, along with his wife, to find out the terrible truth about a man they wanted to believe. But like Bronson noted when watching *Henry Dunbar*, that shock will be short-lived. If the playwright allows the audience to see his guilt beforehand, however, they will sit on the edge of their seats, worrying about the safety of the wife and praying she will uncover the truth before her life is in danger as well.

Read Act I from The *Three Daughters of M. Dupont* by Eugène Brieux (page 123). Based on the private, scheming conversations Brieux allows his audience to overhear, what kind of marriage do you think Julie and Antonin will have? What if Brieux had chosen to hide either Julie or Antonin's family's ulterior motives only to reveal them as a surprise later on? What affect would this have on the intensity of feeling you experience at the close of the first act?

_____

_____

_____

_____

_____

Begin in the Thick of the Action, and Quit When You Are Through!

When writing literature that is meant to be read, the author may include as many scenes and details as he or she sees fit. As long as the plot-line has sufficiently grabbed the reader, he will finish the book regardless of whether this can be accomplished in one sitting or in twenty. This is not an option when writing literature that is meant to be performed. An audience's attention-span is not limitless, and the action (from start to finish) must all take place within a much shorter period of time. This forces the playwright to determine which scenes move the drama along and which are less than essential to the plot.

Turn again to *A March Wind* (page 166). The play opens with Enoch's interest in a broken clock, and he proceeds to take the clock apart. This proves to be vital to the plot. Melia's nervous and insecure behavior is revealed as her uninvited cousin knocks on the door. She panics because her house is cluttered as a result of her husband's work. The play is written in one act, but the playwright manages to emotionally involve and upset her audience, not once, but twice. What seemed at first to be the climax turns out to merely be the catalyst for the climax. Once the misunderstanding has been realized, and the conclusion has been found, the play ends abruptly without a moment of slow or wasted dialog.

What do you see as the top three key moments in *A March Wind*?

1._____

_____

2._____

_____

3._____

_____

No Obstacle, No Drama

In "Play-Making: A Manual of Craftsmanship" Archer examines the prominent dramatic theories of his day, one of which belonged to another well-known critic, Ferdinand Brunetière. According to Brunetière:

> Drama is a representation of the will of man in conflict with the mysterious powers or natural forces which limit and belittle us; it is one of us thrown living upon the stage, there to struggle against fatality, against social law, against one of his fellow-mortals, against himself, if need be, against the ambitions, the interests, the prejudices, the folly, the malevolence of those who surround him.

In other words, Brunetière held to the "no obstacle, no drama" rule. Brunetière did not believe that a piece of literature could be referred to as *drama* without a necessary struggle. In his book, Archer nods to Brunetière in admitting that "[The no obstacle, no drama] theory has a certain practical usefulness, and may well be borne in mind." He asserts that "Many a play would have remained unwritten if the author had asked himself, 'Is there a sufficient obstacle between my characters and the realization of their will?'"

Archer goes on to critique James Bernard Fagan's *The Prayer of the Sword*, which Archer believes is sadly lacking a sufficient obstacle. In Fagan's play, the protagonist is a young man named Andrea who has been raised with the priesthood in mind. When Andrea falls in love with Ilaria, there is a perfect opportunity for suspenseful and emotionally charged struggle. However, before even meeting Ilaria, Andrea reveals that he has already decided against the priesthood. Archer notes, "There was no struggle in his soul between passion and duty; there was no struggle at all in his soul…wherefore the play, which a real obstacle might have converted into a tragedy, remained a sentimental romance—and is forgotten."

> The plain truth seems to be that conflict is *one* of the most dramatic elements in life, and that many dramas--perhaps most--do, as a matter of fact, turn upon strife of one sort or another. But it is clearly an error to make conflict indispensable to drama, and especially to insist--as do some of Brunetière's followers--that the conflict must be between will and will…What, then, is the essence of drama, if conflict be not it? What is the common quality of themes, scenes, and incidents, which we recognize as specifically dramatic? Perhaps we shall scarcely come nearer to a helpful definition than if we say that the essence of drama is *crisis*. A play is a more or less rapidly-developing crisis in destiny or circumstance, and a dramatic scene is a crisis within a crisis, clearly furthering the ultimate event.
>
> William Archer, *Play-Making: A Manual of Craftsmanship*

From what you have seen and read, what do you consider to be the primary essence of a play? Is it will versus will in conflict? Is it merely a crisis, large or small, humorous or serious, that must be overcome before the play's conclusion? Or is it something else? With these theories of Archer and Brunetière in mind, read the one-act plays, *His Return* (page 152) by Percival Wilde and, *Her Tongue* (page 103) by Henry Arthur Jones. What would Brunetière think of the plays? What do you think? Are they memorable despite a formidable obstacle, or are they "easily forgotten" as Archer said of *The Prayer of the Sword*? How would you describe each play's crisis?

Section C: Drama

Her Tongue

a play in one-act

Henry Arthur Jones [1851 – 1929]

CHARACTERS

MISS PATTY HANSLOPE, about thirty

MINNIE BRACE, her cousin

WALTER SCOBELL, a rich Argentine planter

FRED BRACY, Minnie's husband

WAITER

SCENE

Varley's Private Hotel, Southampton

TIME

The Present--a morning in Autumn

[Varley's Hotel, Southampton. A private sitting room furnished in an old-fashioned, rather dingy, comfortable way. A door at back to the right, leading into a passage. A fireplace, right, with fire burning. A large looking-glass over the fireplace. A large bay window all along left, giving a view of a garden, and beyond its wall shipping, masts, big steamer funnels, etc... Left center, toward the window, a large narrow table with a cloth.]

[Discover WAITER, showing in FRED and MINNIE BRACY.]

WAITER: How long should you require the sitting-room, sir?

FRED: (An ordinary Englishman, about thirty-five) Only for an hour or so. My friend is leaving by the Dunstaffnage--what time does she sail?

WAITER: At two o'clock. Will this room suit you, sir?

FRED: Yes; this will do. When my friend comes back, ask him to come here.

WAITER: Yes, sir. (Exit.)

FRED: (Laughing) Well, this is a pretty mad bit of business.

MINNIE: (A well-dressed Englishwoman, about thirty) Not at all! I saw Mr. Scobell was rather struck by Patty at the ball last week. It was lucky she was staying at Southsea and could get over so easily.

FRED: What's the good of bringing her over for an hour? They can't fix up an engagement in that time.

MINNIE: Why not? Mr. Scobell seems to know his own mind.

FRED: Oh, yes!

MINNIE: And he wants to get married.

FRED: Yes; but you're going ahead too fast, old girl.

MINNIE: There isn't much time to waste, is there? He has only another hour in England, and he isn't engaged yet. What did he really say in the smoking room last night?

FRED: Nothing much. Except that he wanted a wife out there, and he wished he'd had an opportunity of seeing more of Patty. And on the strength of that, you telegraph straight off to Patty to come here and meet him.

MINNIE: Naturally! Mr. Scobell will be a very rich man, and I wanted to give poor old Pat a chance.

FRED: She has muddled her love affairs terribly. You might just give Pat a friendly caution.

MINNIE: Her tongue? (FRED nods.) Yes, she does talk.

FRED: And never says anything! But look at her mother!

MINNIE: Oh, aunt's a downright horrid old bore!

FRED: And Patty's just as bad! Poor old Lorry!

MINNIE: Why poor old Lorry?

FRED: Fancy being out alone in the wilds of Argentina, and having nothing to listen to but Patty's tongue for four or five years. (Bursts into a roar of laughter.)

MINNIE: Hush!

[Enter at back, LAWRENCE SCOBELL, about thirty-five, rather heavy, thick-set, stolid, quiet, cautious.]

FRED: So you've turned up, Lorry?

SCOBELL: Yes, there's a mistake about my cabin; wrong number; they've turned another fellow in.

MINNIE: Perhaps you'll have to stay till the next boat.

SCOBELL: (Shakes his head) Can't!

MINNIE: Not even to meet my charming cousin, Patty, and get to know her better?

SCOBELL: (Shakes his head) I must be in Buenos Aires this day three weeks. Miss Hanslope is coming here?

MINNIE: (Taking out an opened telegram) Yes, I've just got her telegram. She says-- (reading): "Delighted to come over, will be at Varley's about twelve." She'll be here directly.

SCOBELL: In your telegram to her you didn't mention it was on my account?

MINNIE: No--at least I said you were sailing by the Dunstaffnage, and wished to say goodbye to her.

SCOBELL: You haven't committed me?

MINNIE: Oh no! But you are--a--interested in Patty?

SCOBELL: Yes, indeed!

MINNIE: And you hope to be--still further interested?

SCOBELL: Yes. I dread the terrible loneliness out there. Not a soul to speak to for weeks together!

MINNIE: Patty is splendid company--isn't she, Fred?

FRED: Delightful! You'll never have a dull moment, old boy.

MINNIE: She has refused three offers in the last six months.

FRED: And I know Bill Garriss is screwing up his pluck to ask her.

MINNIE: (Shakes her head) I'm afraid you don't stand much chance. Still you can but try.

SCOBELL: Thank you. If you will merely give me half an hour alone with Miss Hanslope--

[Enter WAITER.]

WAITER: Mr. Scobell?

SCOBELL: Yes.

WAITER: A clerk from the shipping office wishes to see you about your cabin, sir.

SCOBELL: I'll come to him. (Exit WAITER.) If Miss Hanslope comes, I shall be back in a few minutes. (Exit.)

FRED: Well, Patty can't say we haven't done our best for her!

MINNIE: If only she won't talk too much!

FRED: Yes, Pat's a good-looking girl; if she'd only hold her tongue, nobody would ever guess what a fool she is!

MINNIE: It was her terrible chatter that choked off George Moorcroft--he told me so himself.

FRED: Perhaps Lorry won't find her out--he'll only have half an hour. Let's hope he'll spend all the time in looking at her.

[PATTY'S voice is heard in the passage; a moment or two later the WAITER opens the door for her and stands back; she is heard coming along the passage speaking very rapidly.]

PATTY: (Off) Yes, Mr. and Mrs. Bracy. He's a little fair man with reddish hair and a sandy bristling moustache that he's always curling up at the end, like the German Emperor, and she's a tall dark woman with a Chinchilla muff, and a pointed nose something like my own.

[Sailing into the room, talking all the while. She is a handsome woman about 30, with a perpetual smile, and a perpetual stream of empty irrelevant talk, which flows on in a cackling but not unpleasant voice, and is constantly punctuated by an irritating, meaningless little laugh of three notes; the last note is the highest, so the laugh is never completed, but turns up unexpectedly in another part of the sentence. She has an air of joyous self-complacency, and never suspects herself of being an empty silly fool. She over-emphasizes nearly every word in a sentence, especially unimportant adjectives and adverbs.]

PATTY: (To WAITER) Now, why couldn't you show me in at first instead of making such a fuss about it? (WAITER is going--she continues speaking.) Oh! I've left a waterproof--please look after it.

[WAITER goes off and closes door after him. PATTY goes up, opens it and calls off.]

PATTY: Oh, and an umbrella. (Closes door.) Well, here you are, my dear! (Kissing MINNIE) I've been racing all over the hotel to find you! I do think Southampton is the most stupid place, and the waiters are absolutely the most stupid people under the sun! Well, dear, where is Mr. Scobell? Do you really think now that he is-- (silly little laugh) smitten? I couldn't quite understand your telegram, so I flew upstairs without any breakfast and dressed as quickly as I could. I hope I haven't overdone it-- (glancing at herself in the glass) --because I don't wish Mr. Scobell to think me a dressy, extravagant woman. At the same time I want to look my-- (silly little laugh) sweetest and best. Oh, Fred, how are you? How can Minnie let you wear such awful waistcoats? When I get a husband-- (silly little laugh) I shall take care to---- Where have I put that telegram? (Searching her pockets and a handbag) But you know I thought that night at the ball he was-- (silly little laugh) because he kept on looking at me in a-- (silly little laugh) Well, you know how men look when they really are-- (silly little laugh) Oh, here it is! (Producing the telegram, reading) "You have made a great impression (silly little laugh) on Mr. Scobell. He is most anxious to see you again. (silly little laugh) Meet us at Varley's Hotel, Southampton, early as possible. Your whole future at stake--most important you have an understanding with him before he sails." Do you know I think it was the dearest and sweetest thing in the world for you to spend all that money on a telegram-- (kisses her) --and when it's all settled (silly little laugh) I shall give you my diamond and pearl brooch as a little acknowledgment--darling. You know, the one with the large pearl for the body of the bee--it's my favorite brooch. And I shall work Fred a very handsome waistcoat myself instead of that awful thing he's wearing. And do you really think, eh? (silly little laugh) Mr. Scobell is really, really, really smitten?

MINNIE: We've all but fixed it up for you! You've only got to let him propose and accept him!

PATTY: Thank you, dear. Of course I shall accept him if he gives me the chance.

MINNIE: He's tremendously rich--in a few years he'll be a millionaire.

FRED: A multi-millionaire! You've only got to go out to Argentina for four or five years, Pat, and then come back to London and help him to spend it.

MINNIE: It will be your own fault if you don't bring it off this time!

PATTY: My dear! How can it be my fault when I've simply flown over here without any breakfast to see him? I wonder if I could have just a biscuit, and a glass of sherry?

FRED: Certainly.

PATTY: Not--it might make my nose red. My nose isn't red now, is it? (Glancing at herself in glass) It always gets a little red when I go without breakfast. (Looking at herself in the glass) I almost wish I'd put on my other hat--you know, the large one-- (Her present hat is enormous.) --but I thought it might get dusty--however if he is really-- (silly little laugh) I daresay it will do well enough (silly little laugh), and after all, it isn't what one wears as much as what one is in oneself that really matters--I think I'll take my hat off if you don't think it looks just a little too--too-- (Takes hat off) Yes, I really think that looks better--don't you? (Looking at herself in the glass) Do you know I think I shall hang back at first, and give him just a tiny, tiny little wee bit of a snubbing----

MINNIE: My dear Pat, there's no time for that.

FRED: Take my advice, Pat--come to business at once. The moment Lorry makes you an offer, or even a little before, down on him, and don't give him a chance of escape.

PATTY: Very well. I will. But I hope he won't think I'm throwing myself at him, because it isn't as if I hadn't got other chances. There's George Moorcroft only waiting for me to give him another chance--and I rather fancy Mr. Garriss is hoping I-- (Looking at herself in the glass) --I'm sure my nose is a little red.

FRED: Not a bit! Your nose is all right. It isn't your nose that will do the mischief.

PATTY: What then? What do you mean?

MINNIE: Now, Pat, don't get angry! George Moorcroft told me that the reason he hung back was---- Well, my dear, it was your tongue.

PATTY: My tongue?! My tongue?!! My tongue??!! The reason George Moorcroft holds back is because I've very plainly given him to understand that it's absolutely not the least possible use in the world his coming forward! George Moorcroft! Why, he has the vilest temper. George Moorcroft! (With a little snort)

FRED: Well, never mind George Moorcroft. Lorry Scobell will be here in a moment.

MINNIE: Yes! Now, Patty, for your own sake--take care!

PATTY: Take care of what?

MINNIE: Mr. Scobel is a very cold, quiet, reserved man.

PATTY: Then he'll naturally want somebody who is very gay and lively.

MINNIE: (Looking dubiously at FRED) I don't think Mr. Scobell will like--

PATTY: My dear Minnie, that shows how little you know about human nature. People are always attracted by their opposites. I'm very glad you've told me Mr. Scobell is cold and reserved, because now I know exactly how to manage him. I was going to be a little reserved and standoffish myself, but now, well, I shall be a little, just a little (silly little laugh) free and easy, so as to fit completely into his moods. Why are you two looking at each other like that? Do let me know how to manage my own love affairs. Really any one would think I'd never had (silly little laugh) a proposal before!

FRED: (Solemnly) I hope, Patty, you'll never stand in need of one again!

[SCOBELL enters at back with a steamship ticket in his hand.]

FRED: (To LORRY) Miss Hanslope has just arrived.

PATTY: (Shaking hands eagerly with SCOBELL) How d'ye do? It was so kind of you to wish to see me again. I had a croquet party at the Barringers'--they're really very nice people, and one meets such a lot of nice people there, but the moment I got Minnie's telegram I flew off, and--

FRED: (Has been making signs to PATTY to be quiet--he now bursts in upon her stream of talk) One moment, Patty--Minnie and I have a little shopping to do, and if you'll excuse us-- Lorry, old fellow, I'll order lunch for four, and I'll have it all ready to pop on the table the moment we come in. Come along, Minnie! We must make haste! (Exit.)

[MINNIE kisses PATTY, gives her a warning look and sign, and exits.]

[SCOBELL has gone up to the fireplace.]

PATTY: (Glances at him a moment) So you're really sailing for Argentina today?

SCOBELL: Yes.

PATTY: I've always wished to travel. Of course, we've done Switzerland and the Riviera till we're utterly sick of it. I loathe Switzerland! But I've always had a great desire to explore fresh countries, and camp out, and rough it a great deal, and perhaps do a little pig-sticking--that is if you wouldn't think it a little--just a tiny little bit (silly little laugh)unwomanly. I've such a horror of doing anything unwomanly. When I die I should like my epitaph to be "She never did anything unwomanly." Just that! No more! "She never did anything unwomanly." And perhaps you think pigsticking unwomanly?

SCOBELL: There is no pigsticking in Argentina.

PATTY: Isn't there? Then, of course, that settles the question. Where is Argentina?

SCOBELL: In South America.

PATTY: South America! How awfully interesting! I've always dreamed of South America since I was a schoolgirl, and read about Red Indians, and the Incas, and Pagodas, and the Conquest of Peru. I can't remember who it was that conquered Peru. (A pause.) Pere was conquered, wasn't it? (Pause.) Peru is in South America, isn't it?

SCOBELL: Yes. (She looks at him--a longish pause.)

PATTY: And so you really sail for Argentina this afternoon?

SCOBELL: Yes.

PATTY: I felt so flattered when I got Minnie's telegram to say that you remembered me. And we only met that one night at the ball! But how often one finds that even chance meetings like ours are charged with lifelong consequences, doesn't one?

SCOBELL: Yes.

PATTY: One sees a face in a crowd, or perhaps in a railway carriage, or one hears a distant note of music; or perhaps in the bustle and whirl of a London season a sense of the utter emptiness of things comes over one, and one longs to throw off all the trammels of civilization, and live just a sweet simple existence in some new country--haven't you ever felt like that?

SCOBELL: Not exactly.

[PATTY feels discouraged, and there is a long pause.]

PATTY: So you really must sail for Argentina this afternoon?

SCOBELL: Yes.

[Another long pause. PATTY looks at him and then goes towards table.]

PATTY: (In a colder, less eager voice) I really couldn't understand Minnie's telegram. She said something about your sailing, and you'd like an opportunity of seeing me. You did wish to see me?

SCOBELL: Yes. (Coming up to her) The fact is, I was very lonely out there, and last night at Fred's smoking-room I felt very down in the mouth at the thought of leaving England--and I thought-- (approaching her rather tenderly)

PATTY: Yes? (Approaching him a little)

SCOBEL: I felt-- (approaching her)

PATTY: Yes?

SCOBELL: I thought if I could persuade some nice girl--

PATTY: Yes?

SCOBELL: I dreaded being out there alone--

PATTY: How terrible for you! How absolutely awful! I think there's nothing more dreadful than that feeling of utter solitude and desolation that creeps over one when one is left alone for any long time. What do you do in Argentina?

SCOBELL: I'm developing a large tract of land, cutting it up into farms. I farm one large tract myself.

PATTY: What a perfectly sweet life! Three years ago we went for a month to a farmhouse in Wales, and I used to watch the girl milking the cows every evening. I asked her to let me try one evening, but she didn't understand a word of English, and the cow got rather troublesome, and when I patted her dear little calf she looked quite vicious, as if she was going to toss me. Not that I'm afraid of cows!--Or of anything! In fact I love danger of all kinds! I positively revel in danger! That's my one fault--if it is a fault. And there couldn't be a prettier dress to face dangers and hardships in than a Welse girl's. I wonder if it would be possible to get a Welsh dress in Southampton? No, there isn't time, is there?

SCOBELL: I'm afraid not. (He goes to the corner of table upstage.)

[During the following scene he gradually gets into window--she gradually follows him up, gets on the right side of table, which is on casters; she unconsciously pushes it toward the window until she has hemmed him in the lower bay of the window, with the table diagonally across from middle of window to the corner of the bay, so that he cannot escape. This is done very gradually and quite unconsciously.]

PATTY: (After a pause) What do the women generally wear in Argentina?

SCOBELL: I haven't noticed.

PATTY: But they must wear something! I do think it's so charming when the women of a country adopt some distinctive national costume, like the Tyrolese or the Welse. I believe that some of the Tyrolese women wear a dress that is--a--well, it's really a masculine dress. I couldn't do that! I loathe masculine women, don't you?

SCOBELL: Yes.

PATTY: I think that when once a woman goes out of her own proper sphere and tries to be a man--well, she doesn't succeed, does she?

SCOBELL: No.

PATTY: When a woman has so many attractions of her own, why should she go out of her own proper sphere and try to be a man? Why should she?

SCOBELL: I don't know.

PATTY: I think I shall introduce a national style of dress into Argentina. What are the shops like in Argentina?

SCOBELL: There aren't any shops where I live.

PATTY: No shops?

SCOBELL: It takes three weeks to get to the nearest town.

PATTY: Oh, how delightful! No shops! It must be quite the country.

SCOBELL: (Looking at the steamship ticket in his hand) They've made a mistake in the number of my cabin.

PATTY: Have they? How careless of them! I often ask myself how can people be so stupid? How do you account for there being so many stupid people in the world? (He has been fidgetting--a pause.) What's the climate of Argentina? Is it very hot?

SCOBELL: Rather--in the summer.

PATTY: And I suppose the winters are rather cold? I am so fond of the winter! I think there's nothing more delightful than to gather round the fire on a winter evening, while the logs are crackling on the hearth, and tell ghost stories. I know one or two awfully good ghost stories. Do you know at times I feel I must frighten people! I do! I can't help it! I feel positively wicked! I made a whole party sit up at the Vicar's the other night. The Bishop said I made him feel quite uncomfortable. The dear Bishop! It was too bad of me to frighten him, wasn't it?

SCOBELL: Yes.

PATTY: Are you fond of ghost stories?

SCOBELL: Not very.

PATTY: Then I shall tell you one. Not now--but one of these days I shall suddenly begin a creepy, creepy blood curdler that I reserve for my special friends; and before you expect it, I shall make you positively shudder all over! Positively shudder! Now, don't say I didn't warn you.

SCOBELL: I've got to change my ticket.

PATTY: But I don't know after all if I don't prefer the summer. The delightful long evenings! But really I can make myself happy and contented anywhere. Nothing ever puts me out. If things go wrong, I simply smile, and say all the pleasant things I can think of, and wait till everything comes all right again! (A longish pause.) We didn't settle what dresses I ought to get. And then, of course, there are mother's dresses to think of as well as my own.

SCOBELL: You have a mother?

PATTY: Yes, didn't I tell you? I must have forgotten it. How I wish you could have met her! But, of course, there will be plenty of opportunities, won't there? (Pause--he doesn't reply.) You will like her so much. (Pause.) Everybody says I'm exactly what she was when she was twenty-five. (SCOBELL is fidgetting and looking out of the window. By this time she has pushed the table against the window so that he is quite hemmed in at the lower bay of the window.) I must tell you mother is rather a gay old creature.

SCOBELL: Indeed!

PATTY: Yes. I rather pride myself on my good temper and my constant flow of animal spirits. (silly little laugh) Don't you think I have a rather good supply of animal spirits?

SCOBELL: Yes.

PATTY: I'm nowhere beside mother! She's simply wonderful! Always the life and soul of any company she's in. (Pause.) You've been rather dull and lonely out in Argentina, Fred tells me?

SCOBELL: Not very.

PATTY: Nobody could be dull and lonely for one moment where mother is. What amusements are there in Argentina?

SCOBELL: There aren't any amusements.

PATTY: No amusements?

SCOBELL: Not where I live.

PATTY: Mother is so fond of society, and seeing everything, and going everywhere, and knowing everybody.

SCOBELL: Argentina won't suit her at all.

PATTY: Oh, but of course, if I went to Argentina it would be impossible for me to leave my mother behind! I simply couldn't do it! She is such a dear! Always ready to make herself pleasant and agreeable wherever she is. And she has such a fund of anecdotes and recollections! And so witty and humorous! I love wit and humour in a woman, don't you?

SCOBELL: Yes.

PATTY: I'd far--oh far, rather a woman were witty and humorous than merely beautiful, wouldn't you? Because beauty itself soon fades, and when a woman has beauty and nothing else, well, it's like putting all the goods in the shop window, isn't it? And the moment she loses her good looks--poor creature! What is she? Just a mere bit of faded finery to be thrown aside. I don't wonder that men quickly tire of some women, do you?

SCOBELL: No.

PATTY: Nobody could tire of mother! And she's so ready at repartee--we had my Sunday school children to tea on our lawn, and we invited the new curate, and after tea he took the garden broom and was sweeping up the litter the children had made. "Ah!" my mother said, "new brooms sweep clean!" (SCOBELL doesn't laugh.) Just like that! Quite on the spur of the moment! "New brooms sweep clean!" (SCOBELL doesn't laugh, but stands quite still--an awkward pause. She explains rather sharply.) He was quite a new curate, and so she said "New brooms sweep clean." (A long pause.) You will like my mother. (SCOBELL has been showing signs of restlessness, and glancing out of the window at the ship's funnels. After a pause.) Is anything the matter?

SCOBELL: No. I really must see about my ticket. (Making a slight effort to push the table from the window.)

PATTY: Yes, but--you--haven't--er--a----

SCOBELL: (Taking out his watch) I'd better get across at once.

PATTY: But Minnie said you particularly wished to see me.

SCOBELL: (A little lamely) I thought I should like to have the pleasure of--of saying goodbye.

PATTY: Goodbye? But you sent for me to come from Southsea. I don't understand. Please explain.

SCOBELL: I was agreeably impressed the other night at the ball, and said so to Fred last night--and--in his smoking-room----

PATTY: Yes. Well?

SCOBELL: And on the strength of that Mrs. Bracy telegraphed----

PATTY: Yes, there's her telegram. (Producing the telegram, giving it to him) "Your whole future at stake--most important you have an understanding with him before he sails?" Read it!

SCOBELL: I'm afraid Mrs. Bracy has been indiscreet----

PATTY: Indiscreet! But you said yourself that you were agreeably impressed by me. (Pause. She speaks very sharply.) Did you or did you not say you were agreeably impressed by me?

SCOBELL: At the ball--yes.

PATTY: Yes. Well? And that you would like to see me? (SCOBELL does not reply. She speaks again very sharply.) Did you or did you not say you wished to see me?

SCOBELL: Yes.

PATTY: Yes. Well? Why did you wish to see me?

SCOBELL: (Lamely) I thought we might begin a disinterested friendship----

PATTY: (With a little shriek, getting more and more angry, nearly crying with vexation and losing control over herself.) Disinterested friendship! You couldn't suppose I should hurry over from Southsea for a disinterested friendship!

SCOBELL: I'm very sorry if I have caused you any inconvenience.

PATTY: Inconvenience! I haven't had any breakfast! And I had a most pressing invitation to the Barringers'. They're quite the nicest people in Southsea--one meets everybody there. Instead of that you bring me over here (taking up the telegram which he has put on the table) on the distinct understanding that you intended--I don't understand your conduct, Mr. Scobell. Will you please give me some explanation of it?

SCOBELL: (Making a gentle movement to push the table back so that he can get out.) I must be getting to my boat.

PATTY: Surely, Mr. Scobell, you will not dare to leave me in this terrible uncertainty. Before you go on board we must please have a thorough understanding. (Seats herself resolutely at table. Pause.) Will you or will you not please give me some explanation of your conduct?

SCOBELL: (Getting angry and desperate.) But my boat sails--will you kindly let me pass?

PATTY: Not that I wish to force myself upon you! Please don't think that. I could never stoop to make myself cheap to any man! I'm not driven to that necessity! No! No! A thousand times no! It's simply that my womanly pride and delicacy have been cruelly outraged. It's simply that I owe it to my sense of what is due to an English lady not to be dragged over from Southsea without any breakfast, and then made the sport of your caprice, while you sail off to Argentina, utterly oblivious of your honour, and of the woman you have entangled and deserted!

SCOBELL: Take it easy, my dear lady--take it easy!

PATTY: (Shriek.) My dear lady! My dear lady! You first inveigle me here and then you insult me. Oh, if I had known! Mr. Scobell, surely you will not be so ungentlemanly--so unmanly--but there will come a time when you will vainly remember how recklessly you threw away the happiness that is still within your grasp, if you only choose to pick it up.(Suddenly bursting out.) Oh! What have I said? What have I said? Oh! (With a long wail she bursts into tears, flings herself over the table and sobs.)

[SCOBELL, very uncomfortable, on the other side of the table, watches her with growing embarrassment.]

SCOBELL: My dear Miss Hanslope, I'm terribly sorry--

PATTY: (Wailing from the table.) If you're truly sorry, you can do no less, as a gentleman, than make amends.

SCOBELL: Will you please let me pass out?

PATTY: Then you're prepared to take the consequences?

SCOBELL: Certainly.

PATTY: Very well! Mr. Bracy will be here in a moment to deman a full explanation of your conduct.

SCOBELL: I'll write him about it. Meantime, my lawyers are Beame and Son, Gray's Inn Square. If you have any claim against me, please put your solicitors in communication with them. (Very decidedly) Now, may I pass?

PATTY: (Magnificently) No! How could you suppose that I could degrade myself by making a market of my most sacred feelings and bringing them into a Court of Law! No, the injuries you have done me cannot be paid by money--you have wounded my finest feelings! You have trampled upon--

[Enter MINNIE and FRED at back.]

FRED: Heigho! What's the matter?

PATTY: (Continuing her harangue to SCOBELL) Yes, I refuse you! In the first place our slight acquaintance gave you no right whatever to make me an offer of marriage! And I'm sure the more I knew of you the less I should be inclined to accept you!

FRED: What's the matter?

PATTY: (Losing her self-control, bursting into a fit of rage) I've never been so insulted in my life! (To MINNIE and FRED) How could you bring me over from Southsea only to be annoyed and insulted by this man?

FRED: Lorry! What has he done, Pat?

PATTY: He has called me the most insulting names!

FRED: What names? (Looking at SCOBELL)

PATTY: He said--he said--he said--"Take it easy, my dear lady!" My dear lady! I've never been addressed in such a manner before! Minnie, here is your telegram! Now I want you both to read that over carefully, and say whether it doesn't amount to an offer of marriage. And then before you allow him to sail for Argentina, I want you to ask him plainly whether he intends to carry out his promise, or--where is he?

[She has turned her back to SCOBELL to talk to MINNIE and FRED. Meanwhile SCOBELL has crept under the table and emerges from under it on all fours.]

FRED: (to SCOBELL) Lorry, we'd better clear this up, eh?

SCOBELL: (Getting up) I'll write you fully. Goodbye, old fellow.

FRED: (Embarrassed) You'll stay and have some lunch.

SCOBELL: Haven't a moment. I must catch this boat. Goodbye, Mrs. Bracy!

MINNIE: Goodbye? But can't you explain?

PATTY: (Shrieks out to FRED) You surely won't let him leave this room without an explanation?

SCOBELL: (Hurrying off) Take it easy, my dear lady! Take it easy! (Hurries off.)

FRED: You seem to have muddled it again, Pat!

PATTY: It was all your fault, and Minnie's for bringing me over! (WAITER enters with luncheon ready laid; puts it on table, pulls the table out from the window.) How could you suppose that I should go over to a wretched country like Argentina, where there aren't any shops--after all the really good offers I've refused! You might have had more consideration for me! And without a mouthful of breakfast!

FRED: Well, here's some lunch!

PATTY: And the Barringers sent me such a pressing invitation to their croquet party!(Looks at her watch.) I shall just have time to get back to Southsea. (Puts on her hat.)

MINNIE: You'd much better stay and have some lunch.

PATTY: No, I can get some sandwiches somewhere. I must go. They'll expect me. I mustn't disappoint them! (To WAITER) When does the next train start for Southsea? Come and get me a cab and a Bradshaw. At once! Please! Goodbye, Minnie! Goodbye, Fred! Your friend, Mr. Scobell, must be mad! (To WAITER) Please--a cab and some sandwiches and my waterproof and umbrella! And a Bradshaw! Where are my gloves? (Exit at back.) Is there anybody then who can get ma a cab and some biscuits?--I never was so insulted--and a Bradshaw--do you hear?--a cab and some biscuits and sandwiches!--or anything to eat! And my gloves! (Exit down passage.)

[FRED shrugs his shoulders, points to the lunch. MINNIE and FRED sit down to the table which the WAITER has pulled out into the room. PATTY'S voice is heard dying away along the passage.]

CURTAIN

The Three Daughters of M. Dupont

Eugène Brieux [1858 – 1932]

Translated by St. John Hankin

Abridged

ACT I

A very undistinguished room in a house in a French country town. The time is February. There is in the centre of the room a table, with chairs round it; a fireplace on the left, and window on the right; a piano; lamps; a bronze statuette of Gutenberg; holland covers on the furniture. There are doors to right and left and at the back.

Madame Dupont is discovered alone, darning stockings. Caroline enters and sits to read. After a moment or two Julie comes in.

JULIE: Here I am, maman [she kisses her]. You here, Caro [she does not kiss her]?

MME. DUPONT: Ah, Julie! Sit down, dear, and tell me what you have been doing and whom you have seen.

JULIE: I went to see Madame Leseigneur.

MME. DUPONT: I might have guessed that.

JULIE: Why?

MME. DUPONT: You only go to houses where there are children. And as Madame Leseigneur has six—

JULIE: I wish I were in her place. Only think: André, the youngest, you know, the one who is only six months old?

MME. DUPONT: Yes.

JULIE: He recognized me. There never was such a baby for taking notice.

MME. DUPONT: You talk as if you were a mother yourself.

JULIE: Jean laughed till he cried when he saw what I had brought him. Charles and Pierre were in disgrace because they'd been fighting. But I got their mother to forgive them, so that was all right. To-morrow I shall go to Madame Durand to hear how Jacques is going on. I hear he has the whooping-cough.

MME. DUPONT: [laughing] You ought to have been a nurse.

JULIE: [seriously] No, no. I should have died when I had to leave the first child I had nursed.

MME. DUPONT: Then you should marry.

JULIE: Yes. [Pause, with a sigh] Heigho! You don't know of a husband for me, do you, Caro?

CAROLINE: What sort of one do you want?

JULIE: [seriously] I am getting to the time of life when a woman accepts the first man who offers himself. Choose whatever sort you think best for me [laughing]. What would be your ideal? Someone in business? A captain in the army? Tell me.

CAROLINE: No.

JULIE: Why not?

CAROLINE: If I were to marry, I should choose a worker, a man with a noble aim, a man who would be ready to sacrifice himself to make life a little easier for those who will come after him.

MME. DUPONT: Oh, don't talk like a sentimental novel, Caroline.

CAROLINE: I was not.

MME. DUPONT: Well, I'm sure I've read that somewhere. Besides, at your age one doesn't speak of those things any longer.

JULIE: Talking of that, you know Henriette Longuet?

MME. DUPONT: Yes.

JULIE: She is going to be married.

MME. DUPONT: Indeed?

JULIE: Yes. [Thoughtfully] I'm the last to go. That finishes it!

MME. DUPONT: What do you mean?

JULIE: Nothing.

MME. DUPONT: Were you thinking of M. Jacquemin?

JULIE: How do I know? He has never said anything to me, of course, but I fancied he had noticed me. I didn't care much about him, but he was better than nothing. Better than nothing! [Sighs] It's a stupid sort of world for girls nowadays.

Dupont comes in.

DUPONT: [brimming over with excitement and importance] Ah! Here are the children. Run away, my dears, for a few minutes. I'll call you when I want you.

JULIE: [going with Caroline] Caroline! Do you think it is—?

CAROLINE: [thoughtfully] It does look like it.

They go out together.

MME. DUPONT: Well, what is it?

DUPONT: [with an air of importance] M. and Madame Mairaut will be here in an hour, at six o'clock.

MME. DUPONT: Yes?

DUPONT: [craftily] And do you know why they are coming?

MME. DUPONT: No.

DUPONT: To ask for Julie's hand in marriage. That's all!

MME. DUPONT: For their son?

DUPONT: Well, my dear, it's not for the Sultan of Turkey.

MME. DUPONT: M. Mairaut, the banker.

DUPONT: M. Mairaut, head of the Banque de l'Univers, 14 Rue des Trois-Chapeaux, second floor.

MME. DUPONT: Yes; but—

DUPONT: Now, now, don't excite yourself. Don't lose your head. The thing isn't done yet. Listen. For the last fortnight, at the Merchants' Club, Mairaut has been taking me aside and talking about Julie—asking me this, that, and the other. As you may suppose, I let him run on. To-day we were talking together about the difficulty of marrying one's children. 'I know something of that,' said he. 'So do I,' I said. Then he grinned at me and said: 'Supposing Madame Mairaut and I were to come in one of these days to discuss the question with you and Madame Dupont?' You may imagine my delight. I simply let myself go. But no, when I say I let myself go, I do myself an injustice. I kept a hand over myself all the time. 'One of these days. Next week, perhaps?' I said, carelessly, just like that. 'Why not to-day?' said he. 'As you please,' said I. 'Six o'clock?' 'Six o'clock.' What do you think of that?

MME. DUPONT: But M. Mairaut—the son, I mean—Monsieur—what is his Christian name?

DUPONT: Antonin, Antonin Mairaut.

MME. DUPONT: Antonin, of course. I was wondering. Is M. Antonin Mairaut quite the husband we should choose for Julie?

DUPONT: I know what you mean. His life isn't all that it should be. There's that woman—

MME. DUPONT: So people say.

DUPONT: But we needn't bother about that. There's another matter, however, that is worth considering—though, of course, you haven't thought of it. Women never do think of the really important things.

MME. DUPONT: You mean money? The Mairauts haven't any. They only keep a couple of clerks altogether in their bank. They may have to put up the shutters any day.

DUPONT: Yes: but there's someone else who may put his shutters up first. Antonin's uncle. The old buffer may die. And he has two hundred thousand francs, and never spends a penny.

MME. DUPONT: True. But—

DUPONT: But. But. There you go. You're determined never to see anything that is more than an inch before your nose. I don't blame you for it. Women are like that.

MME. DUPONT: But suppose he disinherits Antonin?

DUPONT: You forget I shall be there. I flatter myself I shall know how to prevent Uncle Maréchal from disinheriting his nephew. Besides, what is Uncle Maréchal?

MME. DUPONT: Antonin's uncle.

DUPONT: You don't understand. I ask you what he is. What is his position, I mean.

MME. DUPONT: He's head clerk at the Prefecture.

DUPONT: Exactly. And he could get me the contract for all the printing work at his office. Thirty thousand francs a year! How much profit does that mean?

MME. DUPONT: Five thousand francs.

DUPONT: Five thousand? Ten thousand! If one is only to make the ordinary trade profit, what's the good of Government contracts?

MME. DUPONT: I'm afraid young M. Mairaut's character—

DUPONT: His character! We know nothing about his character. He has one virtue which nothing can take away from him: he is his uncle's nephew. And his uncle can get me work that will bring in ten thousand francs a year, besides being as rich as Crœsus.

MME. DUPONT: Still, are you sure that he is the right sort of husband for Julie?

DUPONT: He is the right sort of husband for Julie, and the right sort of son-in-law for me.

MME. DUPONT: [dubiously] Well, you know more of these things than I do.

DUPONT: [looks at his watch] Ten minutes past five. Now listen to me. We have very little time, but I feel the ideas surging through my brain with extraordinary clearness. It's only in moments of emergency that I feel myself master of all my faculties, though I flatter myself I'm not altogether a fool at the worst of times. [He sits upon a chair, his hands leaning upon the back of it]. I will explain everything to you, so that you may make as few blunders as possible. We must get old Mairaut to agree that all the money, Julie's and Antonin's, shall be the joint property of them both.

MME. DUPONT: But there will be Julie's dot.

DUPONT: [pettishly] If you keep interrupting we shall never be done. The joint property of them both, on account of Uncle Maréchal's money. Do you understand?

MME. DUPONT: Yes.

DUPONT: That's a blessing. Well, then we shall ask for—

MME. DUPONT: No settlements. I understand.

DUPONT: On the contrary, we shall ask for the strictest settlements on both sides.

MME. DUPONT: But—

DUPONT: You are out of your depth. Better simply listen without trying to understand. [He rises, replaces his chair, and taps her knowingly on the shoulder]. In these cases one should never ask for the thing one wants. One must know how to get the other side to offer it, and be quite pleased to get it accepted. Well, then, I am giving Julie fifty thousand francs as her dot.

MME. DUPONT: Fifty thousand! But Julie has only twenty-five thousand.

DUPONT: That is so. I shall give her twenty-five thousand down and promise the rest for next year.

MME. DUPONT: You can't mean that. You will never be able to keep such a promise. [She rises].

DUPONT: Who knows? If I get the contract from the Prefecture.

MME. DUPONT: We ought to ask Julie what she thinks of this marriage.

DUPONT: We haven't much time, then. Still, call her: and take off these covers [pointing to the chairs].

MME. DUPONT: [she goes towards the door on the right; then returns] But have you thought—

DUPONT: I have thought of everything.

MME. DUPONT: Of everything? What about Angèle and her story?

DUPONT: [pompously] Angèle is no longer my daughter.

MME. DUPONT: Still, we shall have to tell them.

DUPONT: Naturally. Since they know it already.

MME. DUPONT: I am nearly sure it was she I met last time I was in Paris.

DUPONT: You were mistaken.

MME. DUPONT: I don't think so.

DUPONT: In any case, in acting as I did I was doing my duty. I can hold my head up and fear nothing. Call Julie. She will help you to put the room tidy. [Madame Dupont goes out].

DUPONT: [rubbing his hands] I think I've managed things pretty well this time! I think so!

Julie and Madame Dupont come in.

JULIE: Father, is it someone who wants to marry me?

DUPONT: It is. [To Madame Dupont, pointing to the chairs] Take off those covers. [To Julie] You know young M. Mairaut—M. Antonin Mairaut? [He sits down]. You have danced together several times.

JULIE: Yes.

DUPONT: What do you think of him?

JULIE: As a husband?

DUPONT: As a husband. Don't answer in a hurry. Take off that cover from the chair you are sitting on and give it to your mother.

JULIE: [obeying] Have his parents formally proposed for him?

MME. DUPONT: No. But if they should do so your father and I wish to know—

DUPONT: [to Madame Dupont, giving her the last chair cover, which he has taken off himself] Take all these away. [Madame Dupont goes out]. The formal offer has not been made, but it will be soon, in less than an hour.

JULIE: Is that why you are taking all this trouble? [She points to the chairs].

DUPONT: Precisely. We mustn't appear to be paupers or people without social position. [He seizes a bowl in which there are some visiting cards]. Very old, these cards. Very yellow. And the names, too, common rather. I must put that right. [To his wife, who returns] Go down to the printing office and ask Courthezon to give you some printed specimens of our new visiting cards at three francs—no, three francs fifty. And then put that Wagner opera on the piano which someone left to be bound. [Madame Dupont goes. To Julie] I have no desire to influence you, my dear.

JULIE: Still—

DUPONT: [going to the mantelpiece] Still what? Wait while I light the lamp [He strikes a match].

JULIE: Why, it's still quite light.

DUPONT: When one receives visitors one doesn't wait till it is dark.

MME. DUPONT: [coming in and bringing visiting cards and a piano score of an opera] Here are the cards and the music book.

DUPONT: Thanks. [He gives Caroline's hat to Madame Dupont] Take this thing away. And these stockings. Hide them somewhere. You don't want to appear to do your own darning, confound it! Julie, the box of cigars which M. Gueroult sent me when he was elected to the Chamber.

JULIE: [bringing a box] Here it is.

DUPONT: Give it me.

JULIE: You haven't begun it yet.

DUPONT: Wait. [He rummages in his pocket and takes out a knife, which he opens] We must show them that other people besides deputies smoke cigars at five sous. [He opens the box] Without being proud, one has one's dignity to keep up. There! [He takes a handful of cigars and gives them to his daughter] Put those in the drawer so that the box mayn't seem to have been opened on purpose for them. [He arranges the box on the table]. [To his daughter] He is twenty-eight. He is good looking and distinguished. He passed his law examination at Bordeaux. [He puts a fresh ribbon in his coat and looks at himself for a considerable time in the glass]. In a town where I was not known this would be as good as the Legion of Honour. [He turns round]. Well? Have you made up your mind?

JULIE: I should like more time to think it over.

DUPONT: You have still a quarter of an hour.

MME. DUPONT: She would like a few days, perhaps.

DUPONT: That's it. Shilly shally! We are to have the story of that great stupid Caroline over again, are we? No! Your sister, whom you see now an old maid, who will never be married, unless her aunt in Calcutta leaves her some money—your sister, too, had her chance one day. She hum'd and ha'd; she wanted to think it over. And you see the result. That's what thinking it over leads to. Here she is, still on my hands!

MME. DUPONT: You mustn't say that. She earns her own living.

DUPONT: She earns her own living, perhaps; but she remains on my hands all the same. By the way, we had better not say anything to the Mairauts about Caroline's working for money.

MME. DUPONT: They are sure to know.

DUPONT: Not they. What was I saying? Oh, yes. She remains on my hands all the same. And one old maid is quite enough in the family. Two would be intolerable. Remember, my child, you have no dot—at least, none worth mentioning. And as things go nowadays, when one has no dot, one mustn't be too particular.

JULIE: To marry nowadays, then, a girl has to buy her husband?

DUPONT: [shrugs] Well—

JULIE: And there's nothing but misery for girls who have no money.

DUPONT: It's not quite as bad as that. But obviously there is a better choice for those who have a good fortune.

JULIE: [bitterly] And the others must be content with damaged goods, much reduced in price!

DUPONT: There are exceptions, of course. But, as a rule, husbands are like anything else. If you want a good article, you must be prepared to pay for it.

MME. DUPONT: And, even so, one is often cheated.

DUPONT: Possibly. But M. Antonin Mairaut is a very eligible young man. No? If you are waiting for a royal prince, say so. Are you waiting for a prince? Answer me. Come, my child, this is an opportunity you may never see again: a young man, well brought up, with an uncle who is head clerk at the Prefecture and can double my profits by putting the contract for printing in my way, not to speak of other things. And you raise difficulties!

MME. DUPONT: Think, dear. You are four-and-twenty.

DUPONT: And you have had the astonishing good luck to captivate this young fellow—at a ball, it seems.

JULIE: I believe so. He wanted to kiss me in one of the passages. I had to put him in his place.

MME. DUPONT: You were quite right.

DUPONT: I don't say she wasn't—that is, if she didn't overdo it. In his case I'm sure it was only playfulness.

MME. DUPONT: Oh, of course.

JULIE: I only half like him, father.

DUPONT: Well, if you half like him, that's always something. Plenty of people marry without even that.

MME. DUPONT: You don't dislike him, do you, Julie?

JULIE: No.

DUPONT: [triumphantly] Well, then!

JULIE: That's hardly enough, is it?

DUPONT: Come, come, my dear, we must talk seriously. As a child you were full of romantic notions. Thank Heaven, I cured you of that weakness. You know well enough that unhappy marriages are, more often than not, love marriages.

JULIE: [unconvinced] I know, I know. Still, I want to have a husband who loves me.

DUPONT: But he does love you, doesn't he, since you've only just told us that he wanted to kiss you at a ball. You'll lead your husband by the nose, never fear.

JULIE: How do you know?

DUPONT: Never you mind. I know it. And now really we have had enough of this. You think that a whim of yours is to upset all my plans, prevent me from increasing my printing business and retiring next year, as we intended, your mother and I. You think we haven't—I haven't—worked enough, I suppose. You don't wish us to have a little rest before we die? You think I have not earned that rest, perhaps? Answer me! You think I have not earned it?

JULIE: Of course you have, father.

DUPONT: [mollified] Very well, then. Still, I don't want to make you uncomfortable. I don't press you for a definite answer to-day. All I ask is that you won't be obstinate, or refuse to let us present Antonin to you as a possible husband, if his parents make any advances. That is all. You will, then, talk with him, ask him questions. Naturally, you must get to know each other.

MME. DUPONT: Think carefully, my child.

DUPONT: Make up your mind whether you wish to follow the example of that great stupid Caroline.

MME. DUPONT: You are quite old enough to be married. [A pause].

DUPONT: Answer. Aren't you old enough to be married?

JULIE: Quite, father.

DUPONT: Have you any other offers?

MME. DUPONT: Have you any choice?

JULIE: No.

DUPONT: You see!

MME. DUPONT: You see!

DUPONT: Well, then, it's all settled. [He looks at his watch] And only just in time! M. Mairaut is punctuality itself. It's five minutes to six. In five minutes he will be here. [Julie is silent, gazing through the open window. The laughter of children is heard outside. To Madame Dupont, irritably] What's she looking out of that window for?

MME. DUPONT: It's Madame Brichot. She is just going in with her children.

JULIE: [to herself, with a smile of great sweetness, recalling a word which she has just caught while dreaming] Maman!

DUPONT: Well?

JULIE: I will do as you wish.

DUPONT: Ouf! Now go and change your dress.

JULIE: Change my dress?

MME. DUPONT: Of course. You will be supposed to know nothing; but you must be tidy.

JULIE: What am I to put on?

MME. DUPONT: [reflecting] Let me see. [A sudden inspiration] I know. Isn't there a dance at the Gontiers' to-night?

JULIE: But we said we wouldn't go.

MME. DUPONT: [rising, briskly] We are going all the same. Put on your ball dress.

JULIE: Before dinner? Is he marrying my clothes?

MME. DUPONT: No. But you look best in your ball dress. Do as I tell you, dear.

JULIE: Very well. [She goes out.]

DUPONT: Are you really going to this ball?

MME. DUPONT: Certainly not.

DUPONT: Well, then?

MME. DUPONT: M. Antonin is coming.

DUPONT: [understanding] And Julie looks far better when she is—you are quite right. [A bell rings]. There they are! Come into the next room, quick!

MME. DUPONT: Why?

DUPONT: We must keep them waiting a little. It creates an impression. [To the maid, who passes to go to open the door, in an undertone] Ask them to wait a moment.

MAID: Yes, monsieur.

DUPONT: Now, then. [He bustles Madame Dupont out of the room. After a moment M. and Madame Mairaut enter, followed by the maid. Their faces wear a genial smile, which freezes as soon as they see that the room is empty].

MAIRAUT: They are not here?

MAID: I will tell madame. [She goes out].

MME. MAIRAUT: Tell madame! [To her husband] They saw us coming.

MAIRAUT: You think so?

MME. MAIRAUT: Of course. Why was that lamp lighted? Not for an empty room, I imagine! I don't think much of their furniture. Very poor. Very poor. [Lifts up a piece of stuff from the back of an armchair] This chair has been re-covered.

MAIRAUT: [at the bowl with the visiting cards] They know some good people.

MME. MAIRAUT: Let me see. [She looks at the bowl]. Those cards were put there expressly for us not an hour ago.

MAIRAUT: Oh, come!

MME. MAIRAUT: Look! The top ones are all new. The underneath ones are quite yellow.

MAIRAUT: Because the underneath ones are older.

MME. MAIRAUT: Because the underneath ones have been left out ever since New Year's Day, while these are just printed. We must be careful. Above all things, don't you make a fool of yourself.

MAIRAUT: All right.

MME. MAIRAUT: Don't let them think you're set on this marriage.

MAIRAUT: I understand.

MME. MAIRAUT: Get them to offer that all moneys shall be held jointly.

MAIRAUT: Yes.

MME. MAIRAUT: And to work this, insist on separate settlements.

MAIRAUT: Yes.

MME. MAIRAUT: For the rest, do as you usually do. Say as little as possible.

MAIRAUT: But—

MME. MAIRAUT: You know well enough that's the only way you ever do succeed with things.

MAIRAUT: But there's something I want to say to you.

MME. MAIRAUT: Then it's sure to be something stupid. However, we have nothing better to do. Go on.

MAIRAUT: It's what I spoke to you about before. It's been worrying me a good deal. If the Duponts give us their daughter, who has probably a dot of twenty-five thousand francs—

MME. MAIRAUT: Twenty or twenty five thousand, I expect.

MAIRAUT: Well, if they give her to us, who have nothing but the bank, it must be because they don't know that Uncle Maréchal is ruined.

MME. MAIRAUT: Obviously. Nobody knows.

MAIRAUT: It isn't honest not to tell them.

MME. MAIRAUT: Why?

MAIRAUT: Surely, my dear—

MME. MAIRAUT: If you're going to tell them that, we may as well be off at once.

MAIRAUT: You see!

MME. MAIRAUT: I see that we ought to hold our tongues. Oh, yes: we ought. For if you have scruples about injuring the Duponts, I have scruples about injuring Uncle Maréchal.

MAIRAUT: What do you mean?

MME. MAIRAUT: We have no right to betray a secret. I'm sorry you shouldn't have seen that I am quite as particular as you are; only I put my duty to my family before my duty to strangers. If I am wrong, say so.

MAIRAUT: But if they ask us point blank?

MME. MAIRAUT: Then we must consult Uncle Maréchal, since he is the principal person concerned.

MAIRAUT: In spite of all you say it seems to me—[He hesitates. A pause].

MME. MAIRAUT: Well, my dear, which is it to be? If you want us to go, let us go. You are the master. I have never forgotten it. Shall we go?

MAIRAUT: [giving in, after a moment of painful indecision] Now that we are here, what would the Duponts think of us?

MME. MAIRAUT: And then we must remember that the eldest Dupont girl got into trouble and is now living a disreputable life in Paris. That will make them less difficult.

MAIRAUT: Hush!

Madame Dupont and Dupont enter the room. General greetings. 'How do you do, dear madame? How are you? How good of you to call! Sit down,' etc. All sit. Silence.

MME. MAIRAUT: My dear Madame Dupont, I will come straight to the point. The object of our visit is this. M. Mairaut and I think we have observed that mademoiselle, your daughter, has made an impression—how shall I put it? A certain impression on our son.

MAIRAUT: A certain impression. Yes.

MME. MAIRAUT: Antonin will join us here immediately, but of course we have said nothing to him about this.

DUPONT: Julie, of course, has not the least idea—

MME. DUPONT: She is dressing. We are going to the ball at the Gontiers' to-night, and the dear child asked if she might dress before dinner.

DUPONT: Not that she is vain.

MME. DUPONT: Not the least in the world.

DUPONT: [to his wife, in an off-hand tone] She makes her own dresses, doesn't she?

MME. DUPONT: Of course. In this house we don't know what it is to have a bill from the dressmaker.

DUPONT: Yet with all her other occupations she's an excellent musician.

MME. DUPONT: Quite excellent. She has a passion for really good music. She knows Wagner thoroughly.

MME. MAIRAUT: Wagner! Good heavens!

MME. DUPONT: To talk about, I mean.

MME. MAIRAUT: I know your daughter is charming.

MME. DUPONT: And good, too. You would never believe how responsive that poor child is to affection!

DUPONT: [to Mairaut, offering the box] Have a cigar?

MAIRAUT: No, thanks. I never smoke before dinner.

DUPONT: Take one, all the same. You can smoke it afterwards. They are my usual brand, but pretty fair.

MAIRAUT: [taking one] Thank you.

MME. MAIRAUT: If Antonin is not married already it is because his father and I wished him to find a wife who is worthy of him. The question of money, with us, is of secondary importance.

MME. DUPONT: And with us. I'm so glad we agree about that.

MME. MAIRAUT: Antonin might have made quite a number of good matches.

DUPONT: It is just the same with JULIE: In spite of that unfortunate affair in the family.

MAIRAUT: Yes, we know.

MME. MAIRAUT: Unfortunate affair? We have heard nothing of any unfortunate affair. What are you saying, my dear?

MAIRAUT: [mumbling confusedly] I was saying—nothing—I was saying—No, I wasn't saying anything.

MME. MAIRAUT: [to Madame Dupont] Then there has been some unfortunate affair in your family?

DUPONT: Yes. By my first marriage I had two daughters. One, that great fool of a Caroline whom you know.

MME. MAIRAUT: Quite well. She remains unmarried, does she not?

DUPONT: She prefers it. That's the only reason. The other was called Angèle. When she was seventeen she was guilty of an indiscretion which it became impossible to hide. I turned her out of my house. [Quite sincerely] I was deeply distressed at having to do it.

MME. DUPONT: For three days he refused to eat anything.

DUPONT: Yes, I was terribly distressed. But I knew my duty as a man of honor, and I did it.

MME. MAIRAUT: It was noble of you! [She shakes him warmly by the hand].

MAIRAUT: Since you were so fond of her, perhaps it would have been better to keep her with you.

MME. MAIRAUT: My dear, you are speaking without thinking. [To Dupont] And what has become of her?

DUPONT: [lying fluently] She's in India.

MME. DUPONT: In India?

DUPONT: [to Madame Dupont] Yes, with her aunt, a sister of my first wife's. I have had news of her from time to time. [To Madame Mairaut] Indirectly, of course.

MME. MAIRAUT: I repeat, M. Dupont, all this does you honor. [Thoughtfully] Still, some people might feel—However, I don't think this discovery need make us abandon our project at once. Not at once. [To Mairaut] What do you think, my dear?

MAIRAUT: I?

MME. MAIRAUT: You think, as I do, that we must take time to consider, do you not? [A pause]. Without any definite promise on either side, but merely in order to get rid of all money questions, which are most distasteful to me, will you allow me to ask you one question, M. Dupont?

DUPONT: Certainly, Madame MAIRAUT:

MME. MAIRAUT: Have you ever considered [she hesitates] what you would give your daughter?

DUPONT: Oh, yes—roughly, you know.

MAIRAUT: Just so.

MME. MAIRAUT: And the sum is—roughly?

DUPONT: Fifty thousand francs.

MME. MAIRAUT: Fifty thousand francs. [To her husband] You hear, dear, M. Dupont will give his daughter only fifty thousand francs.

MAIRAUT: Yes. [A pause].

MME. MAIRAUT: In cash, of course.

DUPONT: Twenty five thousand at once. Twenty five thousand in six months.

MME. MAIRAUT: [to Mairaut] You hear?

MAIRAUT: Yes.

MME. MAIRAUT: For practical purposes that is only twenty five thousand francs and a promise.

DUPONT: [with dignity] Twenty five thousand francs and my word.

MME. MAIRAUT: Precisely. That is what I said [looking at her husband]. Under these circumstances, we regret very much, but M. Mairaut must decline. It really is not enough.

DUPONT: How much are you giving M. Antonin?

MME. MAIRAUT: Not a sou! On that point we are quite decided and quite frank. As soon as he marries his father will take him into partnership, and his wife's dot will be the capital which he will put into the business.

MAIRAUT: That is the exact position.

MME. MAIRAUT: Antonin will have nothing except what may come to him after our death.

MME. DUPONT: And I am glad to think you are both in excellent health.

MME. MAIRAUT: [modestly] That is so.

MME. DUPONT: [meditatively]. Hasn't your son an uncle, by the way?

MME. MAIRAUT: Yes, madame.

MAIRAUT: Uncle Maréchal.

DUPONT: People say M. Maréchal has a great affection for M. Antonin.

MME. MAIRAUT: Yes.

MAIRAUT: Very great.

DUPONT: He is rich, too, people say.

MME. MAIRAUT: So they say.

MAIRAUT: However, we haven't taken him into account, have we?

MME. DUPONT: Still, M. Maréchal would naturally leave everything to his nephew.

Mairaut & MME. MAIRAUT: [together] Oh, certainly. We can promise that. He will leave him everything he has.

MME. DUPONT: M. Maréchal has considerable influence at the Prefecture, has he not?

MME. MAIRAUT: No doubt. But all this is really beside the mark. At twenty five thousand francs we could not—

DUPONT: I am sorry.

MME. MAIRAUT: We are sorry, too. [She rises, saying to her husband] Come, my dear, we must be taking our leave.

DUPONT: I might, perhaps, go to thirty thousand.

MME. MAIRAUT: I am afraid fifty thousand is the lowest.

DUPONT: Let us split the difference. Thirty thousand and my country house at St. Laurent.

MME. MAIRAUT: But it is flooded two months out of the twelve.

DUPONT: Flooded! Never.

MME. MAIRAUT: [to her husband] Well, my dear, what do you think?

MAIRAUT: Antonin is much attached to Mlle. Julie.

MME. MAIRAUT: Ah, yes, if it were not for that! [Seats herself] My poor boy! [She weeps].

MME. DUPONT: My poor little Julie! [She weeps].

MAIRAUT: [to Dupont] You must excuse her. After all, it is her son.

DUPONT: My dear sir, I quite understand.

MME. MAIRAUT: [wiping her eyes] And, of course, there would be the other twenty five thousand in six months.

MME. DUPONT: Of course.

MME. MAIRAUT: Have you any views as to settlements?

DUPONT: On that point I have very definite ideas.

MAIRAUT: So have I.

DUPONT: The money on each side must be strictly settled.

MAIRAUT: Strictly settled? [A silence of astonishment].

DUPONT: Yes.

MAIRAUT: His and hers?

DUPONT: Certainly. You agree?

MAIRAUT: Oh, yes, I agree, I agree. Unless you preferred—

DUPONT: That all moneys should be held jointly?

MAIRAUT: Perhaps that would be—

DUPONT: Perhaps so. There is something distasteful, I might almost say sordid, about strict settlements.

MAIRAUT: That's it. Something sordid.

DUPONT: They imply a certain distrust.

MAIRAUT: Yes, don't they? Well, that's agreed, then?

DUPONT: Quite. The moneys to be held jointly. All moneys, that is, that may come to them in the future. The first twenty-five thousand, of course, will be settled on JULIE: They will form the dot.

MME. MAIRAUT: The second twenty-five thousand, which you will pay over in six months, to be held jointly.

DUPONT: Yes. We will draw up a little agreement.

MAIRAUT: Quite so.

Antonin Mairaut comes in. He is a handsome youth of twenty-eight, very correct in manner. Greetings are exchanged.

MME. MAIRAUT: Antonin. [To Dupont and Madame Dupont] You allow me?

MME. DUPONT: By all means.

MME. MAIRAUT: [She draws Antonin aside and says to him in a low voice] It's settled.

ANTONIN: How much?

MME. MAIRAUT: Thirty thousand, the house, and twenty five thousand in six months.

ANTONIN: Good.

MME. MAIRAUT: Now you've only the girl to deal with.

ANTONIN: Is she romantic or matter of fact? I don't quite know.

MME. MAIRAUT: Romantic. Raves about Wagner.

ANTONIN: Good heavens!

MME. MAIRAUT: So I said. But once she's married and has children to look after—

ANTONIN: Children! Don't go too fast. Children come pretty expensive nowadays. Troublesome, too.

MME. MAIRAUT: Never mind. Don't cross her now. Later on, of course, you'll be master.

ANTONIN: I rather think so.

MME. MAIRAUT: [returning to Madame Dupont] My dear madame—

MME. DUPONT: Yes?

MME. MAIRAUT: He is afraid he may not please Mlle. JULIE:

DUPONT: Absurd!

MME. MAIRAUT: The amount of the dot, too—

DUPONT: It is my last word. [To his wife] But what is Julie about? [He rings].

MME. DUPONT: [rises] I will go and find her.

A maid enters.

DUPONT: Wait! [To the maid] Ask Mlle. Julie to come here if she is ready.

The maid goes out.

ANTONIN: I must tell you, monsieur and madame, how flattered I am to find that the preliminaries have been settled between you and my parents on this important question. I do not know what will be the issue, but—

MME. DUPONT: It is we, monsieur, who are flattered. But you'll see Julie in a moment. Of course she knows nothing.

MME. MAIRAUT: We might leave them to talk a little together, perhaps?

MME. DUPONT: By all means. We are going to the ball at the Gontiers'. She asked to be allowed—Here she is. [Julie comes in. Madame Mairaut advances to meet her] There is a crease in your dress, dear. [She takes her apart, saying to the Mairauts] Will you excuse me?

JULIE: [in a low tone] Well?

MME. DUPONT: It rests entirely with you. We are going to leave you to talk together. Remember, it may be your last chance. Don't throw it away.

JULIE: I have thought it over and I don't intend to do as Caroline did. So if, after we have had a talk—

MME. DUPONT: You'll have to manage him a little. He has a great eye for business. If you could make him think you would be useful in the bank.

JULIE: But I hate figures.

MME. DUPONT: Once married you will do as you please.

JULIE: They can see you whispering. Go to them. [Madame Dupont goes back to Madame Mairaut].

MME. MAIRAUT: What did she say?

MME. DUPONT: She has not the least suspicion at present.

MME. MAIRAUT: Let us leave them together. [Aloud] My dear M. Dupont, I have long wished to go over a printing office. May we?

DUPONT: [delighted] If you will kindly come this way.

MAIRAUT: Thank you.

MME. MAIRAUT: But there really are too many of us. [Carelessly] The children might stay here, don't you think, madame?

MME. DUPONT: By all means.

They go out.

ANTONIN: [looking at the music on the piano] You are fond of Wagner, mademoiselle.

JULIE: I adore him.

ANTONIN: So do I.

JULIE: What a genius he is.

ANTONIN: Wonderful.

JULIE: For me he is the only composer.

ANTONIN: The greatest, certainly.

JULIE: No: the only one.

ANTONIN: Perhaps so. How nice it is we should have the same tastes in art! [Pause] Er—they have told you nothing, I understand?

JULIE: About what?

ANTONIN: Your parents, I mean. Mine have said nothing either.

JULIE: They have said nothing, of course, but I guessed.

ANTONIN: So did I. Then I may consider myself engaged to you?

JULIE: Oh, not yet. We must know each other better first.

ANTONIN: We have often danced together.

JULIE: Yes. But that's hardly enough.

ANTONIN: It's enough for me. Ever since the first time I saw you at the ball at the Prefecture.

JULIE: No. It was at the band, one Sunday, that your mother first introduced you to me.

ANTONIN: Was it? I forgot.

JULIE: I should like to know more about you. Will you—will you let me ask you some questions? It is not usual, perhaps, but—

ANTONIN: Certainly. Pray ask them.

JULIE: Are you fond of children?

ANTONIN: Passionately.

JULIE: Really and truly?

ANTONIN: Really and truly.

JULIE: I am quite crazy about them. For me children mean happiness. They are the one thing worth living for [wistfully]. But I think I have a higher idea of marriage than most girls. I want to have my mind satisfied as well as my heart.

ANTONIN: So do I.

JULIE: A marriage that is a mere business partnership seems to me horrible.

ANTONIN: Horrible! That's just the word.

JULIE: And tell me, are you very fond of society?

ANTONIN: Not particularly. Are you?

JULIE: No.

ANTONIN: I am delighted to hear it. The fact is I am sick to death of parties and balls. Still, if it were necessary for business reasons: if it would help to get business for the bank, you wouldn't mind?

JULIE: Of course not. What kind of business do you do at your bank?

ANTONIN: Oh, the usual kind.

JULIE: I have often read what is put up on the wall, Current Accounts, Bourse Quotations.

ANTONIN: Coupons cashed.

JULIE: That must be very interesting.

ANTONIN: Would you take an interest in all that?

JULIE: Of course. When I was little my father used to make me help him with his books.

ANTONIN: But now?

JULIE: Now, unfortunately, he has a clerk. I am sorry.

ANTONIN: Do you know that you are charming?

JULIE: So you told me once before.

ANTONIN: Yes: at that ball. You had on a dress just like this one. You are beautiful. Beautiful. [He seizes her hand].

JULIE: [a little troubled] Please.

ANTONIN: Come. We are engaged, as good as married. Give me one kiss.

JULIE: No. No.

ANTONIN: Won't you?

JULIE: [frightened] No, I tell you.

The Mairauts and Duponts come in again.

DUPONT: And when I have the contract from the Prefecture I shall double my business.

MAIRAUT: Excellent. Excellent.

MME. MAIRAUT: We must be going, dear madame. We have stayed far too long already. Are you coming, Antonin?

ANTONIN: [to Julie, aloud, bowing profoundly] Mademoiselle. [In a low voice] My beloved Julie. [To his mother] She's charming. I was charming, too, by the way. Wagner, children, every kind of romantic idiocy. And she believed me. [Aloud to Dupont] M. and Madame Dupont, my parents will have the honor of calling upon you to-morrow to ask on my behalf for the hand of Mlle. JULIE:

DUPONT: Till to-morrow, then. Till to-morrow. [To Antonin] All sorts of messages to your uncle, if you see him.

ANTONIN: I shall not fail. [He bows. The Mairauts take their leave].

DUPONT: [to Julie] That's all right, then?

JULIE: Yes. I really do like him. I think I managed him pretty well too. Wagner. The bank. He thinks I've a perfect passion for banking.

DUPONT: [laughing] Good. You're my own daughter. Kiss me. And your father? He managed pretty well, I think. I have arranged that all moneys except your dot shall be held by you both jointly; so that if you are divorced, or if you die after Uncle Maréchal, your dot will come back to us, and half whatever he leaves. I call that a good day's work. And at dessert we'll drink a bottle of the best to the health of Madame Antonin Mairaut.

MME. DUPONT: [embracing her] My poor little daughter.

DUPONT: Poor, indeed! She's a very lucky girl. I wonder where that great stupid Caroline has got to. [He calls] Caroline. She is never here when one wants her. [He calls again] Caroline. [Caroline appears] Here she is. Great news. Your sister is engaged to be married.

CAROLINE: JULIE: Is it true?

JULIE: Yes.

CAROLINE: Ah!

DUPONT: Is that all you have to say?

CAROLINE: I am very glad, very glad. [She bursts into tears].

DUPONT: [astonished] What's wrong with her? Crying! And she's not even asked who he is. She's to marry M. Antonin Mairaut, nephew of M. Maréchal.

MME. DUPONT: Don't cry like that, my dear.

JULIE: CAROLINE:

CAROLINE: [trying to restrain her sobs] Don't mind me. It is only because I love you, dear. Now you at least will be happy.

JULIE: [musing] Yes.

DUPONT: [to himself] The moral of all this is that that little affair of Angèle's is costing me an extra five thousand francs and my house at St. Laurent.

His Return

a play in one-act

Percival Wilde [1887-1953]

[The nicely furnished boudoir in Mrs. Hartley's home in a small Northwestern town. There are three doors. The central one leads into the hall; that on the right into the interior of the house; that on the left into a bathroom. There is the furniture one would expect; a dressing table, a chaise-lounge, two or three dainty chairs, and a pier-glass at one side. On the dressing table are two large framed photographs.]

[At the rise of the curtain the stage is empty. There is a pause. Then there enters John Hartley, a man of thirty-five or forty, dressed in a Canadian uniform.]

[He is very much excited. He is returning home after an absence of years. He enters as if he expects to find his wife here. She is not. He is disappointed, but he takes visible pleasure in going about the room, identifying the many familiar objects which it contains. He stops *abruptly at the sight of two portraits on his wife's dressing table, one of him, one of her. He takes up her picture, deeply affected, and kisses it.]*

[There is a pause. Then he hears steps coming, and straightens up expectantly.]

[The maid enters.]

THE MAID: *[looking at him in surprise]* How--how did you get in here?

HARTLEY: *[smiling]* Why, I walked upstairs.

THE MAID: Yes, yes, I know that. But how did you get into the house? I didn't hear the bell ring.

HARTLEY: I opened the door. *[As she looks her surprise, he shows a latchkey.]* With this.

THE MAID: *[with sudden comprehension]* O-oh! Then you--you're the master! *[Hartley nods and smiles.]* You're Captain Hartley! I'm so glad to see you! Why, I've heard all about you, and your medals, and being wounded, for three years! *[Timidly.]* Might I--might I shake hands with you, Captain?

HARTLEY: Why, of course!

[He shakes hands.]

THE MAID: *[rubbing her hand delightedly]* I never thought that I'd shake hands with a real hero!

HARTLEY: Hero? Bosh! They're *all* heroes over there! I'm just unlucky--wounded--sent home.

THE MAID: Nevertheless, the town's mighty proud of you!

HARTLEY: Shucks! I don't care about the town! Tell me: how is *she?*

THE MAID: The missis?

[He nods eagerly. The maid starts abruptly, aghast.]

HARTLEY: *[frightened]* What is it? What's wrong?

THE MAID: She doesn't expect you until five o'clock!

HARTLEY: *[laughing]* I took an earlier train.

THE MAID: *[dismayed]* But why did you do that?

HARTLEY: Why? Is it so difficult to understand?

THE MAID: It was wrong.

HARTLEY: Wrong?

THE MAID: Don't you see? She wants to be dressed: to look her nicest, to receive you.

HARTLEY: *[laughing]* Well, what of that?

THE MAID: She'd be simply heartbroken if she knew that you'd gotten here, and she wasn't ready! You see, it's--it's something very special.

HARTLEY: *[beginning to understand]* Oh, something very special?

[The door downstairs is heard to close.]

THE MAID: Here she is now!

HARTLEY: *[delighted]* Oh!

THE MAID: You won't spoil her pleasure?

HARTLEY: [sincerely] God forbid! [He goes to the right-hand door.] Remember--half an hour upstairs will seem almost as long as three years over there!

[He goes out. The maid waits until she hears approaching footsteps. Then she, too, goes. There is a pause. Then Helen Hartley enters in a street dress.]

HELEN: [turning, and calling to a person following her] Come right in, Sylvia.

[Sylvia enters. She is a pretty, brainless, young girl.]

SYLVIA: Mrs. Hartley--

HELEN: [correcting her] Helen.

SYLVIA: Helen dear, will you do me a favor?

HELEN: [smiling] Who's the man?

SYLVIA: Your husband.

HELEN: What?

[She takes off her hat.]

SYLVIA: May I stay here--till he comes?

HELEN: [shaking her head gently] No, dear.

SYLVIA: I'm simply dying to meet him!

HELEN: Do you want me to tell you a secret? So am I! [As Sylvia pouts.] I haven't seen him in three years.

SYLVIA: I've never seen him at all!

HELEN: *[simply]* I'm his wife.... Child, child, when you've been married as long as I have, you will understand--if--if you and the lucky man who gets you love each other as dearly as-- well, as *we* do!

[She takes up Hartley's photograph.]

SYLVIA: Oh, but we will!

HELEN: *[smiling]* That's right! Be happy! Be as happy as I have been! *[She pauses.]* There are moments in life that are like no other moments. There was one in my life when he asked me a question, and I said yes; and there was another when we knelt together in church; and there was another, but that wasn't so pleasant, when I waved goodbye to him from the station platform, when he joined the Canadians three years ago-- *[She pauses.]* And there will be a wonderful moment, a moment for which I have been living ever since, when he comes home to me. *[Kindly.]* Don't you see? There mustn't be any third person here? Just he--and I!

SYLVIA: *[contritely]* I'm so sorry, Mrs. Hartley.

HELEN: *[with an abrupt change of manner]* Now, now! Don't call me Mrs. Hartley! It makes me feel so old! Ugh!

SYLVIA: *[smiling and kissing her]* Helen, dear!

HELEN: And don't be so respectful! I don't like it when young girls are so respectful to me; treat me just as they would their mothers! I'm not old! I'm only thir--I'm only-- *[She breaks off.]* Well, it's nobody's business how old I am, is it?

SYLVIA: Of course not!

HELEN: *[slowly]* Not that there's any secret about it.... *[She smiles at Sylvia.]* But what I wouldn't give to be your age again! *[Tapping Sylvia's cheek.]* It didn't take paint to put *that* color on, did it?

SYLVIA: *[embarrassed]* Oh, Mrs. Hartley!

HELEN: *[resignedly]* There you go again: Mrs. Hartley! *[Sighing.]* I suppose it's the right thing, anyhow, isn't it?

SYLVIA: You old darling! *[Helen winces at the word. Sylvia picks up her wraps.]* You want me to go now, don't you?

HELEN: *[looking at her shrewdly]* Would you like to help me dress?

SYLVIA: *Would I?*

HELEN: Then I'll read you his last letter! *[She rings for the maid.]*

SYLVIA: From over there?

HELEN: *[shaking her head]* No; written the moment he landed here--to let me know when he'd arrive.

[The maid enters.]

THE MAID: Yes, ma'am?

HELEN: Bring me the dress. You know which one?

THE MAID: *[smiling]* I know, Mrs. Hartley.

[She goes to the clothes closet.]

HELEN: *[turning to Sylvia]* The same dress I wore the day I said goodbye to him at the train!

SYLVIA: What a charming idea!

HELEN: *[producing a letter]* His letter suggested it. Listen: "My own dearest girl--" *[She reads to herself: looks up.]* No, I can't read the beginning. *[She reads a little further silently.]* No, I really can't. *[She goes ahead.]* Ah! Here's something!

SYLVIA: *[with eager anticipation]* Yes?

HELEN: *[reading]* "The weather on the trip home was lovely."

SYLVIA: How intensely exciting!

HELEN: It's not very satisfactory, is it? *[By this time the maid has changed her shoes. She indicates them.]* The same shoes I wore that day! *[She reverts to the letter.]* Ah!

SYLVIA: Yes?

HELEN: *[after an instant's hesitation]* I'm going to read this to you. Some day you may get letters like it. *[She reads.]* "Do you know what image has been in my mind every minute for the last three years? Do you know what picture was before my eyes as I lay in that shell hole, wounded, expecting every instant to be my last? It was your face, dear, as the train pulled out of the station, your face, dear, and your smile, your smile put on to encourage me, for God knows there was no smile in my heart--that day. Every detail is as distinct as if you stood before me as I write--the little dress you wore: it was always my favorite-- *[She indicates the dress in the maid's hands.]* --the hat: the one of the kind that came down over the side of your face-- *[She indicates it.]* Do you remember how it was in the way when--" *[She drops her voice so that it is inaudible, and continues.]*

SYLVIA: What was that last, Helen?

HELEN: "Every detail; yes, every detail--"

SYLVIA: But the hat? What did he say about the hat?

HELEN: [Rises. By this time the maid has unhooked her dress.] This is the hat. Don't you like it? [She thrusts it into Sylvia's hands, and changes quickly into the second dress.]

SYLVIA: [putting down the hat, and looking at the dress] Do you know, I used to have a dress something like that? [She watches the maid attempt to hook it up.] That's not the way to do it! Mayn't I hook you up, Helen?

HELEN: If you'd like to.

[She nods to the maid, who goes out.]

SYLVIA: [taking the maid's place] I'll feel that I had some share in preparing for him!

HELEN: [dreamily] His favorite dress!

SYLVIA: [working very hard: panting] Mrs. Hartley!

HELEN: Well?

SYLVIA: I believe -- I believe -- you've grown stout!

HELEN: What?

SYLVIA: I can't close more than half of the hooks!

HELEN: [horrified] I never thought of trying it on until today! [She hurries to the pier glass, followed by Sylvia. She looks: then, in horror.] Oh-h!

SYLVIA: [laughing] What?

HELEN: Oh! Oh!

SYLVIA: Helen! Just because you've gotten stout?

HELEN: It's not that! Oh, no! It's not that! It's because I've gotten old! Come here: stand beside me: look at yourself next to me! Do you see?... It's come! It's come! I always knew it *would* come--not gradually, so that I wouldn't know it, but all of a sudden, without a moment's notice--all at once! It was only three years ago that I said goodbye to him, and I wore this dress. I was a young wife. Today he's coming home to find me an old woman!

SYLVIA: *[frightened]* Why, Mrs. Hartley, that dress looks very becoming!

HELEN: It would--on you. Don't lie to me, please! I've lied to myself enough! I've painted and powdered and dined and danced with the youngest of them! But it had to come to an end. I knew it had to come to an end. But I hoped--*how* I hoped that it would not come to an end before today!

SYLVIA: Helen, dear -- why -- why --

HELEN: You can't say anything. There's nothing anybody can say. *I* used to say to myself that he'd find me as young, as beautiful, as the day I waved goodbye to him at the station. Now--now I know that will never be. *[With horror.]* He'll come home to find an old woman sitting opposite him at his own table! *[She weeps.]*

SYLVIA: *[nervously, after a pause]* Helen dear, you can't be over--

HELEN: *[interrupting]* I can't be--but I am. They always are "over!" *[She pauses.]* You know, it's not that I care what other people think: I don't give *that* for their opinions! He's the only one that counts. He used to love my youth; my freshness--and now, if he wants youth and freshness, he'll have to go somewhere else to get it!... *[She shakes her head bitterly.]* Jealous? I have always hated jealous women! But today I understand: today I too am jealous, jealous!

SYLVIA: Mrs. Hartley!

HELEN: *[coming to a hysterical calm]* I don't mean you, child. Of course not! You'll pardon me, won't you? Just the excitement--the excitement of knowing that he was coming home. *[She has led the way to the door.]* You will go now, Sylvia?

SYLVIA: I'm so sorry, Mrs. Hartley!

[She goes.]

HELEN: *[closing the door after her]* So sorry! So sorry!

[She laughs bitterly; walks to the dressing table; takes up the letter: reads it over again with obviously tragic feelings.]

THE MAID: *[entering]* Ma'am!

HELEN: *[wearily]* Yes?

THE MAID: He's come!

HELEN: *[taken aback]* What?

THE MAID: He's just come in!

HELEN: *[An instant of indecision. Her first impulse is to rush to the door.]* Tell him to wait!

THE MAID: *[astonished]* To wait?

HELEN: You heard what I said? And come back when you've told him.

[The maid goes. Even before she has crossed the threshold, Helen has torn off the dress, and flung a wrap around her shoulders. She rushes to the table, sits down, and begins rubbing off her paint madly. The maid returns.]

HELEN: Bring me my black and gold!

THE MAID: *[astonished]* Your black and gold?

HELEN: And quickly!

THE MAID: Yes, Ma'am.

[She hurries to the closet, and takes out a third gown.]

HELEN: Put me into it.

THE MAID: But I thought -- but I thought --

HELEN: *[hysterically]* That I was going to wear the other one? How absurd! What on earth made you think that? *[The maid stares at her, simply dumbfounded.]* Never mind. I'm so excited that I don't quite know what I'm saying. You can wear the other dress, can't you?

THE MAID: *[incredulously]* The blue and white?

HELEN: Yes.

THE MAID: Yes'm. I can wear it.

HELEN: Then take it. It's yours.

THE MAID: Oh, thank you, ma'am.

HELEN: Now--I'm ready. Show him in.

[The maid goes off with the dress. Immediately she is out of sight. Helen rushes off through the left-hand door. There is a pause. Then Hartley enters softly.]

HARTLEY: Helen! Helen dear! *[He advances into the room.]* Where are you? Where are you, dear?

[Helen returns. She has finished removing every vestige of paint and powder from her face. She has suddenly become herself--a beautiful woman.]

HARTLEY: Helen! *[They rush into an embrace.]* Isn't it wonderful to be home again?

HELEN: John!

HARTLEY: To walk the streets of my own town! To stand under the roof of my own house!

HELEN: Is that all, John?

HARTLEY: *[shaking his head with a smile]* No; that isn't all.

HELEN: Say it, John! Say it!

HARTLEY: To feel your arms around my neck! To feel your lips pressing mine! *[He kisses her.]* Do you realize what I've been through for three years?

HELEN: We'll try to forget that.

HARTLEY: We'll try! *[He holds her off at arm's length.]* And now!

HELEN: Now!

HARTLEY: Let me look at you!

HELEN: *[in a strained voice, after a little pause]* Well?

HARTLEY: *[surprised at her tone]* What is it?

HELEN: *[excitedly]* Tell me what I know already! Let me say it for you! That I've grown old, old, old! *[He tries to interrupt. She continues without a break.]* You are not the only one who suffered these three years! I suffered! God knows how I suffered! For any reason--for no reason--when your letters didn't come--when the newspapers told of heavy fighting--when I stayed awake all night, worrying my soul out, I suffered, I suffered too!

HARTLEY: My dear!

HELEN: Let me finish! These wrinkles -- do you see them? These lines -- they were not here three years ago -- do you know why I have them? They are for you, you, you! It's not the men alone who go through hell! It's the women they leave behind them!

HARTLEY: *[taking her in his arms violently]* My dear, dear girl! How I should love every wrinkle in your face--if there were any! Only there aren't!

HELEN: John!

HARTLEY: You old? That is what comes of looking too much in your mirror! A woman is only as old as she looks in the eyes of her lover!

HELEN: *[almost gasping]* And I?

HARTLEY: I have never seen you look so young, so beautiful, so altogether charming!

HELEN: John!

HARTLEY: Yes?

HELEN: Look what I've found!

HARTLEY: What?

HELEN: *[with childish delight]* A gray hair--in your moustache!

HARTLEY: *[laughing]* I've grown old, haven't I? *[As they separate an instant, a surprised look comes into his eyes.]* Helen!

HELEN: What is it?

HARTLEY: *[clapping his hands together]* By Jove! What a fool I was not to see it!

HELEN: See what?

HARTLEY: And after the maid warned me that you had a surprise in store for me!

HELEN: *[utterly bewildered]* What is it, John?

HARTLEY: *[triumphantly]* You're wearing the same dress you wore the day you saw me off at the station!

[She falls into his arms, laughing happily.]

CURTAIN

A March Wind

a play in one-act
Alice Brown

CHARACTERS

MELIA, a middle-aged New England woman

ENOCH, her husband

ROSIE, Enoch's child

JOSIAH PEASE, Melia's cousin

[A farmhouse kitchen comfortably furnished, the kettle boiling on the stove, a plain sofa, a clock on the mantel, etc... MELIA, a handsome, middle-aged woman in print dress and apron, is scouring tins at a table. ENOCH, a gentle-looking middle-aged man, virile, but with the worn appearance of an artisan who has worked too hard, stands before the mantel clock regarding it absorbedly, starting the pendulum, moving the hands, etc... ROSIE is putting her doll to bed on the sofa.]

MELIA: *[To Enoch.]* What's the matter with it?

ENOCH: Dunno yet. She's balky.

MELIA: When it give up strikin' I lost all patience. Let's cart it off into the attic an' buy us one o' them little nickel ones.

ENOCH: Oh, I guess we'll give her a chance. *[Lifts it down carefully.]* Should you jest as soon I'd bring in that old shoemaker's bench out o' the shed? It's low, an' I could reach my tools off'n the floor.

MELIA: Law, yes. It's a good day to clutter up. There won't be nobody in.

[Exit Enoch. Rosie runs up to Melia.]

ROSIE: Dolly's asleep.

MELIA: [Fondly.] Somebody's 'most asleep herself. She ain't had no nap today. You cover up with mother's red shawl an' go bylow.

[Enter Enoch, with bench.]

ENOCH: [Having arranged himself on the bench, a clutter of clock and tools on the floor before him.] There! Now, sirree, sir, I'll see 'f I can 'tend to ye.

MELIA: [Proudly.] You can if anybody. Never see sich a hand with tools.

ROSIE: [Who has been wandering about, singing a little song, brings up at Melia's side again.] Dolly's asleep now.

MELIA: Ain't you goin' bylow? I know what little folks want. They want suthin' to do. You go fetch the button box out o' that lower drawer. Then you set down on your cricket an' sort 'em out. The white ones are white cows, an' the black ones are black cows, an' they're all goin' to pastur'. [Rosie runs delightedly to obey.] Enoch, there ain't a soul been in today.

ENOCH: [Speaking absorbedly, as he takes the clock apart with a delicate care.] Well, I can stand it if you can.

MELIA: [Laughing.] Three's company--in this house.

ROSIE: [Seating herself on her cricket and pouring the buttons in her lap.] Black cows. White cows.

MELIA: Yes, black cows an' white cows.

ROSIE: Where's the pastur'?

MELIA: Rosie's apron pockets. The black cows are goin' into one pocket, the white cows into t'other.

ENOCH: I kinder thought Elbridge True'd be over today 'bout them cows.

MELIA: Which you goin' to swap?

ENOCH: Ain't much to choose. He's got a mighty nice Alderney, an' if he's goin' to sell milk next year he'll be glad to get two good milkers instead. I guess we can trade.

MELIA: [Glancing from the window.] I wouldn't go out such a day as this, cows or no cows. My! how them trees rock. Ain't this a wind! Makes me as nervous as a witch.[Laughing.] You know folks say if anything's goin' to happen it's on a day like this when the wind's been blowin' all night an' got everybody's nerves on edge.

ENOCH: [Absorbed in his work and talking half absently.] 'T was a day about like this, a year ago, when Rosie an' me come along the road an' I asked if you didn't want a hired man.

MELIA: So 't was. Don't put the buttons on your mouth, Rosie. Sort 'em out pretty an' drive 'em off to pastur'.

ENOCH: [Going musingly on.] "I want to hire out," I says. "I've got two to feed," says I, "Rosie an' me." [Slyly.] Remember what you says, Melia?

MELIA: [Confused and laughing.] There! Don't call up that old tale. When I think on't in the night my face burns like fire.

ENOCH: [Laughing quietly.] You says, says you, "I don't hire tramps."

MELIA: *[Defensively.]* Well, what if I did, Enoch? What if I did? You stood there starin' down on Rosie's hood. You didn't once lift your eyes. But minute you give me a look, I says right off, "You come in an' I'll git the little girl some milk."

ENOCH: So ye did, Melia. So you did. An' I sawed wood all that arternoon, an' when I appeared, to git Rosie an' take the road ag'in, she was sound asleep covered over with your red shawl.

ROSIE: *[Over her buttons.]* Now the white cows' goin' to pastur'. Now the black cows' comin' home.

MELIA: I says to you, "Don't you wake her up. I'll put her to bed byme-by."

ENOCH: An' so't went on from day to day. An' 't wa'n't a month 'fore we found out how we prized one another, an' we was man an' wife.

MELIA: *[Dropping her scouring cloth.]* There! I dropped my dish cloth.

ENOCH: Sign of a stranger?

MELIA: Sure sign. *[She laughs.]*

ENOCH: What you laughin' at?

MELIA: I was thinkin' how there hadn't been a soul in today, an' the month after we was married they come from fur an' near.

ENOCH: *[With a wild amusement.]* Swarmed like bees, didn't they?

MELIA: Flew like blackbirds, an' every one of 'em lighted right down here.

ENOCH: Clattered like 'em, too.

MELIA: Now let's not go back to that, makes me so hot. I'm mad as fire only thinkin' on't. Mebbe I shouldn't be so mad if the wind wa'n't blowin so.

ENOCH: *[Indulgently.]* There! there! 't was only human natur'. They'd heerd you'd married a tramp, an' 't was meat an' drink to 'em to see how't worked.

MELIA: Didn't find out much, did they?

ENOCH: No, you was as short as pie crust.

ROSIE: *[Precipitating herself on him.]* Father, here's a white cow rolled away. You come get her for me.

ENOCH: Byme-by. Father's got his clock to pieces now. He can't tend to little girls.

[Melia picks up the button.]

ROSIE: Father, you lemme take your soldier button for a great big ox.

ENOCH: No. Can't have that.

ROSIE: O father, please.

[Enoch shakes his head and goes absorbedly on with his work.]

MELIA: *[Surprised.]* Why, Enoch, give it to the child. Whatever 't is, you give it to her.

ENOCH: Can't do that, Melia.

MELIA: Can't give her a button? Well, I never. Why not?

ENOCH: I could any other button, but this one I promised to wear as long's I lived.

MELIA: *[With interest.]* Why, I never see it on ye.

ENOCH: No. I sewed it on inside here. *[Throws back his coat and turns out his waistcoat pocket for her to see.]*

MELIA: *[Amused, but with growing interest.]* Why, ye don't sew it into ever weskit you got, do ye?

ENOCH: *[Laughing indulgently.]* I ain't had many new weskits, for quite a few years.

MELIA: *[Walking back and forth at her work, she suddenly feels the significance of the situation. She stops short, and speaks with a quickly growing excitement.]* Enoch, I ain't asked you no questions about--'bout anything, have I?

ENOCH: No.

MELIA: Well, now I do. Who'd you make that promise to?

ENOCH: *[Looking at Rosie in trouble, and then at Melia. Speaks with hesitation.]* A--a woman.

MELIA: Well, she's got a name, ain't she?

ENOCH: *[Still indicating Rosie.]* I dunno's I want to speak it jest now. There's little pitchers--

MELIA: *[Touched.]* If it's a name you can't speak afore Rosie--

ENOCH: *[Gravely.]* It *is* a name I can't speak afore Rosie.

ROSIE: *[Rushing at him in high glee.]* Why can't you? Why can't you? *[Instantly forgets her interest and returns to her game.]*

MELIA: *[With decision, trying to control herself.]* Yes. Why can't you?

ENOCH: *[Laughing, yet in a troubled way and seeking to recall her.]* One button ain't no great matter.

MELIA: It ain't the button. It's--it's-- *[Stops on the verge of tears.]*

ENOCH: You think it's queer I promised to wear it? Well, 'Melia, a promise is a promise, ain't it?

MELIA: *[Bitterly.]* There's promises you made to--to me--before the minister.

ENOCH: *[Gravely.]* Well, if I didn't keep all my promises, how'd you be sure I'd keep the ones to you?

[A knock at the door. 'Melia stands transfixed.]

MELIA: My land! Who's that? Rosie, you run to the sidelight an' peek. I hope to my soul 't ain't company, a day like this. *[Rosie jumps up, loosens her clutch on her pinafore, and the buttons fall and roll in wild confusion. She stands looking at them, aghast.]* Oh, my soul an' body!

ENOCH: *[After the brief trouble of his scene with Melia, he has gone back to his work in relief, and now glances up at Rosie in a mild reproach.]* See there now, what ye done.

[Rosie relinquishes the problem of the buttons and exits to "peek."]

MELIA: *[Listening.]* Now, who should you s'pose 't could be? *[Knock repeated.]*

ENOCH: Mebbe it's Elbridge about them cows.

MELIA: No, 't ain't. He'd walk right in. *[Enter Rosie.]*

ROSIE: *[With importance, as the bearer of news.]* It's a man. He's got on a blue coat 'n' a fuzzy hat. He's got a big nose.

MELIA: *[In despair.]* Enoch, do you know what's happened?

ENOCH: *[Absently.]* Them buttons? I'll pick 'em up byme-by, when I git this cog trued. Rosie 'n' me'll do it together.

MELIA: Buttons! I ain't talkin' about buttons. You know who that is out there? It's Cousin Josiah Pease.

ENOCH: *[Amiably, though without interest.]* Is it? Want me to go to the door?

MELIA: Go to the door? No, I don't want nobody to go to the door till this room's cleared up. If 't wa'n't so everlastin' cold, I'd take him right into the front room an' blaze a fire. But ye couldn't keep him there, more'n ye could a hornet.

ENOCH: *[Abstractedly.]* Oh, you have him right in here where it's good an' warm.

MELIA: *[Advancing on him.]* You gether up them tools an' things, an' I'll help carry out the bench.

ENOCH: Look out. You'll joggle. No, I guess I won't move. If he's any kind of a man he'll know what 'tis to clean a clock.

MELIA: *[Imploringly.]* Don't you see, Enoch? This room looks like the Old Boy an' so do you, an' he'll go home an' tell all the folks.

ENOCH: *[Absently.]* Tell 'em what?

MELIA: He's been livin' with Cousin Sarah, out west, an' minute he gits back, here he is to spy out the land. *[In renewed despair.]* Enoch, you wake up. He's come to find out.

ENOCH: *[At sea, yet absorbed in the clock.]* Find out what?

MELIA: You stop mullin' over that clock, an' you hear to me. He's come to find out--about us.

ENOCH: *[Bewildered.]* What's he want to know? Whatever 'tis, why don't ye tell him an' git rid of him?

MELIA: It's about you, Enoch. Don't you see?

ENOCH: *[Indulgently.]* Law, there ain't nothin' about me 't would take a man long to find out. I guess you better ask him in. Don't you let him bother ye.

MELIA: *[Superbly.]* He don't bother me an' I will let him in.

[Exit Melia, walking over buttons with a tragic dignity. Rosie gives a little cry, regards her buttons sorrowfully, picks up a few, relinquishes the enormous task, and kneels to put a forefinger on Enoch's tools.]

ENOCH: *[Mildly.]* No! no!

[Rosie goes to the sofa and covers her doll with her handkerchief for a quilt. Enter Melia and JOSIAH PEASE--he is a spare lantern-jawed old man, sharp-eyed and hateful. He bustles up to the fire and struggles out of his coat.]

JOSIAH: There! There, Melia! Can't begin to talk till I git he't through. *[Rubbing his hands unctuously at the stove.]* That your man?

[Melia gets the broom and begins sweeping buttons ruthlessly. Rosie rushes to the rescue and, unafraid of the broom, gets in its way and clutches at buttons as she can as they whirl by.]

MELIA: That's my husband. Enoch, here's Cousin Josiah Pease.

ENOCH: *[Looking up mildly and putting out a hand which Josiah does not see.]* Pleased to meet you, sir. I'd git up, but you see I'm tinkerin' a clock.

JOSIAH: *[Drawing a chair close to the stove and hovering.]* You a clock mender by trade?

ENOCH: No, not to say by trade.

JOSIAH: *[With a consuming curiosity.]* Ain't got no trade, have ye?

ENOCH: *[Mildly.]* Oh, I've got a kind of an insight into one or two.

JOSIAH: No reg'lar trade, have ye? *[Enoch shakes his head.]* That's what I thought. *[Melia is putting tins together with a clash.]* Law, Melia, to think o' your bein' married.

MELIA: *[Coldly.]* Good many folks marry, fust an' last. There's been quite a few couples since Adam an' Eve.

JOSIAH: *[With a toothless laugh.]* Adam an' Eve! Adam an' Eve! Yes, yes. Garden of Eden. Got turned out, didn't they. Got turned out.

MELIA: *[With a cold acidity.]* I b'lieve I've heerd some tales about a snake round there.

JOSIAH: So there was! So there was! Risky business, gittin' married. Well, Melia, I never'd ha' thought it o' you.

ENOCH: *[Arriving at a fortunate conclusion with the clock, and bursting out.]* There ye be.

JOSIAH: No, I never'd ha' thought o' your marryin'--your time o' life.

MELIA: *[Starting nervously and frowning at him.]* You never'd ha' thought it o' me? Well, I never'd ha' thought it o' myself. Ye don't know what ye'll do till you've tried.

JOSIAH: *[With a hideous joviality.]* Love will go where it's sent if it hits the pigpen.

MELIA: What do you mean by that?

JOSIAH: Oh, I's only thinkin' on't over. I do a good deal o' thinkin' fust an' last, an' when I stepped into this door I says to myself: "It's Natur', that's all 'tis, Natur'. Natur' says to folks, 'You up an' marry, an' if there ain't nobody else for 'em to marry they'll pitch upon the most unsignifyin' creatur's that ever stepped."

MELIA: *[In a cold rage.]* I dunno what there is about this house to start ye off on a tack like that.

JOSIAH: *[Speciously.]* Law, no. I'm a thoughtful man, that's all. Things come into my head.

MELIA: *[Curtly.]* You had your dinner?

JOSIAH: *[Ingratiatingly.]* I ain't had a bite since six o'clock this mornin'.

MELIA: I'll make ye a cup o' tea. *[Does it rapidly and grudgingly and sets food on the table.]*

JOSIAH: Your hair looks real thick, Melia. I warrant 't ain't all your own.

MELIA: *[Stopping suddenly and facing him.]* Josiah Pease, I know your tricks. You was always one to hector an' thorn anybody till they flew all to pieces an' didn't care what they said, an' mebbe 't would prove to be what you was itchin' to find out. For all the world like that March wind blowin' outside there.

JOSIAH: Law, Melia, I never had such a thought. I was jest lookin' at your hair. Ain't a grey thread in it. *[In a tone mysteriously lowered, pointing to Enoch.]* He's a leetle mite gray. Gittin' along in years, ain't he?

MELIA: *[Curtly.]* I never inquired.

JOSIAH: [Mumbling over the stove.] Well! Well! [Rousing.] Melia, ain't you ever had your teeth out?

MELIA: [Coldly.] My teeth'll last me quite a spell yet. So'll my tongue.

JOSIAH: They looked real white an' firm last time I see 'em, but ye never can tell what's goin' on underneath.

[From without a jovial "Whoa!" Enoch hastily puts his tools aside, rises and peers from the window.]

ENOCH: There's Elbridge True. He's come round to trade for them cows. [Takes out his watch and looks at it.] 'Most time to feed the hens, Melia. You keep the water bilin' so't I can give 'em some warm dough. [Exit Enoch.]

JOSIAH: [Alive with curiosity.] Whose watch was that he took out o' his pocket?

MELIA: [Coldly.] His, I suppose. Whose should it be?

JOSIAH: I could ha' took my oath that was your Gran'ther Baldwin's gold watch. You git a look at it, fust chance you find, an' see 'f you don't think so, too.

MELIA: [Violently.] Do you s'pose if Gran'ther Baldwin's watch is in my husband's pocket, 't is for any reason except I put it there?

JOSIAH: [Soothingly.] I know how ye feel. Stan' by him as long as ye can--but, Melia, you git that watch back.

MELIA: There. You draw up an' I'll give you some tea an' have it over.

JOSIAH: [Obeying, greedily and in haste. Points his fork testingly at a dish.] What do ye call that?

MELIA: Fried pork an' apples. We had it left.

JOSIAH: I dunno when I've tasted pork an' apples. We used to call that livin' pretty nigh the wind.

[Rosie, attracted by food, has slipped up to the table and with difficulty reached over to get a bit of bread.]

MELIA: *[Harshly.]* You've had your dinner. Go an' se' down.

[Rosie looks at her in amazement, drops the bread and goes quietly off to nurse her doll.]

JOSIAH: *[Pointing at her with his fork.]* That his gal?

MELIA: *[Perversely.]* Whose?

JOSIAH: His. Your man's.

MELIA: Yes.

JOSIAH: *[Eating rapidly.]* Mother dead?

MELIA: Josiah Pease, I never thought a poor insignificant creatur' like you could rile me so. Mother dead? Ain't I been an' married her father?

JOSIA: Law, Melia, do se' down. You give me a mite o' that butter whilst I eat. I'll be bound you thought the woman was dead, or ye wouldn't ha' took such a step.

MELIA: Do you think everybody's scamps an' raskils?

JOSIAH: *[Soothingly.]* Course he told ye t'other woman was dead. Course you b'lieved him. All I meant was, did ye see her death in the paper, or the matter o' that?

MELIA: *[Violently.]* No.

JOSIAH: Well, there now! I'm dretful sorry. There was a woman down Tiverton way--I heerd on't only yisterdy--she took in a tramp to pick her apples, an' next thing the neighbors knew, there she laid, front o' the fireplace, as it might ha' been there *[pointing with his knife]* head split open as neat as ever you see.

MELIA: If anybody's head's split open in this house 't won't be mine nor *[tenderly]* my husband's neither.

JOSIAH: So I say, Melia. Don't ye do nothin' ye could be hauled up for. When ye find ye can't stan' folks no longer, you jest open the door an' tell 'em to cut.

MELIA: *[Meaningly.]* I will.

JOSIAH: He ain't made no mention of any other woman, has he?

MELIA: *[Hysterically.]* Another woman! What are you talkin' about another woman for? Seems if you was the snake in the garden, come to put words into my mouth.

JOSIAH: *[With greedy satisfaction.]* There is another woman, then? He owns to't! What'd he say about her, Melia? What'd he say?

MELIA: *[Tortured, yet fascinated.]* He didn't say nothin'. Nor I ain't said nothin'. What do you think you're draggin' out o' my lips. It's p'ison, that's what it is--p'ison words--p'ison thoughts.

JOSIAH: *[Soothingly.]* There, there, Melia, you can talk to me. I'm your own kin.

MELIA: *[In horror at herself.]* O my God! Have I got to be like you?

JOSIAH: If there's another woman, ye know, Melia, he's said the same things to her 't he has to you. He's made her the same promises--

MELIA: *[Wildly.]* Promises! Promises! Don't you remind me o' that word!

JOSIAH: Where's he gone?

MELIA: *[Getting hold of herself.]* He's gone out to look at a cow.

JOSIAH: Find he's sellin' things off pretty fast?

MELIA: More tea?

JOSIAH: You kep' your bank stock in your own name?

MELIA: Here's the sugar.

JOSIAH: Your father left consid'able. I guess he'd turn in his grave if he could know 't was goin' to waste.

MELIA: Butter?

JOSIAH: *[Ingratiatingly.]* If you had the courage to kinder put things into my hands so't I could manage for ye, I'd do it in a minute.

MELIA: You finished?

JOSIAH: *[Leaning back in his chair and looking up at her.]* Melia, you do look terribly tried.

MELIA: Ain't you finished?

JOSIAH: No, no. I'll take my time. Got suthin' on your mind, ain't ye, Melia? Kind o' worried?

MELIA: *[Going to the window.]* Blows harder 'n' harder. It's an awful wind.

JOSIAH: *[Following her.]* Find he's a drinkin' man?

MELIA: *[Controlling herself with difficulty.]* You'll have hard work to git home 'fore dark.

JOSIAH: I thought mebbe he'd harness up. *[Suddenly attracted by what he sees from the window.]* What's that? What's that? I'll be buttered if he ain't been an' traded off both your cows.

MELIA: *[Pouncing upon his coat and holding it out for him.]* Here's your coat.

JOSIAH: *[Still absorbed at the window.]* My Lord, Melia! Be you goin' to stan' there an' let them two cows walk off from under your nose? If he's got anything to boot, he's put it into his pocket, an' when it comes out o' there 't'll go onto somebody's back--an' 't won't be yourn.

MELIA: Here's your coat, I tell you. Git into it as quick as ever you can.

JOSIAH: *[Recalled to his own plight. Helplessly.]* I was in hopes he'd harness up.

MELIA: Here. Put t'other arm in fust.

JOSIAH: I was in hopes--

MELIA: This your neck hankercher? *[Summarily ties it.]* Here's your hat.

JOSIAH: I was in hopes--

MELIA: Got your mittins? *[Snatches them from his pocket and thrusts them on him.]*Here they be. This way. *[Goes to the door and throws it open.]*

JOSIAH: *[Feebly.]* I ain't finished my dinner.

MELIA: This is the door you come to by your own will, an' this is the door you'll go out of by mine. Come. Come, Josiah Pease, out you go. *[Exit Josiah tremblingly. She calls to him.]* Josiah Pease, this is the end. I've done with ye, egg an' bird. *[Closes the door and goes swiftly back to the window. Rosie comes and lays a hand on her skirt, and Melia stoops and hugs her violently.]* You little lamb! You never see mother carry on like that, did ye? Well, I'll warrant you never will ag'in so long as Josiah Pease keeps out o' here. *[Kisses Rosie and lets her go. Laughs a little to herself, half crying.]* My soul! I'd ruther see a hornet. I feel as if I's stung all over an' if anybody laid a finger on me I'd scream right out! Don't seem as if Josiah Pease could ha' done it all. I guess some on't 's that aggravatin' wind. *[Enter Enoch in high feather.]*

ENOCH: *[Jovially.]* Well, I've made us a good trade. Company gone? Se' down whilst I tinker, an' I'll tell ye all about it. Yes, I made us a good trade.

[Melia watches him in growing excitement while, not looking at her, he seats himself on his bench and tenderly takes up his work.]

MELIA: *[Suddenly, with shrill violence.]* You've made a good trade, have you? You've sold my cows an' had 'em drove off the place without if or but. That's what you call a good trade.

ENOCH: *[Rising, aghast.]* Melia! Why, Melia!

MELIA: Ever since you set foot in this house it's been the same. Have I had my say once?

ENOCH: Why, Melia, I thought 't was all as smooth as silk.

MELIA: Here we be on my own farm. Be I the mistress of it? No. You took the head o' things an' you've kep' it.

ENOCH: *[Dazed.]* Don't seem as if I took it--that way. Seems as if you give it to me.

MELIA: *[With rising violence.]* 'T was all mine. Now what's mine's yourn.

ENOCH: *[With a recalling tenderness.]* I didn't have anything to bring ye, Melia. If I had, 't would ha' been all yourn.

MELIA: *[Bitterly.]* If you'd had anything, you wouldn't ha' been a tramp.

ENOCH: *[Touching her arm gently and smiling at her.]* Then I might never ha' come this way. 'T wa'n't such a bad thing to be a tramp, if it brought me to this door.

MELIA: *[Repelling his touch.]* A tramp! I'm the laughin' stock of the town. There ain't a man or woman in it that don't know I've married a tramp.

ENOCH: *[Looks at her a moment, as if really to understand, and turns to his bench.]* I guess I'll move this back where 't was. *[Exit with bench. Enters and rapidly picks up his tools, putting them in a drawer. Melia watches him coldly, and then begins clearing away Cousin Josiah's meal. As she works she sings "The Bailiff's Daughter" in a high, angry voice. Enoch sets the clock again on its shelf.]* I'll leave the clock as 't is. If any kind of a tinker comes along, he wouldn't find it any the wuss for what I've done. *[Takes his hat from the nail.]* Goodbye, Melia.

MELIA: *[Coldly.]* Where you bound for?

ENOCH: *[Taking out his watch.]* I can ketch the four o'clock down by the crossin'. *[Is about to restore the watch to his pocket, but with a sudden thought, lays it on the table.]*That's your watch. I like to forgot. Reminds me--*[pulling out a roll of bills]* This money's yourn too.

MELIA: *[In growing trouble.]* Mine? What makes it mine?

ENOCH: I got it to boot, tradin' them cows. *[Selects some of the money and puts it in his pocket.]* Here's two eighty-seven. That's mine. He paid it to me for fixin' his pump. Goodbye, Melia. You've been good to me. Better'n anybody ever was in the world.

MELIA: *[Uneasily following him a step to the door.]* Where you goin'?

ENOCH: *[Reassuringly.]* I dunno--yet.

MELIA: *[Bitterly.]* On the tramp?

ENOCH: I s'pose ye could call it that--till I pick up suthin' to do.

[Exit Enoch. Melia runs to the window and looks after him, to the door, opens it and then shuts it again. Stands motionless, her hands tense at her side. Suddenly relaxes and gives a little scornful laugh.]

MELIA: Well, that's over. *[Goes on clearing the table. Stops suddenly.]* He's gone. It's over. *[Enter Rosie with a red shawl pinned about her, to make a long skirt.]* Rosie! Rosie! He's gone. You're father's gone. He's forgot you. Take off that thing. *[Snatches off the shawl.]* Here's your hood. *[Snatches it from a nail.]* On with it, quick.

ROSIE: Where's father?

MELIA: He's gone, I tell you, an' he's forgot to take you with him. *[Snatches the child's coat from a nail and puts her into it.]* Here! In with you. When we git outdoor, I'll carry ye.

ROSIE: Where we goin'?

MELIA: *[Bitterly.]* Down to the crossin'. Then you're goin' with your father an' I'm comin' home--alone. *[Enter Enoch. Wildly.]* Enoch! Enoch! In the name of God have you come back? *[Rushes to him and throws her arms about him.]*

ENOCH: *[Gently drawing her arms from his neck.]* There! There! Don't take on so.

MELIA: O Enoch, you've come home. If it's only for a minute, you're in this house ag'in.

ENOCH: I jest turned back for Rosie. Mebbe you won't believe it, but I forgot her.

MELIA: *[Putting out her hand and touching his sleeve.]* I can see you. I can touch your coat. If you should walk out o' that door now, I've had you a minute more.

ENOCH: Rosie, git your mittins.

MELIA: Don't lay up anything ag'inst me. You couldn't if you knew.

ENOCH: *[Gently.]* Knew what?

MELIA: He talked about you. He said things. I couldn't stand 'em.

ENOCH: *[Sternly.]* Did you believe 'em?

MELIA: No, as I'm a livin' woman, no! I've been nervous as a witch all day--that wind out there, blowin', set me all on edge--an' then he pitched upon you.

ENOCH: *[To Rosie.]* You run along an' father'll come. *[Rosie hesitates, takes up her doll and lays it down.]* Yes, you take that with ye. I guess nobody'd grudge ye that. *[Exit Rosie slowly, with the doll.]* You see, Melia, I couldn't stan' bein' less'n other men be jest because the woman had the money an' I hadn't.

MELIA: Money! Money! That word betwixt you an' me?

ENOCH: I don't know but 't was kind o' queer about the cows, but somehow you set me at the head o' things, an' if there was a trade to make, seemed kind o' nat'ral for me to make it.

MELIA: So you're goin' to punish me. You're goin' away.

ENOCH: Why, I got to, dear. We couldn't live together nohow, feelin' as you do.

MELIA: We've lived together a whole year.

ENOCH: Yes, an' it's been all springtime, birds singin' an' flowers in bloom. But springtime passes. *[Musingly.]* I thought mebbe this wouldn't. Mebbe you thought so, too. Or I thought if it did, 't would be summer an' the flowers brighter yet. An' then the leaves fallin', an' we layin' down amongst 'em, an' then the snow to cover us. But together, that's what I thought, together. *[Recovering himself.]* I'm dreamin', ain't I? Dreamin' out loud. Well, Melia, I got to look at ye once more, so I won't never forgit. I ain't likely to, though. I ain't likely to. *[Looks at her long and tenderly, and turns away with a sigh.]* Goodbye, Melia. God Almighty bless you.

[He has reached the door and she calls him piercingly.]

MELIA: Enoch! *[He halts.]* You've made up your mind. You're goin' on the tramp.

ENOCH: Yes. That's what it amounts to.

MELIA: Then you've got to take me with you. Talkin' won't make you see that what I said never meant no more than that wind out there blowin' up trouble an' not meanin' to. The farm's come between us. Let's leave it. If you tramp, I'll tramp. If you work out, so'll I.

ENOCH: *[Returning. Incredulously.]* Would you go with me?

MELIA: I'm goin'. Here, take your watch. *[Thrusts it into his coat pocket.]*

ENOCH: Goin' with me? S'pose I say you mustn't?

MELIA: I'll foller on behind. Here's your money. Take it. *[Thrusts it into his coat pocket.]*

ENOCH: To walk an' walk, to find no work mebbe. 'Most al'ays a little hungry. Sometimes cold.

MELIA: Three's company, you an' me an' Rosie. We'll laugh an' sing.

ENOCH: Don't ye want to pack up some things an' git on a bunnit?

MELIA: No.

ENOCH: Don't ye want to leave the key with some o' the neighbors?

MELIA: I don't want anything in the world but you.

ENOCH: *[Stepping forward, arms outstretched and then dropping them and speaking wistfully.]* You sure you think enough o' me? You didn't a minute ago.

MELIA: *[Wildly.]* 'T was because I thought so much o' you, not because I didn't. Can't you understand that? *[Losing control of herself.]* O what's the use of excusin' myself! It's that button. It all goes back to that. An' that aggravatin' wind.

ENOCH: *[Dazed.]* Rosie lose a button? *[Light breaking on him.]* Why, Melia, you can't mean that old soldier button on my weskit.

MELIA: *[In shame and tumultuous emotion.]* 'T wa'n't the button. No, no, 't wa'n't that. You might be sewed all over buttons. But you said 't was a woman, an' you said you promised her, an' you said she couldn't be talked about afore Rosie--

ENOCH: *[Sternly.]* Melia, let's stop right here. She was Rosie's mother an' she can't be talked about afore Rosie, because if I've got any pity in me for that little creatur' I'm goin' to wipe out o' her mind the foul words she's heard an' the blows she's had from the woman that brought her into the world.

MELIA: Enoch! Enoch!

ENOCH: An' if I said I was goin' to keep a promise made to that poor creatur' that's dead, 't was because every promise she made to me she broke--the promise to be faithful, to put by the liquor that turned her into a beast--oh! *[in disgust]*. An' because my promises to her are broken as hers be to me--I promised to love her an' I don't. I promised to make Rosie love her an' I can't--why, I s'pose I thought if there was some poor miserable little promise I could keep, I'd be the more a man for doin' it.

MELIA: *[In a wild compassion.]* Oh, if I'd known! If I'd only known! You never'll forgive me. No, you never can.

ENOCH: *[In a rapt tenderness.]* Why, who is it that's makin' Rosie forgit the mother that's dead? 'T ain't me. It's you.

MELIA: *[Timidly.]* Me, Enoch?

ENOCH: Now she sees what mothers be. Who is it 's makin' me forgit all them old days when I cursed God for bringin' me into the world?

MELIA: *[In an incredulous hope.]* Not me, Enoch? It ain't me?

ENOCH: *[Laughing tenderly.]* Want I should throw away the old soldier button, darlin'?

MELIA: *[In growing hope and thankfulness.]* No, no, Enoch, no! You keep your promise. We'll have it to remind us, you an' me. 'T ain't yourn. It's ours.

ENOCH: *[Taking her in his arms.]* Spring an' summer, darlin' an' then the snow.

MELIA: *[Happily.]* The snow now, if it covers both of us together.

ENOCH: There ain't anything in my life I couldn't tell you. You say the word an' I'll go over every day of it.

MELIA: *[Laughing.]* There's only one thing you've got to say--jest one.

ENOCH: Name it, darlin' dear.

MELIA: Whose cows were them you sold today?

ENOCH: *[Laughing.]* That ain't fair. I'll take the money for one of 'em, if you say so, or I'll own it don't make no difference whose they be. But as to lyin'--

MELIA: Say it. Whose were they?

ENOCH: Mine.

[Rosie enters timorously, and each holds out a hand to her. She runs to them delighted.]

CURTAIN

Section D: Exercises in Drama

CREATIVITY EXERCISE: Fifteen minute free-write. Set a timer for fifteen minutes; then go and take a seat. Pick up a pen, and write about something, anything, until the timer chimes. Don't stop. Begin with the writing prompt, and if you get stumped, begin to write a recent conversation you've overheard or been a part of. Have fun! (C3 Scale)

Prompt: "I hope you plan to stay for dinner!" she said sternly from the kitchen window.

Exercise 1: Read Genesis chapters 37 and 39-50. Write a one-page paper describing the literary devices used in the retelling of Joseph's life. Note the characterization of Joseph, the story's conflict, climax, foreshadowing, and use of juxtaposition. (C1 Scale)

Exercise 2: Outline the introduction, rising action, climax, falling action and conclusion in Joseph's story. (C3 Scale)

Exercise 3: Choose one main character from a play you've read in this unit. Complete a character sketch of what you know, and of what you assumed while reading, about the character. Whether or not the character's physical appearance is mentioned, you formulated his/her appearance in your mind while reading. Include this in your sketch outline. When you've finished the sketch, write a paragraph focused on characterization through one or more of the methods discussed in sub-section four. (C1 Scale)

Exercise 4: Create a character who is loosely based on someone you know or have known. Complete a thorough sketch of your character. (C3 Scale)

Exercise 5: With permission, record the first minute or two of a conversation. Transcribe the conversation and finish it as it might have happened. Stay true to the dialect and personality of the speakers. Write a minimum of two pages of new dialog. Mark the beginning of the added text. (C1 Scale)

Exercise 6: In Exercise 4 of Unit I, you wrote a limerick about a funny experience. Creating new characters and situations if you need to, write a one-act play based on the memory. (C1 Scale)

Exercise 7: The suggestion for a play might come anywhere—a newspaper article, a history book, an incident witnessed at a local restaurant, a heart-thumping adventure, or a comical misunderstanding. Outline the introduction, rising action, climax, falling action and conclusion of a play you might like to write starring the character you created in Exercise 4. (C3 Scale)

Unit III: Creative Nonfiction

Section A: What is Creative Nonfiction?

Nonfiction writing may be persuasive (in which the author tries to influence the reader), informational (in which the author explains something to the reader), autobiographical (in which the author writes about himself), or biographical (in which the author writes about someone else). The term "creative nonfiction" can refer to any type of nonfiction: a blog, an essay, a journal entry, a book, a research paper, etc. The only true requirement of nonfiction is that the facts presented be completely accurate. For a piece of nonfiction to qualify as "creative nonfiction," however, it must also be well-written and engaging.

The "creative" label does not give the writer license to lie. A writer of creative nonfiction should take advantage of *every* literary technique employed by fiction writers, playwrights, and poets; he should write narratives that are compelling and vividly put. But a writer of creative nonfiction, spurred by the beauty and pain of life itself, should write with the primary goal of engrossing his reader in life's truths—not in half-truths or exaggerations.

The nonfiction writer is, himself, enthralled by the wonders of life. He is a professor and a student. He is an appreciator of life as teacher, and he is taught by the quietest gurgling of the river as well as the raging oppressions of injustice.

> He should tell of the kind and wholesome and beautiful elements of our life; he should tell unsparingly of the evil and sorrow of the present, to move us with instances: he should tell of wise and good people in the past, to excite us by example; and of these he should tell soberly and truthfully, not glossing faults, that we may neither grow discouraged with ourselves nor exacting to our

neighbours. So the body of contemporary literature, ephemeral and feeble in itself, touches in the minds of men the springs of thought and kindness, and supports them (for those who will go at all are easily supported) on their way to what is true and right. And if, in any degree, it does so now, how much more might it do so if the writers chose! There is not a life in all the records of the past but, properly studied, might lend a hint and a help to some contemporary. There is not a juncture in to-day's affairs but some useful word may yet be said of it. Even the reporter has an office, and, with clear eyes and honest language, may unveil injustices and point the way to progress. And for a last word: in all narration there is only one way to be clever, and that is to be exact. To be vivid is a secondary quality which must presuppose the first; for vividly to convey a wrong impression is only to make failure conspicuous. But a fact may be viewed on many sides; it may be chronicled with rage, tears, laughter, indifference, or admiration, and by each of these the story will be transformed to something else.

Robert Louis Stevenson, *Essays in the Art of Writing*

Section B: Reading and Writing Creative Nonfiction

1. Literary Devices

Analogy:

Analogy is the mental linking of two ideas for the purpose of increased understanding. In various places in the Bible, God is called a potter while people are referred to as clay. The metaphors, "God is a potter," and "We are clay" are used in an analogy and reveal many things about the Creator and His relationship to His creation.

Analogies are used to teach and to explain. A mother might tell her children, "Bread isn't done until it's been through the fire; so life's trials make us complete and ready." There are few ways in which people can be compared to bread; still, this analogy is helpful in explaining the benefits of suffering. The language of analogy is seen in parables and allegories which both make use of resemblance/correspondence between ideas.

Anti-Climax:

The term anti-climax refers to a literary form of backpedaling away from perceived climax to something disappointing or more mundane. When done accidentally, the reader is left feeling let-down and disappointed. When done purposefully, an anticlimactic moment can produce laughter and/or sighs of relief.

Anti-climax may be used at any point in a story. An example of anti-climax replacing the reader's feared climax is as follows:

In the opening lines of a story, a wife wakes from a very intense nightmare in which her husband has been hit by a car. As she wakes, she realizes that her husband has already caught the bus to work. She tries to call to warn him, but he's left his phone behind. As the story unfolds, we read as the frantic wife attempts to reach her husband through all possible means. We read as the unaware husband makes his way through his day, and we're gripped by the story as he barely avoids death on a few occasions (none of which he notices). As we approach the climax, the wife has driven herself downtown to her husband's office to check on him. He steps off the curb just as she pulls up in front. Nearly missing him, she slams on her brakes. Oblivious, he walks to the driver's window, kisses his wife, and says, "Thanks for picking me up."

Narrative:

A narrative is the telling of a story, true or fictitious, in a logical order. A narrative is not the story itself but the way the story is told. The narrator will focus on some elements of the story more than others; he will prolong some moments and eliminate others altogether. Therefore the opinions of the narrator will dramatically shape the narrative. A narrative might be a first-hand account, or it might be the reflections of a third-person observer. The gospels of Matthew, Mark, Luke, and John are narrative accounts of Jesus' life on earth.

Point of View:

The angle in which something is seen is called the point of view. In literature, point of view refers to the viewpoint of the narrator.

1. In the first person point of view, the narrator is speaking for himself. First person employs the pronouns "I" and "we". Example:

"In the next section, I will attempt to explain Brunetière's theory of dramatic literature."

2. In the second person point of view, the narrator is directly addressing his audience. Second person uses the pronoun "you". Example:

"As you can see, there is a great deal to be learned from the literary mechanics of Scripture."

3. In the third person point of view, the narrator is telling about something or someone. Third person employs character names and pronouns such as "he," "she," "it," and "they". Example:

"As Mr. Archer rounded the corner, he could see that his guests had already arrived."

2. The Elements of Style

In 1918, William Strunk, Jr. wrote a book that has stood the test of time. *The Elements of Style* is a useful read for any writer, but we'll focus on one particular section: "Elementary Principles of Composition". The ten principles Strunk calls elementary are:

1. Make the paragraph the unit of composition: one paragraph to each topic.

2. As a rule, begin each paragraph with a topic sentence; end it in conformity with the beginning.

3. Use the active voice.

4. Put statements in positive form.

5. Omit needless words.

6. Avoid a succession of loose sentences.

7. Express co-ordinate ideas in similar form.

8. Keep related words together.

9. In summaries, keep to one tense.

10. Place the emphatic words of a sentence at the end.

1 - 2. Make the paragraph the unit of composition: one paragraph to each topic. Begin each paragraph with a topic sentence; end it in conformity with the beginning.

A paragraph should be a cohesive unit. Everything contained within the paragraph should make sense when compared to the paragraph's introductory sentence; before moving on to a new point and paragraph, the current paragraph should be nicely concluded. These rules apply to entire papers, and each paragraph within a paper, alike.

If writing a paper about a play, the first paragraph might introduce the play and state what the writer intends to prove throughout the remainder of the paper. For example, the writer might break down the play by plot point (though his paper will vary depending on whether he's set out to prove something about the play or simply to tell about it). If the writer intends to prove a point, the outline might look something like this:

I. Essay on Alice Brown's *A March Wind*

Paragraph 1: Introduce the play and its author:

Alice Brown's *A March Wind* is a play about the strength of words, secret insecurities, and the power we give to both...

Paragraph 2: Play's Introduction: Discuss the introduction of the play in relation to the introductory statement.

Paragraph 3: Rising Action: Discuss the rising action of the play in relation to the introductory statement.

Paragraph 4: Climax: Discuss the climax of the play in relation to the introductory statement.

Paragraph 5: Falling action: Discuss the falling action of the play in relation the introductory statement.

Paragraph 6: Play's Conclusion: Discuss the conclusion of the play in relation to the introductory statement.

Paragraph 7: Restate and prove the introductory statement.

3. Use the active voice.

After insisting on the active voice, Strunk explains that the passive voice exists for a reason and is oftentimes unavoidable. However,

...it should be avoided wherever you can. (Passive)

...you should avoid it wherever you can. (Active)

Example:

The movie was enjoyed by the entire family. (Passive)

The entire family enjoyed the movie. (Active)

Strunk includes the following example:

The dramatists of the Restoration are little esteemed today. (Passive)
Modern readers have little esteem for the dramatists of the Restoration. (Active)

In the **active voice**, the subject of the sentence *performs* the action. In the **passive voice**, the subject *receives* the action. Strunk explains that the passive voice would be correct in an essay about the dramatists, and the active voice would be correct in an essay about modern readers.

4. Put statements in positive form.

Strunk insists that "the reader is dissatisfied with being told only what is not; he wishes to be told what is."

Example: Don't say, "*Not* honest" when the word "dishonest" exists; the latter strikes a harder point.

Weaker	Stronger
not well	ill, unwell, sickly, infirmed
not hard-working	lazy, slothful, lackadaisical, apathetic
not loving	hateful, vengeful, resentful ruthless, merciless

5. Omit needless words.

Strunk writes, "A sentence should contain no unnecessary words, a paragraph no unnecessary sentences…This requires not that the writer make all his sentences short, or that he avoid all detail and treat his subjects only in outline, but that every word tell." Strunk urges writers to avoid common expressions that violate this rule; and in fact, common expressions generally act as filler more than as necessary statements. For example:

Overly wordy	Succinct
In spite of the fact that	Although
He is a man who	He
This is a subject which	This subject
Call your attention to the fact that	Remind you

6. Avoid a succession of loose [structurally repetitive] sentences.

Strunk refers to the tiresome repetition of a particular type of sentence (two co-ordinate clauses, the second introduced by a conjunction or relative); however, the immediate and continual repetition of *any* type of sentence should be avoided.

Tiresome Repetition
The winter was harsh, and the children grew weary. Snow covered the ground, and not a single blade of grass could be seen. The mornings were cold, and everyone stayed in bed long after sunrise. The sun set early, and it took every last bit of warmth.
Sentence Structure Variety
The winter was harsh, and the children grew weary. Snow covered the ground until not a single blade of grass could be seen. The mornings were cold; everyone stayed in bed long after sunrise. The sun set early taking with it every last bit of warmth.

7. Express co-ordinate ideas in similar form.

Under point seven, Strunk advises writers to remember to keep their lists and comparisons in like-form with each other. For example:

Discordant
In the olden days, people used to wait months for a letter, while now we can check our computers for e-mail.
Parallel
In the olden days, people waited months for a letter; today, we check our computers for instant, electronic mail.

Discordant	Parallel
The French, the Italians, Spanish, and Portuguese	The French, the Italians, the Spanish, and the Portuguese
In spring, summer, or in winter	In spring, summer, or winter

	Or
	In spring, in summer, or in winter
to explain the procedure, to prevent damage, and equip students	to explain the procedure, to prevent damage, and to equip students

8. Keep related words together.

Strunk writes, "The position of the words in a sentence is the principal means of showing their relationship. The writer must therefore, so far as possible, bring together the words, and groups of words, that are related in thought, and keep apart those which are not so related."

For example, Wadsworth is the one giving the description, so it is important not to separate him from that action:

Separated	Related
Wordsworth, in the fifth book of The Excursion, gives a minute description of this church.	In the fifth book of The Excursion, Wordsworth gives a minute description of this church.

The writer is attempting to say that *some* members were missing:

Unclear	Clear
All the members were not present.	Not all the members were present.

Be careful with the placement of prepositional phrases! It was the *look* that indicated mischief.

Separated	Related
There was a look in his eye that boded mischief.	In his eye was a look that boded mischief.

9. In summaries, keep to one tense.

Unless relevant to the subject of the essay, the writer should avoid switching back and forth between tenses. For example:

Switched Tense
I climbed out of the car, limped through the door, and sat down to eat a quiet dinner, but instead she ambushes me with a surprise party!
Uniform Tense
I climbed out of the car, limped through the door, and sat down to eat a quiet dinner, but instead she ambushed me with a surprise party!

10. Place the emphatic words of a sentence at the end [or at the beginning, but rarely in the middle].

The most striking positions in a sentence are the opening and closing words.

Weaker	Stronger
All he felt was hate for the man.	Hate is all he felt for the man. Or All he felt for the man was hate.

3. The Art of Writing

In the posthumously published *Essays in the Art of Writing* [1905], Robert Louis Stevenson [1850-1894] speaks to the mechanics of literature. In doing so he says that he is, in essence, "taking down the picture from the wall and looking on the back."

1. *Choice of Words*:

The first thing Stevenson discusses is an author's choice of words. Stevenson compares words, "the commodity of everyday life," to the randomly sized building blocks one would find in a nursery. "It is with blocks of just such arbitrary size and figure that the literary architect is condemned to design the palace of his art...It is, indeed, a strange art to take these blocks...and by tact of application touch them to the finest meanings and distinctions."

Stevenson refers to these blocks, or the "dialect of life," as the things that put writers at a disadvantage to architects, sculptures, painters, and designers. While other artists work with mediums that are malleable and elastic, the writer must create a mosaic out of concretely sized materials that are not only pre-defined but have a specific and narrower meaning for each individual generation. This makes the choosing of words a serious undertaking for the writer.

2. *The web*:

The magical weaving of words is what Stevenson calls *the web*. It is this web that makes literature and music comparable arts; while simple, everyday communication cannot be compared with music. Stevenson explains the spinning of the web as the clever way an author weaves into the fullness of his point by ringing around and around it in ever tightening circles—the way a spider weaves a web. While his meaning is at first unclear, the end result is evident.

> Communication may be made in broken words, the business of life be carried on with substantives alone; but that is not what we call literature; and the true business of the literary artist is to plait or weave his meaning, involving it around itself; so that each sentence, by successive phrases, shall first come into a kind of knot, and then, after a moment of suspended meaning, solve and clear itself.

3. *Rhythm of the Phrase*:

In order to successfully master the composition of what Stevenson calls a "comely sentence," it is imperative the writer be a student of poetry. The poet observes accented and unaccented syllables; he notes the rhythm of a line. The poet understands meter— therefore he knows how to lean into it (for poetry) and how to steer around it (for prose).

> Each phrase of each sentence, like an air or a recitative in music, should be so artfully compounded out of long and short, out of accented and unaccented, as to gratify the sensual ear. And of this the ear is the sole judge. It is impossible to lay down laws… Prose must be rhythmical, and it may be as much so as you will; but it must not be metrical. It may be anything, but it must not be [metered] verse.

4. *Contents of the Phrase*:

As Stevenson analyzes the elements that make up a sentence, he does not focus on the intellectual content but rather on letters and the sounds they produce. The difference between a choppy phrase and an eloquent one depends as much on the sound of the words as on their meaning.

> One sound suggests, echoes, demands, and harmonizes with another; and the art of rightly using these concordances is the final art in literature...The beauty of the contents of a phrase, or of a sentence, depends implicitly upon alliteration and upon assonance. The vowel demands to be repeated; the consonant demands to be repeated; and both cry aloud to be perpetually varied. You may follow the adventures of a letter through any passage that has particularly pleased you; find it, perhaps, denied a while, to tantalize the ear; find it fired again at you in a whole broadside.

Stevenson concludes that it is the job of the writer to keep ear-pleasing phrases flowing from his pen. The prose writer should avoid falling into the strict meters intended for poetry, and he should artfully combine both breath and speech so that what he is composing is music in the mouth (and to the ear) of the reader. The writer should do all this, Stevenson says, while paying careful attention to each and every word he chooses. It is no wonder Stevenson finds writing to be an "intricate affair," and he wonders, as most writers do, "if perfect sentences are rare, and perfect pages *rarer*."

Read Twain's "Two Ways of Seeing a River" (page 218) and Isabella Bird's "Letter I" (page 220). Both of these selections are vividly descriptive. Bird's letter, however, is about *telling* while Twain's essay is about *teaching*. Bird returns immediately from an experience that was too beautiful not to share, and she shares it in detail with a friend. Twain, while still composing sentences full of imagery, looks back over time and reports something of life that he has learned.

Note ways that the four points presented by Stevenson are applied in both selections.

Nonfiction

"Two Ways of Seeing a River"

1. _____

_____

_____

2. _____

_____

_____

3. _____

_____

_____

4. _____

_____

_____

"Letter I"

1. _____

_____

_____

2. _____

_____

_____

3. _____

_____

_____

4. _____

_____

_____

4. Writing from Personal Experience

Writer and professor, Elisabeth Morris [1870-1964], discusses the problems facing writers of nonfiction, and reality-based fiction, in her 1917 essay, "The Literary Uses of Experience". To the writer of fiction, Morris warns against basing characters too closely on actual people—as by doing so one is likely to lose most of his friends. It is wise, according to Morris, to write from memory more than direct dictation of life—to create a separation of time between the life one is living and the life one is writing about.

Morris recommends memory as editor, because memory is far more artistic than an individual's immediate perceptions. There is magic in memory, Morris says:

> Children are following a true instinct when they beg for a story "about something you remember, that happened a long time ago," for the things that we thus remember have a way of gathering into themselves any flavor of poetic feeling that may be in our nature. What is it, then, that memory does? For one thing, it selects. In our immediate perceptions we often cannot see the woods for the trees. Memory knows no such trouble. Its trees are often blurred, but its woods stretch far and blue, dark-shadowed and full of meanings. For another, it distances. Through it we escape from the importunity of practical issues. Memory knows no practical issues; things are clear but we cannot alter them, they are real but we can neither seize nor avoid them.

It is only by holding a thing at a distance that we are truly able to understand the complexities of it, and life is no different. If it is the writer's desire to teach and inspire (as is often the case with the writer of nonfiction) and not simply to narrate an experience, he must give himself time to truly understand the lesson for himself.

> The pressure upon the artist urging him to serve green fruit instead of waiting for it to ripen, has, of course, never been so great as now. But there is, I believe, pressure of another sort, far stronger and far more respectable, arising naturally and inevitably out of our present habits of thought. With the enormous growth of scientific interest—interest in facts, and faith in what they may lead us to—we have developed a reverence for accuracy, patience, thoroughness, and discrimination.

In *Narrative of the Life of Frederick Douglass*, Mr. Douglass tells the story of his life as vividly as if his childhood had happened yesterday. The memories that stand firm in Frederick's adult mind are the same memories that impact his readers—and likely for similar reasons. Douglass includes seemingly commonplace things (like clothing and sleeping quarters), and if he'd written his journal as a child he'd probably have overlooked many of those details. Not being distanced from them, they wouldn't have seemed unusual or particularly impactful. Having the benefit of life behind him, he could allow his memory to select the scenes that would best teach and provoke his readers.

Read chapters four and five from *Narrative of the Life of Frederick Douglass* with Elisabeth Morris' advice in mind. What scenes and details do you find to be the most impactful?

_____

_____

_____

_____

_____

Section C: Creative Nonfiction

Narrative of the Life of Frederick Douglass, an American Slave. Written by Himself:

Frederick Douglass [1818-1895]

Chapter IV

MR. HOPKINS remained but a short time in the office of overseer. Why his career was so short, I do not know, but suppose he lacked the necessary severity to suit Colonel Lloyd. Mr. Hopkins was succeeded by Mr. Austin Gore, a man possessing, in an eminent degree, all those traits of character indispensable to what is called a first-rate overseer. Mr. Gore had served Colonel Lloyd, in the capacity of overseer, upon one of the out-farms, and had shown himself worthy of the high station of overseer upon the home or Great House Farm. Mr. Gore was proud, ambitious, and persevering. He was artful, cruel, and obdurate. He was just the man for such a place, and it was just the place for such a man. It afforded scope for the full exercise of all his powers, and he seemed to be perfectly at home in it. He was one of those who could torture the slightest look, word, or gesture, on the part of the slave, into impudence, and would treat it accordingly. There must be no answering back to him; no explanation was allowed a slave, showing himself to have been wrongfully accused. Mr. Gore acted fully up to the maxim laid down by slaveholders,--"It is better that a dozen slaves suffer under the lash, than that the overseer should be convicted, in the presence of the slaves, of having been at fault." No matter how innocent a slave might be--it availed him nothing, when accused by Mr. Gore of any misdemeanor. To be accused was to be convicted, and to be convicted was to be punished; the one always following the other with immutable certainty. To escape punishment was to escape accusation; and few slaves had the fortune to do either, under the overseership of Mr. Gore. He was just proud enough to demand the most debasing homage of the slave, and quite servile enough to crouch, himself, at the feet of the master. He was ambitious enough to be contented with nothing short of the highest rank of overseers, and persevering enough to reach the height of his ambition. He was cruel enough to inflict the severest punishment, artful enough to descend to the lowest trickery, and obdurate enough to be insensible to the voice of a reproving conscience. He was, of all the overseers, the most dreaded by the slaves. His presence was painful; his eye flashed confusion; and seldom was his sharp, shrill voice heard, without producing horror and trembling in their ranks.

Mr. Gore was a grave man, and, though a young man, he indulged in no jokes, said no funny words, seldom smiled. His words were in perfect keeping with his looks, and his looks were in perfect keeping with his words. Overseers will sometimes indulge in a witty word, even with the slaves; not so with Mr. Gore. He spoke but to command, and commanded but to be obeyed; he dealt sparingly with his words, and bountifully with his whip, never using the former where the latter would answer as well. When he whipped, he seemed to do so from a sense of duty, and feared no consequences. He did nothing reluctantly, no matter how disagreeable; always at his post, never inconsistent. He never promised but to fulfil. He was, in a word, a man of the most inflexible firmness and stone-like coolness.

His savage barbarity was equaled only by the consummate coolness with which he committed the grossest and most savage deeds upon the slaves under his charge. Mr. Gore once undertook to whip one of Colonel Lloyd's slaves, by the name of Demby. He had given Demby but few stripes, when, to get rid of the scourging, he ran and plunged himself into a creek, and stood there at the depth of his shoulders, refusing to come out. Mr. Gore told him that he would give him three calls, and that, if he did not come out at the third call, he would shoot him. The first call was given. Demby made no response, but stood his ground. The second and third calls were given with the same result. Mr. Gore then, without consultation or deliberation with any one, not even giving Demby an additional call, raised his musket to his face, taking deadly aim at his standing victim, and in an instant poor Demby was no more. His mangled body sank out of sight, and blood and brains marked the water where he had stood.

A thrill of horror flashed through every soul upon the plantation, excepting Mr. Gore. He alone seemed cool and collected. He was asked by Colonel Lloyd and my old master, why he resorted to this extraordinary expedient. His reply was, (as well as I can remember,) that Demby had become unmanageable. He was setting a dangerous example to the other slaves,--one which, if suffered to pass without some such demonstration on his part, would finally lead to the total subversion of all rule and order upon the plantation. He argued that if one slave refused to be corrected, and escaped with his life, the other slaves would soon copy the example; the result of which would be, the freedom of the slaves, and the enslavement of the whites. Mr. Gore's defence was satisfactory. He was continued in his station as overseer upon the home plantation. His fame as an overseer went abroad. His horrid crime was not even submitted to judicial investigation. It was committed in the presence of slaves, and they of course could neither institute a suit, nor testify against him; and thus the guilty perpetrator of one of the bloodiest and most foul murders goes unwhipped of justice, and uncensured by the community in which he lives. Mr. Gore lived in St. Michael's, Talbot county, Maryland, when I left there; and if he is still alive, he very probably lives there now; and if so, he is now, as he was then, as highly esteemed and as much respected as though his guilty soul had not been stained with his brother's blood.

I speak advisedly when I say this,--that killing a slave, or any colored person, in Talbot county, Maryland, is not treated as a crime, either by the courts or the community. Mr. Thomas Lanman, of St. Michael's, killed two slaves, one of whom he killed with a hatchet, by knocking his brains out. He used to boast of the commission of the awful and bloody deed. I have heard him do so laughingly, saying, among other things, that he was the only benefactor of his country in the company, and that when others would do as much as he had done, we should be relieved of "the d--d n--s."

The wife of Mr. Giles Hick, living but a short distance from where I used to live, murdered my wife's cousin, a young girl between fifteen and sixteen years of age, mangling her person in the most horrible manner, breaking her nose and breastbone with a stick, so that the poor girl expired in a few hours afterward. She was immediately buried, but had not been in her untimely grave but a few hours before she was taken up and examined by the coroner, who decided that she had come to her death by severe beating. The offence for which this girl was thus murdered was this:-- She had been set that night to mind Mrs. Hick's baby, and during the night she fell asleep, and the baby cried. She, having lost her rest for several nights previous, did not hear the crying. They were both in the room with Mrs. Hicks. Mrs. Hicks, finding the girl slow to move, jumped from her bed, seized an oak stick of wood by the fireplace, and with it broke the girl's nose and breastbone, and thus ended her life. I will not say that this most horrid murder produced no sensation in the community. It did produce sensation, but not enough to bring the murderess to punishment. There was a warrant issued for her arrest, but it was never served. Thus she escaped not only punishment, but even the pain of being arraigned before a court for her horrid crime.

Whilst I am detailing bloody deeds which took place during my stay on Colonel Lloyd's plantation, I will briefly narrate another, which occurred about the same time as the murder of Demby by Mr. Gore.

Colonel Lloyd's slaves were in the habit of spending a part of their nights and Sundays in fishing for oysters, and in this way made up the deficiency of their scanty allowance. An old man belonging to Colonel Lloyd, while thus engaged, happened to get beyond the limits of Colonel Lloyd's, and on the premises of Mr. Beal Bondly. At this trespass, Mr. Bondly took offence, and with his musket came down to the shore, and blew its deadly contents into the poor old man.

Mr. Bondly came over to see Colonel Lloyd the next day, whether to pay him for his property, or to justify himself in what he had done, I know not. At any rate, this whole fiendish transaction was soon hushed up. There was very little said about it at all, and nothing done. It was a common saying, even among little white boys, that it was worth a half-cent to kill a "n--," and a half-cent to bury one.

Chapter V

As to my own treatment while I lived on Colonel Lloyd's plantation, it was very similar to that of the other slave children. I was not old enough to work in the field, and there being little else than field work to do, I had a great deal of leisure time. The most I had to do was to drive up the cows at evening, keep the fowls out of the garden, keep the front yard clean, and run of errands for my old master's daughter, Mrs. Lucretia Auld. The most of my leisure time I spent in helping Master Daniel Lloyd in finding his birds, after he had shot them. My connection with Master Daniel was of some advantage to me. He became quite attached to me, and was a sort of protector of me. He would not allow the older boys to impose upon me, and would divide his cakes with me.

I was seldom whipped by my old master, and suffered little from anything else than hunger and cold. I suffered much from hunger, but much more from cold. In hottest summer and coldest winter, I was kept almost naked--no shoes, no stockings, no jacket, no trousers, nothing on but a coarse tow linen shirt, reaching only to my knees. I had no bed. I must have perished with cold, but that, the coldest nights, I used to steal a bag which was used for carrying corn to the mill. I would crawl into this bag, and there sleep on the cold, damp, clay floor, with my head in and feet out. My feet have been so cracked with the frost, that the pen with which I am writing might be laid in the gashes.

We were not regularly allowanced. Our food was coarse corn meal boiled. This was called mush. It was put into a large wooden tray or trough, and set down upon the ground. The children were then called, like so many pigs, and like so many pigs they would come and devour the mush; some with oyster-shells, others with pieces of shingle, some with naked hands, and none with spoons. He that ate fastest got most; he that was strongest secured the best place; and few left the trough satisfied.

I was probably between seven and eight years old when I left Colonel Lloyd's plantation. I left it with joy. I shall never forget the ecstasy with which I received the intelligence that my old master (Anthony) had determined to let me go to Baltimore, to live with Mr. Hugh Auld, brother to my old master's son-in-law, Captain Thomas Auld. I received this information about three days before my departure. They were three of the happiest days I ever enjoyed. I spent the most part of all these three days in the creek, washing off the plantation scurf, and preparing myself for my departure.

The pride of appearance which this would indicate was not my own. I spent the time in washing, not so much because I wished to, but because Mrs. Lucretia had told me I must get all the dead skin off my feet and knees before I could go to Baltimore; for the people in Baltimore were very cleanly, and would laugh at me if I looked dirty. Besides, she was going to give me a pair or trousers, which I should not put on unless I got all the dirt off me. The thought of owning a pair of trousers was great indeed! It was almost a sufficient motive, not only to make me take off what would be called by pig-drovers the mange, but the skin itself. I went at it in good earnest, working for the first time with the hope of reward.

The ties that ordinarily bind children to their homes were all suspended in my case. I found no severe trial in my departure. My home was charmless; it was not home to me; on parting from it, I could not feel that I was leaving anything which I could have enjoyed by staying. My mother was dead, my grandmother lived far off, so that I seldom saw her. I had two sisters and one brother, that lived in the same house with me; but the early separation of us from our mother had well nigh blotted the fact of our relationship from our memories. I looked for home elsewhere, and was confident of finding none which I should relish less than the one which I was leaving. If, however, I found in my new home hardship, hunger, whipping, and nakedness, I had the consolation that I should not have escaped any one of them by staying. Having already had more than a taste of them in the house of my old master, and having endured them there, I very naturally inferred my ability to endure them elsewhere, and especially at Baltimore; for I had something of the feeling about Baltimore that is expressed in the proverb, that "being hanged in England is preferable to dying a natural death in Ireland." I had the strongest desire to see Baltimore. Cousin Tom, though not fluent in speech, had inspired me with that desire by his eloquent description of the place. I could never point out anything at the Great House, no matter how beautiful or powerful, but that he had seen something at Baltimore far exceeding, both in beauty and strength, the object which I pointed out to him. Even the Great House itself, with all its pictures, was far inferior to many buildings in Baltimore. So strong was my desire, that I thought a gratification of it would fully compensate for whatever loss of comforts I should sustain by the exchange. I left without a regret, and with the highest hopes of future happiness.

We sailed out of Miles River for Baltimore on a Saturday morning. I remember only the day of the week, for at that time I had no knowledge of the days of the month, nor the months of the year. On setting sail, I walked aft, and gave to Colonel Lloyd's plantation what I hoped would be the last look. I then placed myself in the bows of the sloop, and there spent the remainder of the day in looking ahead, interesting myself in what was in the distance rather than in things nearby or behind.

In the afternoon of that day, we reached Annapolis, the capital of the State. We stopped but a few moments so that I had no time to go on shore. It was the first large town that I had ever seen, and though it would look small compared with some of our New England factory villages, I thought it a wonderful place for its size--more imposing even than the Great House Farm!

We arrived at Baltimore early on Sunday morning, landing at Smith's Wharf, not far from Bowley's Wharf. We had on board the sloop a large flock of sheep; and after aiding in driving them to the slaughterhouse of Mr. Curtis on Louden Slater's Hill, I was conducted by Rich, one of the hands belonging on board of the sloop, to my new home in Alliciana Street, near Mr. Gardner's ship-yard, on Fells Point.

Mr. and Mrs. Auld were both at home, and met me at the door with their little son Thomas, to take care of whom I had been given. And here I saw what I had never seen before; it was a white face beaming with the most kindly emotions; it was the face of my new mistress, Sophia Auld. I wish I could describe the rapture that flashed through my soul as I beheld it. It was a new and strange sight to me, brightening up my pathway with the light of happiness. Little Thomas was told, there was his Freddy,--and I was told to take care of little Thomas; and thus I entered upon the duties of my new home with the most cheering prospect ahead.

I look upon my departure from Colonel Lloyd's plantation as one of the most interesting events of my life. It is possible, and even quite probable, that but for the mere circumstance of being removed from that plantation to Baltimore, I should have to-day, instead of being here seated by my own table, in the enjoyment of freedom and the happiness of home, writing this Narrative, been confined in the galling chains of slavery. Going to live at Baltimore laid the foundation, and opened the gateway, to all my subsequent prosperity. I have ever regarded it as the first plain manifestation of that kind providence which has ever since attended me, and marked my life with so many favors. I regarded the selection of myself as being somewhat remarkable. There were a number of slave children that might have been sent from the plantation to Baltimore. There were those younger, those older, and those of the same age. I was chosen from among them all, and was the first, last, and only choice.

I may be deemed superstitions, and even egotistical, in regarding this event as a special interposition of divine Providence in my favor. But I should be false to the earliest sentiments of my soul, if I suppressed the opinion. I prefer to be true to myself, even at the hazard of incurring the ridicule of others, rather than to be false, and incur my own abhorrence. From my earliest recollection, I date the entertainment of a deep conviction that slavery would not always be able to hold me within its foul embrace; and in the darkest hours of my career in slavery, this living word of faith and spirit of hope departed not from me, but remained like ministering angels to cheer me through the gloom. This good spirit was from God, and to him I offer thanksgiving and praise.

Two Ways of Seeing a River

Mark Twain [1835-1910]

Now when I had mastered the language of this water and had come to know every trifling feature that bordered the great river as familiarly as I knew the letters of the alphabet, I had made a valuable acquisition. But I had lost something, too. I had lost something which could never be restored to me while I lived. All the grace, the beauty, the poetry had gone out of the majestic river! I still keep in mind a certain wonderful sunset which I witnessed when steamboating was new to me. A broad expanse of the river was turned to blood; in the middle distance the red hue brightened into gold, through which a solitary log came floating, black and conspicuous; in one place a long, slanting mark lay sparkling upon the water; in another the surface was broken by boiling, tumbling rings, that were as many-tinted as an opal; where the ruddy flush was faintest, was a smooth spot that was covered with graceful circles and radiating lines, ever so delicately traced; the shore on our left was densely wooded, and the somber shadow that fell from this forest was broken in one place by a long, ruffled trail that shone like silver; and high above the forest wall a clean-stemmed dead tree waved a single leafy bough that glowed like a flame in the unobstructed splendor that was flowing from the sun. There were graceful curves, reflected images, woody heights, soft distances; and over the whole scene, far and near, the dissolving lights drifted steadily, enriching it, every passing moment, with new marvels of coloring.

I stood like one bewitched. I drank it in, in a speechless rapture. The world was new to me, and I had never seen anything like this at home. But as I have said, a day came when I began to cease from noting the glories and the charms which the moon and the sun and the twilight wrought upon the river's face; another day came when I ceased altogether to note them. Then, if that sunset scene had been repeated, I should have looked upon it without rapture, and should have commented upon it, inwardly, in this fashion: This sun means that we are going to have wind to-morrow; that floating log means that the river is rising, small thanks to it; that slanting mark on the water refers to a bluff reef which is going to kill somebody's steamboat one of these nights, if it keeps on stretching out like that; those tumbling "boils" show a dissolving bar and a changing channel there; the lines and circles in the slick water over yonder are a warning that that troublesome place is shoaling up dangerously; that silver streak in the shadow of the forest is the "break" from a new snag, and he has located himself in the very best place he could have found to fish for steamboats; that tall dead tree, with a single living branch, is not going to last long, and then how is a body ever going to get through this blind place at night without the friendly old landmark?

No, the romance and the beauty were all gone from the river. All the value any feature of it had for me now was the amount of usefulness it could furnish toward compassing the safe piloting of a steamboat. Since those days, I have pitied doctors from my heart. What does the lovely flush in a beauty's cheek mean to a doctor but a "break" that ripples above some deadly disease? Are not all her visible charms sown thick with what are to him the signs and symbols of hidden decay? Does he ever see her beauty at all, or doesn't he simply view her professionally, and comment upon her unwholesome condition all to himself? And doesn't he sometimes wonder whether he has gained most or lost most by learning his trade?

Letter I

Isabella Bird [1831-1904]

Lake Tahoe, September 2

I have found a dream of beauty at which one might look all one's life and sigh. Not lovable, like the Sandwich Islands, but beautiful in its own way! A strictly North American beauty—snow splotched mountains, huge pines, red-woods, sugar pines, silver spruce; a crystalline atmosphere, waves of the richest colour; and a pine-hung lake which mirrors all beauty on its surface. Lake Tahoe is before me, a sheet of water twenty-two miles long by ten broad, and in some places 1,700 feet deep. It lies at a height of 6,000 feet and the snow-crowned summits which wall it in are from 8,000 to 11,000 feet in altitude. The air is keen and elastic. There is no sound but the distant and slightly musical ring of the lumberer's axe.

It is a weariness to go back, even in thought, to the clang of San Francisco, which I left in its cold morning fog early yesterday, driving to the Oakland ferry through streets with side-walks heaped with thousands of cantaloupe and water-melons, tomatoes, cucumbers, squashes, pears, grapes, peaches, apricots—all of startling size as compared with any I ever saw before. Other streets were piled with sacks of flour, left out all night, owing to the security from rain at this season. I pass hastily over the early part of the journey, the crossing the bay in a fog as chill as November, the number of "lunch baskets," which gave the car the look of conveying a great picnic party, the last view of the Pacific, on which I had looked for nearly a year, the fierce sunshine and brilliant sky inland, the look of long rainlessness, which one may not call drought, the valleys with sides crimson with the poison oak, the dusty vineyards, with great purple clusters thick among the leaves, and between the vines great dusty melons lying on the dusty earth. From off the boundless harvest fields the grain was carried in June, and it is now stacked in sacks along the track, awaiting freightage. California is a "land flowing with milk and honey." The barns are bursting with fullness. In the dusty orchards the apple and pear branches are supported, that they may not break down under the weight of fruit; melons, tomatoes, and squashes of gigantic size lie almost unheeded on the ground; fat cattle, gorged almost to repletion, shade themselves under the oaks; superb "red" horses shine, not with grooming, but with condition; and thriving farms everywhere show on what a solid basis the prosperity of the "Golden State" is founded. Very uninviting, however rich, was the blazing Sacramento Valley, and very repulsive the city of Sacramento, which, at a distance of 125 miles from the Pacific, has an elevation of only thirty feet. The mercury stood at 103 degrees in the shade, and the fine white dust was stifling.

In the late afternoon we began the ascent of the Sierras, whose saw-like points had been in sight for many miles. The dusty fertility was all left behind, the country became rocky and gravelly, and deeply scored by streams bearing the muddy wash of the mountain gold mines down to the muddier Sacramento. There were long broken ridges and deep ravines, the ridges becoming longer, the ravines deeper, the pines thicker and larger, as we ascended into a cool atmosphere of exquisite purity, and before 6 P.M. the last traces of cultivation and the last hardwood trees were left behind.

At Colfax, a station at a height of 2,400 feet, I got out and walked the length of the train. First came two great gaudy engines, the Grizzly Bear and the White Fox, with their respective tenders loaded with logs of wood, the engines with great, solitary, reflecting lamps in front above the cow guards, a quantity of polished brass-work, comfortable glass houses, and well-stuffed seats for the engine-drivers. The engines and tenders were succeeded by a baggage car, the latter loaded with bullion and valuable parcels, and in charge of two "express agents." Each of these cars is forty-five feet long. Then came two cars loaded with peaches and grapes; then two "silver palace" cars, each sixty feet long; then a smoking car, at that time occupied mainly by [Chinese men]; and then five ordinary passenger cars, with platforms like all the others, making altogether a train about 700 feet in length. The platforms of the four front cars were clustered over with Digger Indians, with their squaws, children, and gear. They are perfect savages, without any aptitude for even aboriginal civilization, and are altogether the most degraded of the ill-fated tribes which are dying out before the white races. They were all very diminutive, five feet one inch being, I should think, about the average height, with flat noses, wide mouths, and black hair, cut straight above the eyes and hanging lank and long at the back and sides. The squaws wore their hair thickly plastered with pitch, and a broad band of the same across their noses and cheeks. They carried their infants on their backs, strapped to boards. The clothing of both sexes was a ragged, dirty combination of coarse woolen cloth and hide, the moccasins being unornamented. They were all hideous and filthy, and swarming with vermin. The men carried short bows and arrows, one of them, who appeared to be the chief, having a lynx's skin for a quiver. A few had fishing tackle, but the bystanders said that they lived almost entirely upon grasshoppers. They were a most impressive incongruity in the midst of the tokens of an omnipotent civilization.

The light of the sinking sun from that time glorified the Sierras, and as the dew fell, aromatic odors made the still air sweet. On a single track, sometimes carried on a narrow ledge excavated from the mountain side by men lowered from the top in baskets, overhanging ravines from 2,000 to 3,000 feet deep, the monster train snaked its way upwards, stopping sometimes in front of a few frame houses, at others where nothing was to be seen but a log cabin with a few [Chinese men] hanging about it, but where trails on the sides of the ravines pointed to a gold country above and below. So sharp and frequent are the curves on some parts of the ascent, that on looking out of the window one could seldom see more than a part of the train at once. At Cape Horn, where the track curves round the ledge of a precipice 2,500 feet in depth, it is correct to be frightened, and a fashion of holding the breath and shutting the eyes prevails, but my fears were reserved for the crossing of a trestle bridge over a very deep chasm, which is itself approached by a sharp curve. This bridge appeared to be overlapped by the cars so as to produce the effect of looking down directly into a wild gulch, with a torrent raging along it at an immense depth below. Shivering in the keen, frosty air near the summit pass of the Sierras, we entered the "snow-sheds," wooden galleries, which for about fifty miles shut out all the splendid views of the region, as given in dioramas, not even allowing a glimpse of "the Gem of the Sierras," the lovely Donner Lake. One of these sheds is twenty-seven miles long. In a few hours the mercury had fallen from 103 degrees to 29 degrees, and we had ascended

6,987 feet in 105 miles! After passing through the sheds, we had several grand views of a pine forest on fire before reaching Truckee at 11 P.M. having traveled 258 miles. Truckee, the center of the "lumbering region" of the Sierras, is usually spoken of as "a rough mountain town," and Mr. W. had told me that all the roughs of the district congregated there, that there were nightly pistol affrays in bar-rooms, etc., but as he admitted that a lady was sure of respect, and Mr. G. strongly advised me to stay and see the lakes, I got out, much dazed, and very stupid with sleep, envying the people in the sleeping car, who were already unconscious on their luxurious couches. The cars drew up in a street—if street that could be called which was only a wide, cleared space, intersected by rails, with here and there a stump, and great piles of sawn logs bulking big in the moonlight, and a number of irregular clap-board, steep-roofed houses, many of them with open fronts, glaring with light and crowded with men. We had pulled up at the door of a rough Western hotel, with a partially open front, being a bar-room crowded with men drinking and smoking, and the space between it and the cars was a moving mass of loafers and passengers. On the tracks, engines, tolling heavy bells, were mightily moving, the glare from their cyclopean eyes dulling the light of a forest which was burning fitfully on a mountain side; and on open spaces great fires of pine logs were burning cheerily, with groups of men round them. A band was playing noisily, and the unholy sound of tom-toms was not far off. Mountains—the Sierras of many a fireside dream—seemed to wall in the town, and great pines stood out, sharp and clear cut, against a sky in which a moon and stars were shining frostily.

It was a sharp frost at that great height, and when an "irrepressible [man]," who seemed to represent the hotel establishment, deposited me and my carpetbag in a room which answered for "the parlor," I was glad to find some remains of pine knots still alight in the stove. A man came in and said that when the cars were gone he would try to get me a room, but they were so full that it would be a very poor one. The crowd was solely masculine. It was then 11:30 P.M., and I had not had a meal since 6 A.M.; but when I asked hopefully for a hot supper, with tea, I was told that no supper could be got at that hour; but in half an hour the same man returned with a small cup of cold, weak tea, and a small slice of bread, which looked as if it had been much handled.

I asked the [man] about the hire of horses, and presently a man came in from the bar who, he said, could supply my needs. This man, the very type of a Western pioneer, bowed, threw himself into a rocking-chair, drew a spittoon beside him, cut a fresh quid of tobacco, began to chew energetically, and put his feet, cased in miry high boots, into which his trousers were tucked, on the top of the stove. He said he had horses which would both "lope" and trot, that some ladies preferred the Mexican saddle, that I could ride alone in perfect safety; and after a route had been devised, I hired a horse for two days. This man wore a pioneer's badge as one of the earliest settlers of California, but he had moved on as one place after another had become too civilized for him, "but nothing," he added, "was likely to change much in Truckee." I was afterwards told that the usual regular hours of sleep are not observed there. The accommodation is too limited for the population of 2,000, which is masculine mainly, and is liable to frequent temporary additions, and beds are occupied continuously, though by different occupants, throughout the greater part of the twenty-four hours. Consequently I found the bed and room allotted to me quite tumbled looking. Men's coats and sticks were hanging up, miry boots were littered about, and a rifle was in one corner. There was no window to the outer air, but I slept soundly, being only once awoke by an increase of the same din in which I had fallen asleep, varied by three pistol shots fired in rapid succession.

This morning Truckee wore a totally different aspect. The crowds of the night before had disappeared. There were heaps of ashes where the fires had been. A sleepy German waiter seemed the only person about the premises, the open drinking saloons were nearly empty, and only a few sleepy-looking loafers hung about in what is called the street. It might have been Sunday; but they say that it brings a great accession of throng and jollity. Public worship has died out at present; work is discontinued on Sunday, but the day is given up to pleasure. Putting a minimum of indispensables into a bag, and slipping on my Hawaiian riding dress over a silk skirt, and a dust cloak over all, I stealthily crossed the plaza to the livery stable, the largest building in Truckee, where twelve fine horses were stabled in stalls on each side of a broad drive. My friend of the evening before showed me his "rig," three velvet-covered side-saddles almost without horns. Some ladies, he said, used the horn of the Mexican saddle, but none "in the part" rode cavalier fashion. I felt abashed. I could not ride any distance in the conventional mode, and was just going to give up this splendid "ravage," when the man said, "Ride your own fashion; here, at Truckee, if anywhere in the world, people can do as they like." Blissful Truckee! In no time a large grey horse was "rigged out" in a handsome silver-bossed Mexican saddle, with ornamental leather tassels hanging from the stirrup guards, and a housing of black bear's-skin. I strapped my silk skirt on the saddle, deposited my cloak in the corn-bin, and was safely on the horse's back before his owner had time to devise any way of mounting me. Neither he nor any of the loafers who had assembled showed the slightest sign of astonishment, but all were as respectful as possible.

Once on horseback my embarrassment disappeared, and I rode through Truckee, whose irregular, steep-roofed houses and shanties, set down in a clearing and surrounded closely by mountain and forest, looked like a temporary encampment; passed under the Pacific Railroad; and then for twelve miles followed the windings of the Truckee River, a clear, rushing, mountain stream, in which immense pine logs had gone aground not to be floated off till the next freshet, a loud-tongued, rollicking stream of ice-cold water, on whose banks no ferns or trailers hang, and which leaves no greenness along its turbulent progress. All was bright with that brilliancy of sky and atmosphere, that blaze of sunshine and universal glitter, which I never saw till I came to California, combined with an elasticity in the air which removed all lassitude, and gives one spirit enough for anything. On either side of the Truckee great sierras rose like walls, castellated, embattled, rifted, skirted and crowned with pines of enormous size, the walls now and then breaking apart to show some snow-slashed peak rising into a heaven of intense, unclouded, sunny blue. At this altitude of 6,000 feet one must learn to be content with varieties of coniferæ, for, except for aspens, which spring up in some places where the pines have been cleared away, and for cotton-woods, which at a lower level fringe the streams, there is nothing but the bear cherry, the raspberry, the gooseberry, the wild grape, and the wild currant. None of these grew near the Truckee, but I feasted my eyes on pines which, though not so large as the Wellingtonia of the Yosemite, are really gigantic, attaining a height of 250 feet, their huge stems, the warm red of cedar wood, rising straight and branchless for a third of their height, their diameter from seven to fifteen feet, their shape that of a larch, but with the needles long and dark, and cones a foot long. Pines cleft the sky; they were massed wherever level ground occurred; they stood over the Truckee at right angles, or lay across it in prostrate grandeur. Their stumps and carcasses were everywhere; and smooth "shoots" on the sierras marked where they were shot down as "felled timber," to be floated off by the river. To them this wild region owes its scattered population, and the sharp ring of the lumberer's axe mingles with the cries of wild beasts and the roar of mountain torrents.

The track is a soft, natural, wagon road, very pleasant to ride on. The horse was much too big for me, and had plans of his own; but now and then, where the ground admitted to it, I tried his heavy "lope" with much amusement. I met nobody, and passed nothing on the road but a freight wagon, drawn by twenty-two oxen, guided by three fine-looking men, who had some difficulty in making room for me to pass their awkward convoy. After I had ridden about ten miles the road went up a steep hill in the forest, turned abruptly, and through the blue gloom of the great pines which rose from the ravine in which the river was then hid, came glimpses of two mountains, about 11,000 feet in height, whose bald grey summits were crowned with pure snow. It was one of those glorious surprises in scenery which make one feel as if one must bow down and worship. The forest was thick, and had an undergrowth of dwarf spruce and brambles, but as the horse had become fidgety and "scary" on the track, I turned off in the idea of taking a short cut, and was sitting carelessly, shortening my stirrup, when a great, dark, hairy beast rose, crashing and snorting, out of the tangle just in front of me. I had only a glimpse of him, and thought that my imagination had magnified a wild boar, but it was a bear. The horse snorted and plunged violently, as if he would go down to the river, and then turned, still plunging, up a steep bank, when, finding that I must come off, I threw myself off on the right side, where the ground rose considerably, so that I had not far to fall. I got up covered with dust, but neither shaken nor bruised. It was truly grotesque and humiliating. The bear ran in one direction, and the horse in another. I hurried after the latter, and twice he stopped till I was close to him, then turned round and cantered away. After walking about a mile in deep dust, I picked up first the saddle-blanket and next my bag, and soon came upon the horse, standing facing me, and shaking all over. I thought I should catch him then, but when I went up to him he turned round, threw up his heels several times, rushed off the track, galloped in circles, bucking, kicking, and plunging for some time, and then throwing up his heels as an act of final defiance, went off at full speed in the direction of Truckee, with the saddle over his shoulders and the great wooden stirrups thumping his sides, while I trudged ignominiously along in the dust, laboriously carrying the bag and saddle-blanket.

I walked for nearly an hour, heated and hungry, when to my joy I saw the ox-team halted across the top of a gorge, and one of the teamsters leading the horse towards me. The young man said that, seeing the horse coming, they had drawn the team across the road to stop him, and remembering that he had passed them with a lady on him, they feared that there had been an accident, and had just saddled one of their own horses to go in search of me. He brought me some water to wash the dust from my face, and re-saddled the horse, but the animal snorted and plunged for some time before he would let me mount, and then sidled along in such a nervous and scared way, that the teamster walked for some distance by me to see that I was "all right." He said that the woods in the neighborhood of Tahoe had been full of brown and grizzly bears for some days, but that no one was in any danger from them. I took a long gallop beyond the scene of my tumble to quiet the horse, who was most restless and troublesome.

Then the scenery became truly magnificent and bright with life. Crested blue-jays darted through the dark pines, squirrels in hundreds scampered through the forest, red dragon-flies flashed like "living light," exquisite chipmunks ran across the track, but only a dusty blue lupin here and there reminded me of earth's fairer children. Then the river became broad and still, and mirrored in its transparent depths regal pines, straight as an arrow, with rich yellow and green lichen clinging to their stems, and firs and balsam pines filling up the spaces between them, the gorge opened, and this mountain-girdled lake lay before me, with its margin broken up into bays and promontories, most picturesquely clothed by huge sugar pines. It lay dimpling and scintillating beneath the noonday sun, as entirely unspoilt as fifteen years ago, when its pure loveliness was known only to trappers and Indians. One man lives on it the whole year round; otherwise early October strips its shores of their few inhabitants, and thereafter, for seven months, it is rarely accessible except on snowshoes. It never freezes. In the dense forests which bound it, and drape two-thirds of its gaunt sierras, are hordes of grizzlies, brown bears, wolves, elk, deer, chipmunks, martens, minks, skunks, foxes, squirrels, and snakes. On its margin I found an irregular wooden inn, with a lumber-wagon at the door, on which was the carcass of a large grizzly bear, shot behind the house this morning. I had intended to ride ten miles farther, but, finding that the trail in some places was a "blind" one, and being bewitched by the beauty and serenity of Tahoe, I have remained here sketching, reveling in the view from the veranda, and strolling in the forest. At this height there is frost every night of the year, and my fingers are benumbed.

The beauty is entrancing. The sinking sun is out of sight behind the western Sierras, and all the pine-hung promontories on this side of the water are rich indigo, just reddened with lake, deepening here and there into Tyrian purple. The peaks above, which still catch the sun, are bright rose-red, and all the mountains on the other side are pink; and pink, too, are the far-off summits on which the snow-drifts rest. Indigo, red, and orange tints stain the still water, which lies solemn and dark against the shore, under the shadow of stately pines. An hour later, and a moon nearly full—not a pale, flat disc, but a radiant sphere—has wheeled up into the flushed sky. The sunset has passed through every stage of beauty, through every glory of color, through riot and triumph, through pathos and tenderness, into a long, dreamy, painless rest, succeeded by the profound solemnity of the moonlight, and a stillness broken only by the night cries of beasts in the aromatic forests.

I.L.B. (1879)

Section D: Exercises in Creative Nonfiction

CREATIVITY EXERCISE: Fifteen minute free-write. Set a timer for fifteen minutes; then go and take a seat. Pick up a pen, and write about something, anything, until the timer chimes. Don't stop. Begin with the writing prompt; have fun! (C3 Scale)

Prompt: I was born on…

Exercise 1: In chapter five of Frederick Douglass' narrative, he tells of the hope he felt at his first sight of Sophia Auld. The juxtaposition of his warm welcome by the Aulds and the life he had experienced and witnessed previously allow us to grasp the joy he felt at that moment. Write a two to five page narrative about a personal experience in which a terrifying or tragic moment is juxtaposed with a lighthearted or happy one. Write your first draft without thought to technique, and then edit your own writing according to the rules and guidelines presented in sub-sections 2 and 3. Submit the final draft. (C2 Scale)

Exercise 2: Take a walk around your backyard or a hike through the woods. Pay attention to every sound, smell, and sight that you see. As soon as you arrive back home, sit down and write a letter to Isabella Bird. (C1 Scale)

Exercise 3: In Exercise 6 of Unit I, you wrote a poem about a special memory. Write a two to five page short story about the events behind that poem. Write the story in the third person point of view. (C2 Scale)

Exercise 4: Looking back over your life, and allowing memory to work as editor, what do you see? What do you feel qualified to teach or share? Write a two to five page first-person narrative in which you impart a truth or lesson that you have learned through life experience. Try to use analogy in your writing. (C2 Scale)

Exercise 5: Using the plot outline you wrote in Unit II, write the story of Joseph's life. Do not add to the content of the story, but be very creative in the retelling. Write from the point of view of your choice. (C2 Scale)

Unit IV: Fiction

Section A: What is Fiction?

Fiction has been categorized in a variety of ways. For the purpose of this text, we will deal only with two broad classifications: fiction realism and fiction fairy-tale (sometimes referred to as romantic fiction). While fairy-tale style fiction may involve superhuman powers, futuristic sciences, aliens, fairies, elves, talking animals, and even more otherworldly things, the truths put forth by fairy-tale fiction are no less true than the truths put forth by fiction that is *real.* As literary critic, Clayton Hamilton [1881–1946], states in *A Manual of the Art of Fiction* [1918], "The purpose of fiction is to embody certain truths of human life in a series of imagined facts."

The created world of the fiction writer may look very much like his own, or it may climb from the corners of his wildest imagination. Regardless of the actuality or the unfathomability of the world he has designed, the writer should structure his world around laws and theories that reveal something of humankind.

It is the goal of every serious novelist not only to entertain but to teach. The novelist does not present his theories or doctrines like those who instruct through essays; the novelist shows his truths through the lives of imaginary people—people that he has created from a diligent study of life around him. Because one could never get away with writing as boldly or directly about the thoughts, motivations, and lives of actual people, the novelist, through his created world, can potentially report truer stories than the biographical writer of nonfiction.

Fiction, to borrow a figure from chemical science, is *life distilled*. In the author's mind, the actual is first evaporated to the real, and the real is then condensed to the imagined. The author first transmutes the concrete actualities of life into abstract realities; and then he transmutes these abstract realities into concrete imaginings. Necessarily, if he has pursued this mental process without a fallacy, his imaginings will be true; because they represent realities, which in turn have been induced from actualities. If the general laws of life which the novelist has thought out be true laws, and if his imaginative embodiment of them be at all points thoroughly consistent, his characters will be true men and women in the highest sense. They will not be actual, but they will be real.

Clayton Hamilton, *A Manual of the Art of Fiction*

Section B: Reading and Writing Fiction

1. Literary Devices

Allegory:

An allegory involves the comparison of something abstract with something concrete and familiar. Metaphors and similes are used to write an allegory. Essentially, an allegory is an expanded metaphor. A writer uses allegory to garner the reader's interest in two separate ways: 1) in the concrete events, characters, and setting presented 2) in the ideas which the concrete things are conveying. Allegories may be political, moral, satirical, personal, or a combination of these. Nathaniel Hawthorne's, *The Celestial Railroad* (page 270), is a perfect example of allegory. In fact, it is an allegory based on an allegory, as Hawthorne wrote his piece as a modern response to John Bunyan's *The Pilgrim's Progress*.

Anachronism:

Anachronism is derived from the Greek "anachronous," meaning "against time". An out of place accent, speech pattern, invention, style of dress, etc. are all possible ways an author might slip into unintended anachronism. Anachronism is usually due to the writer's failure to thoroughly research the setting in which his story takes place. A famous *oops* of anachronism is found in Act 2, Scene 1 of William Shakespeare's play *Julius Caesar*:

"Brutus: Peace! Count the clock.

Cassius: The clock has stricken three."

The setting of this play is 44 AD, and mechanical clocks had yet to be invented.

Archaism:

Archaism is the term used when a written phrase, word, or spelling is considered outdated. "Thee," "thou," and other Old English words and phrases commonly found in the King James' Version of the Bible are thought to be archaic and should be avoided by modern writers.

Flashback:

A flashback is an interruption of the chronological sequence of a story in order to take the reader back to an earlier point in time. Flashbacks are used by the writer at crucial points in the narrative in order to inform the reader of pertinent information. Flashback scenes provide the reader with context as to the thoughts and motivations of the characters. Dream sequences and memories are two methods sometimes used to present flashbacks.

Irony:

There are several different types of irony, the most common being situational irony, cosmic irony, dramatic irony, and sarcasm.

Situational irony occurs when the outcome is completely different than what was expected. If the officer instructing a class on gun-safety were to accidentally fire his gun, the situation would be very ironic.

Cosmic irony happens when one tempts fate and loses. A good example of cosmic irony is the sinking of that "unsinkable ship," the *Titanic*.

Dramatic irony occurs when the reader or audience is allowed to know more than the characters they are observing. Unable to step in and warn them, the reader is left with a sense of irony as their silent pleas of "No, don't marry him!" or "Turn back, it's a trap!" are ignored.

Sarcasm is a commonly used form of irony. When a person uses sarcasm, they verbally attack (whether in fun or rudeness) by pretending to compliment instead. "Oh, that was a brilliant plan!" is an example of a sarcastic response to a failed idea.

Symbolism:

Symbolism is the use of symbols, actions, or words to signify deeper ideas. As well as having a place in literature, we deal with symbolism in everyday life. A hand extended outward is, in our culture, a symbol for friendship or a sign that a deal is being made; a smile is a symbol of affection; a heart-shaped drawing is a symbol of love and friendship. In art and literature, symbolism is generally less pronounced. For example, the black bird in Edgar Allan Poe's "The Raven" is a symbol of death and loss. In the movie trilogy, *Star Wars*, Luke is dressed in light colors and Darth Vader is dressed in black, symbolizing good versus evil.

2. Fiction's Burden of Proof

If an author desires to write true fiction—or fiction that speaks truth to the reader—he should carefully study the world around him. He should train himself to look at and to listen to everything that crosses his path. Simple watching will not be enough, however, for he must care deeply about the things that he studies. Curiosity and compassion will cause experiences to knock at his door; he will learn to see beauty in things that others ignore and pass by. It is only through this sympathetic observation that he will understand the complexity of the world around him. Once he has this knowledge, he will have something *true* to say.

Fiction Realism

> One can speak best from one's own taste, and I may therefore venture to say that the air of reality (solidity of specification) seems to me to be the supreme virtue of a novel--the merit on which all its other merits...helplessly and submissively depend. If it be not there, they are all as nothing, and if these be there, they owe their effect to the success with which the author has produced the illusion of life. The cultivation of this success, the study of this exquisite process, form, to my taste, the beginning and the end of the art of the novelist. They are his inspiration, his despair, his reward, his torment, his delight. It is here, in very truth, that he competes with life; it is here that he competes with his brother the painter in his attempt to render the look of things, the look that conveys their meaning, to catch the colour, the relief, the expression, the surface, the substance of the human spectacle.
>
> Henry James, *The Art of Fiction*

The writer of realistic fiction chooses to teach through imitation of the actual facts found in life. His characters are true to recognizable location, class, dialect, upbringing, etc. He doesn't merely retell stories with names changed to protect the innocent; he *patterns* stories after his real life experiences and observations. This writer's goal is to take what life has taught him and to teach that to his reader. If he does this well, the reader will agree that his tale is truth. But if his characters stray from or break the laws which surround their imagined existence, no amount of narrated explanation and excuse will satisfy the reader. The writer will be labeled a liar. Though the reader understands he is not reading *truth,* he is unwilling to swallow anything less believable.

Of course, because it is true to real life, the reader *wants* to observe as the characters grow and change. It is not stagnation that proves believability. Character is everything in literary fiction, and character development tells the reader that the author has thought through both his story and the affect it will have on his characters. When an author truly understands his characters he can fully present their motivations and effectively write their dialog. Credibility is always an issue. The reader wants to see that the actions and thoughts of the characters are believable for each stage in the story, and the reader also wants to know that the characters are being irrevocably changed in a way that is logical within the story. The reader does not need to understand the life of an 18th century painter to judge whether or not the writer has realistically portrayed it, and he does not have to *be* an 18th century painter to judge the credibility of such a character's actions. The reader will continually and thoroughly judge what is and what is not credible to the story—he will base this judgment on his own life experience and on the facts presented by the writer.

The writer of biographical fiction imagines the lives of actual people; he creates living stories from dusty fact. He does not change his subject; he fills in forgotten blanks so that his subject is resurrected and known by a modern audience. He does his best to accurately represent his character, and he avoids misrepresentation at every turn. Mr. Hamilton says of the biographical writer that "he makes fiction of his heroes in order most emphatically to tell the truth about them," and this is absolutely correct. This attentiveness is especially important for the writer of biblical fiction.

Careful adherence to character should guide all writers of fiction, not only those who speak for an actual human being. Once a character is created, whether by God or by the writer, nothing that falsely portrays that character should ever be written about them. The reader of fiction is as upset by a feeling of falsehood as the reader of nonfiction. In fact, it is much easier to upset the reader of fiction. Whereas real people may be nonsensical to the point where no good plot could be written about them, fictional characters are called upon and created because of their ability to make sense of the world.

The same devotion to *truth* should also pertain to plot. It is not enough to write about something that *has* happened, as life is not always believable. When writing realistic fiction, it's better to write about something that *does* happen—something to which the reader will be able to relate. The laws of life must win.

> The romantic says, "These things are so, because I know they are"; and unless we reject him at once and in entirety as a colossal liar, we are almost doomed to take his word in the big moments of his story. But the realist says, "These things are so, because they are supported by actual facts similar to the imagined facts in which I clothe them"; and we may answer at any point in the story, "Not at all! On the very basis of the facts you show us, we know better than to take your word." In other words, when the reader disbelieves a romance, he does so by instinct, without necessarily knowing why; but when he disbelieves a realistic novel, he does so by logic, with the evidence before him.
>
> Clayton Hamilton, *A Manual of The Art of Fiction*

Fiction Fairy-Tale

Regarding character, character development, and the higher, moral laws of life, the writer of fairy-tale fiction must approach his craft with the same care as the writer of realistic fiction. However, the fairy-tale fiction writer cares little of the basic, everyday facts of life. His animals talk, and his human-like figures have giftings and abilities that drop children's jaws in rapture and envy. The writer of fairy-tale fiction transports the reader to another place—a place far, far away. And he need not tell his readers exactly *how* they've arrived there, only that they have. The fairy-tale writer paints in large sweeping strokes of analogy and brightly colored allegory. This does not, however, remove the burden of proof from the writer of fairy-tale fiction. What his analogies teach us, what his bizarre characters show us, are the same truths put forth by the writer of realistic fiction. The packaging is different, but the lessons are the same.

Robert Louis Stevenson understood that there is an element of evil in the heart of man. To illustrate this point in a way that's left a lasting impression upon the face of literature, Stevenson abandoned the facts of everyday life and instead wrote *Dr. Jekyll and Mr. Hyde,* a bold tale that wildly illustrates (by exaggeration) the truths he had learned in real life.

Just because elephants were created with trunks and did not obtain them in a whacky and dangerous manor does not mean that Rudyard Kipling lied when he wrote his fable, "The Elephant's Child" (page 288). And, while the story is unusual, the reader never has the feeling that he is being lied to. This is because Mr. Kipling is clearly not interested in presenting to the reader the actual facts of life (and the reader is not expecting to read them); Mr. Kipling is interested in telling a story about the unpopularity, the danger, and the remarkable benefits of curiosity.

In *The Celestial Railroad* (page 270), Hawthorne creates characters like Mr. Smooth-it-away; and when Apollyon rides upon the train with smoke coming out of his mouth, no one but the narrator seems bothered by it. Many attributes of Hawthorne's characters are not common to actual people; still, they further the point of his story. This is essentially what good romantic/fairy-tale fiction is all about: the writer sits down to write a truth, but he tells a fable to make the points even clearer than he might have through an everyday tale. What do you believe Hawthorne was attempting to illustrate through *The Celestial Railroad*?

_____

_____

_____

_____

_____

3. Narrative, Description, and Dialog

In *A Manual of the Art of Fiction*, Mr. Hamilton states that well-written fiction is the careful combining of three other forms of writing: narrative, description, and dialog. Because of the necessary weaving of these three different forms, Hamilton, and many others, have dubbed fiction to be the most difficult literary genre. Everything we've learned so far in this text will apply to fiction writing.

Narrative

To master the art of narrative, the writer should first learn to begin a story and to tell it through to the end. Letter-writing is good narrative practice. Another simple exercise is to choose one random event and then to look back over the days, weeks, or years in order to explain how that event came to be—and then to look into the future to logically envision what might happen next.

When a writer encounters an unusually well-dressed person, an out-of-breath woman quickly walking through the grocery store, or a man and a woman colliding in the street and spilling the man's newly poured coffee...the writer will not merely notice the event. Every event consists of three components: the thing that happens (the action), the people involved in the happening (the actors), and the time and place where the thing occurs (the setting). Upon witnessing an event, a diligent writer will create a narrative. *Why is that person dressed so nicely in the middle of the day? Where did they come from, and where are they going now?* The writer will always wonder. *Perhaps the man with the coffee was in such a hurry because he'd purchased it for his overly demanding employer. Perhaps the man has often wondered why he continues to work for such a person. But on this particular day, his work ethic was greatly rewarded as he literally ran into his future wife. Yes!* This scenario would satisfy the writer's imagination.

After the writer has outlined his entire story (as he sees it in that moment), he should look again and determine which events are essential to his narrative. *This happened because this happened before it, and because this happened, this will happen afterwards*: the writer must always be on the lookout for events connected by cause and effect. Once the writer has chosen his scenes and the order in which they occur, once he understands his introduction, his rising action, his climax, his falling action and his conclusion, he may begin writing his story at any point he chooses. In "An Unpremeditated Ceremony" (page 261), L.M. Montgomery briefly resorts to flashback via memory to catch us up in an otherwise chronological story.

Though it is almost never a mistake to start a story from the beginning, in the example of the fortunate coffee incident, the writer might choose to begin his story just before, and leading into, the swell of the climax. In the midst of the climax, he might then stop before the reader is allowed to know whether angry screams or understanding laughter follow the couple's collision. The writer may flash-back as far as he deems necessary to reveal relevant information about the man and the woman. He may then proceed with the rising action and again lead the reader to that event in the street where he first opened his story. Upon approaching the climactic scene for the second time, the reader (who has by this point been convinced that the man and the woman are a perfect match) will be anxious to see the couple "meet".

Description

A narrative is a description of events (fiction or non-fiction) as they happened. The narrative, in itself, is not descriptive. The narrative is continually moving forward, but from time to time it is necessary to stop the progression of the story and to welcome the reader by describing something—object, landscape, person, experience, situation, emotion, etc. The goal of descriptive writing is to paint a rich image that sticks in the mind, impacts the emotions, and appeals to the senses of the reader.

When pausing the narrative to be descriptive, it is important to avoid words that attempt to say without actually saying. If the writer states that the morning was lovely, the reader will not necessarily be convinced. If the writer describes the morning in such a way as to evoke, "Oh, how lovely!" from the reader, the scene will be far more impacting.

Dialog

Dialogue is the most expansive and tiring [form to read], and [it] should frequently be relieved by the condensed narrative, which is simple and easy reading. Description should seldom be given in chunks, but rather in touches of a brief and delicate kind, and with the aim of being suggestive rather than full and detailed.

Clayton Hamilton, *A Manual of the Art of Fiction*

Because listening to and reading dialog are entirely different experiences, the dialog in a story is somewhat different from the dialog in a play. Dialog in a story should be the description of an exchange with snippets of actual conversation, whereas dialog in a play is the full report of what is said.

The best way to master dialog as an element by itself is to practice the type of activity found in Exercise 5 of Unit II—to become a student of conversation. To learn how to most effectively weave that conversation into a story, it is essential to study the novels of writers like Dickens. A wonderful example of the blending of narrative, description, and dialog is found in Chapter II of Dickens' *Mugby Junction,* "Barbox Brothers and Co." (page 245).

4. Rules to Write By

Taken from two lists written by Sherwin Cody and Mark Twain, here are eighteen parting rules to keep in mind when writing:

1. Use words which are in themselves expressive.

2. Place those words in emphatic positions in the sentence.

3. Vary the length and form of successive sentences so that the reader or hearer shall never be wearied by monotony.

4. Use figures of speech, or constant comparison and illustration, thus making words suggest ten times more.

5. Keep persistently at one idea, though from every possible point of view and without repetition of any kind, till that idea has sunk into the mind of the hearer and has been fully comprehended.

6. Remember that a tale shall accomplish something and arrive somewhere.

7. Remember that all events of a tale should be necessary parts of the tale and should help to develop it.

8. Remember that the characters in a tale should be alive, except in the case of corpses, and that always the reader should be able to tell the corpses from the others!

9. Remember that the characters in a tale, both dead and alive, should exhibit a sufficient excuse for being there.

10. Remember that when the characters are talking, the talk should sound like human talk, and be talk such as human beings would be likely to talk in the given circumstances. The talk should have a discoverable meaning, also a discoverable purpose; it should show of relevancy, remain in the neighborhood of the subject in hand, and be interesting to the

reader. It should help out the tale and stop when the people cannot think of anything more to say.

11. When you describe a character, remember that the conduct and conversation of that character should justify your description.

12. When a character talks like a well-educated rich man in the beginning of a paragraph, he should not talk like an illiterate servant in the end of it (and vice versa).

13. Remember to make the reader feel a deep interest in the characters and in their fate; make the reader love the good people in the tale and hate the bad ones.

14. The characters in a tale should be so clearly defined that the reader can tell beforehand what each will do in a given emergency.

15. Say what you are proposing to say, not merely come near it.

16. Use the right word, not its second cousin.

17. Do not omit necessary details.

18. Use good grammar.

What have you learned from this course that you feel should be added to this list?

_____

_____

_____

_____

Section C: Fiction

Mugby Junction, Chapter II--Barbox Brothers and Co.

Charles Dickens [1812-1870]

Although he had arrived at his journey's end for the day by noon, he had since insensibly walked about the town so far and so long that the lamp-lighters were now at their work in the streets, and the shops were sparkling up brilliantly. Thus reminded to turn towards his quarters, he was in the act of doing so, when a very little hand crept into his, and a very little voice said:

"Oh! if you please, I am lost!"

He looked down, and saw a very little fair-haired girl.

"Yes," she said, confirming her words with a serious nod. "I am indeed. I am lost!"

Greatly perplexed, he stopped, looked about him for help, descried none, and said, bending low, "Where do you live, my child?"

"I don't know where I live," she returned. "I am lost."

"What is your name?"

"Polly."

"What is your other name?"

The reply was prompt, but unintelligible.

Imitating the sound as he caught it, he hazarded the guess, "Trivits."

"Oh no!" said the child, shaking her head. "Nothing like that."

"Say it again, little one."

An unpromising business. For this time it had quite a different sound.

He made the venture, "Paddens?"

"Oh no!" said the child. "Nothing like that."

"Once more. Let us try it again, dear."

A most hopeless business. This time it swelled into four syllables. "It can't be Tappitarver?" said Barbox Brothers, rubbing his head with his hat in discomfiture.

"No! It ain't," the child quietly assented.

On her trying this unfortunate name once more, with extraordinary efforts at distinctness, it swelled into eight syllables at least.

"Ah! I think," said Barbox Brothers with a desperate air of resignation, "that we had better give it up."

"But I am lost," said the child, nestling her little hand more closely in his, "and you'll take care of me, won't you?"

If ever a man were disconcerted by division between compassion on the one hand, and the very imbecility of irresolution on the other, here the man was. "Lost!" he repeated, looking down at the child. "I am sure I am. What is to be done?"

"Where do you live?" asked the child, looking up at him wistfully.

"Over there," he answered, pointing vaguely in the direction of his hotel.

"Hadn't we better go there?" said the child.

"Really," he replied, "I don't know but what we had."

So they set off, hand-in-hand. He, through comparison of himself against his little companion, with a clumsy feeling on him as if he had just developed into a foolish giant. She, clearly elevated in her own tiny opinion by having got him so neatly out of his embarrassment.

"We are going to have dinner when we get there, I suppose?" said Polly.

"Well," he rejoined, "I--Yes, I suppose we are."

"Do you like your dinner?" asked the child.

"Why, on the whole," said Barbox Brothers, "yes, I think I do."

"I do mine," said Polly. "Have you any brothers and sisters?"

"No. Have you?"

"Mine are dead."

"Oh!" said Barbox Brothers. With that absurd sense of unwieldiness of mind and body weighing him down, he would have not known how to pursue the conversation beyond this curt rejoinder, but that the child was always ready for him.

"What," she asked, turning her soft hand coaxingly in his, "are you going to do to amuse me after dinner?"

"Upon my soul, Polly," exclaimed Barbox Brothers, very much at a loss, "I have not the slightest idea!"

"Then I tell you what," said Polly. "Have you got any cards at your house?"

"Plenty," said Barbox Brothers in a boastful vein.

"Very well. Then I'll build houses, and you shall look at me. You mustn't blow, you know."

"Oh no," said Barbox Brothers. "No, no, no. No blowing. Blowing's not fair."

He flattered himself that he had said this pretty well for an idiotic monster; but the child, instantly perceiving the awkwardness of his attempt to adapt himself to her level, utterly destroyed his hopeful opinion of himself by saying compassionately: "What a funny man you are!"

Feeling, after this melancholy failure, as if he every minute grew bigger and heavier in person, and weaker in mind, Barbox gave himself up for a bad job. No giant ever submitted more meekly to be led in triumph by all-conquering Jack than he to be bound in slavery to Polly.

"Do you know any stories?" she asked him.

He was reduced to the humiliating confession: "No."

"What a dunce you must be, mustn't you?" said Polly.

He was reduced to the humiliating confession: "Yes."

"Would you like me to teach you a story? But you must remember it, you know, and be able to tell it right to somebody else afterwards."

He professed that it would afford him the highest mental gratification to be taught a story, and that he would humbly endeavour to retain it in his mind. Whereupon Polly, giving her hand a new little turn in his, expressive of settling down for enjoyment, commenced a long romance, of which every relishing clause began with the words: "So this," or, "And so this." As, "So this boy;" or, "So this fairy;" or, "And so this pie was four yards round, and two yards and a quarter deep." The interest of the romance was derived from the intervention of this fairy to punish this boy for having a greedy appetite. To achieve which purpose, this fairy made this pie, and this boy ate and ate and ate, and his cheeks swelled and swelled and swelled. There were many tributary circumstances, but the forcible interest culminated in the total consumption of this pie, and the bursting of this boy. Truly he was a fine sight, Barbox Brothers, with serious attentive face, and ear bent down, much jostled on the pavements of the busy town, but afraid of losing a single incident of the epic, lest he should be examined in it by-and-by, and found deficient.

Thus they arrived at the hotel. And there he had to say at the bar, and said awkwardly enough; "I have found a little girl!"

The whole establishment turned out to look at the little girl. Nobody knew her; nobody could make out her name, as she set it forth--except one chamber-maid, who said it was Constantinople--which it wasn't.

"I will dine with my young friend in a private room," said Barbox Brothers to the hotel authorities, "and perhaps you will be so good as to let the police know that the pretty baby is here. I suppose she is sure to be inquired for soon, if she has not been already. Come along, Polly."

Perfectly at ease and peace, Polly came along, but, finding the stairs rather stiff work, was carried up by Barbox Brothers. The dinner was a most transcendant success, and the Barbox sheepishness, under Polly's directions how to mince her meat for her, and how to diffuse gravy over the plate with a liberal and equal hand, was another fine sight.

"And now," said Polly, "while we are at dinner, you be good, and tell me that story I taught you."

With the tremors of a Civil Service examination upon him, and very uncertain indeed, not only as to the epoch at which the pie appeared in history, but also as to the measurements of that indispensable fact, Barbox Brothers made a shaky beginning, but under encouragement did very fairly. There was a want of breadth observable in his rendering of the cheeks, as well as the appetite, of the boy; and there was a certain tameness in his fairy, referable to an under-current of desire to account for her. Still, as the first lumbering performance of a good-humoured monster, it passed muster.

"I told you to be good," said Polly, "and you are good, ain't you?"

"I hope so," replied Barbox Brothers.

Such was his deference that Polly, elevated on a platform of sofa cushions in a chair at his right hand, encouraged him with a pat or two on the face from the greasy bowl of her spoon, and even with a gracious kiss. In getting on her feet upon her chair, however, to give him this last reward, she toppled forward among the dishes, and caused him to exclaim, as he effected her rescue: "Gracious Angels! Whew! I thought we were in the fire, Polly!"

"What a coward you are, ain't you?" said Polly when replaced.

"Yes, I am rather nervous," he replied. "Whew! Don't, Polly! Don't flourish your spoon, or you'll go over sideways. Don't tilt up your legs when you laugh, Polly, or you'll go over backwards. Whew! Polly, Polly, Polly," said Barbox Brothers, nearly succumbing to despair, "we are environed with dangers!"

Indeed, he could descry no security from the pitfalls that were yawning for Polly, but in proposing to her, after dinner, to sit upon a low stool. "I will, if you will," said Polly. So, as peace of mind should go before all, he begged the waiter to wheel aside the table, bring a pack of cards, a couple of footstools, and a screen, and close in Polly and himself before the fire, as it were in a snug room within the room. Then, finest sight of all, was Barbox Brothers on his footstool, with a pint decanter on the rug, contemplating Polly as she built successfully, and growing blue in the face with holding his breath, lest he should blow the house down.

"How you stare, don't you?" said Polly in a houseless pause.

Detected in the ignoble fact, he felt obliged to admit, apologetically: "I am afraid I was looking rather hard at you, Polly."

"Why do you stare?" asked Polly.

"I cannot," he murmured to himself, "recall why.--I don't know, Polly."

"You must be a simpleton to do things and not know why, mustn't you?" said Polly.

In spite of which reproof, he looked at the child again intently, as she bent her head over her card structure, her rich curls shading her face. "It is impossible," he thought, "that I can ever have seen this pretty baby before. Can I have dreamed of her? In some sorrowful dream?"

He could make nothing of it. So he went into the building trade as a journeyman under Polly, and they built three stories high, four stories high; even five.

"I say! Who do you think is coming?" asked Polly, rubbing her eyes after tea.

He guessed: "The waiter?"

"No," said Polly, "the dustman. I am getting sleepy."

A new embarrassment for Barbox Brothers!

"I don't think I am going to be fetched to-night," said Polly. "What do you think?"

He thought not, either. After another quarter of an hour, the dustman not merely impending, but actually arriving, recourse was had to the Constantinopolitan chamber-maid: who cheerily undertook that the child should sleep in a comfortable and wholesome room, which she herself would share.

"And I know you will be careful, won't you," said Barbox Brothers, as a new fear dawned upon him, "that she don't fall out of bed?"

Polly found this so highly entertaining that she was under the necessity of clutching him round the neck with both arms as he sat on his footstool picking up the cards, and rocking him to and fro, with her dimpled chin on his shoulder.

"Oh, what a coward you are, ain't you?" said Polly. "Do you fall out of bed?"

"N--not generally, Polly."

"No more do I."

With that, Polly gave him a reassuring hug or two to keep him going, and then giving that confiding mite of a hand of hers to be swallowed up in the hand of the Constantinopolitan chamber-maid, trotted off, chattering, without a vestige of anxiety.

He looked after her, had the screen removed and the table and chairs replaced, and still looked after her. He paced the room for half an hour. "A most engaging little creature, but it's not that. A most winning little voice, but it's not that. That has much to do with it, but there is something more. How can it be that I seem to know this child? What was it she imperfectly recalled to me when I felt her touch in the street, and, looking down at her, saw her looking up at me?"

"Mr. Jackson!"

With a start he turned towards the sound of the subdued voice, and saw his answer standing at the door.

"Oh, Mr. Jackson, do not be severe with me! Speak a word of encouragement to me, I beseech you."

"You are Polly's mother."

"Yes."

Yes. Polly herself might come to this, one day. As you see what the rose was in its faded leaves; as you see what the summer growth of the woods was in their wintry branches; so Polly might be traced, one day, in a careworn woman like this, with her hair turned grey. Before him were the ashes of a dead fire that had once burned bright. This was the woman he had loved. This was the woman he had lost. Such had been the constancy of his imagination to her, so had Time spared her under its withholding, that now, seeing how roughly the inexorable hand had struck her, his soul was filled with pity and amazement.

He led her to a chair, and stood leaning on a corner of the chimney-piece, with his head resting on his hand, and his face half averted.

"Did you see me in the street, and show me to your child?" he asked.

"Yes."

"Is the little creature, then, a party to deceit?"

"I hope there is no deceit. I said to her, 'We have lost our way, and I must try to find mine by myself. Go to that gentleman, and tell him you are lost. You shall be fetched by-and-by.' Perhaps you have not thought how very young she is?"

"She is very self-reliant."

"Perhaps because she is so young."

He asked, after a short pause, "Why did you do this?"

"Oh, Mr. Jackson, do you ask me? In the hope that you might see something in my innocent child to soften your heart towards me. Not only towards me, but towards my husband."

He suddenly turned about, and walked to the opposite end of the room. He came back again with a slower step, and resumed his former attitude, saying: "I thought you had emigrated to America?"

"We did. But life went ill with us there, and we came back."

"Do you live in this town?"

"Yes. I am a daily teacher of music here. My husband is a book-keeper."

"Are you--forgive my asking--poor?"

"We earn enough for our wants. That is not our distress. My husband is very, very ill of a lingering disorder. He will never recover--"

"You check yourself. If it is for want of the encouraging word you spoke of, take it from me. I cannot forget the old time, Beatrice."

"God bless you!" she replied with a burst of tears, and gave him her trembling hand.

"Compose yourself. I cannot be composed if you are not, for to see you weep distresses me beyond expression. Speak freely to me. Trust me."

She shaded her face with her veil, and after a little while spoke calmly. Her voice had the ring of Polly's.

"It is not that my husband's mind is at all impaired by his bodily suffering, for I assure you that is not the case. But in his weakness, and in his knowledge that he is incurably ill, he cannot overcome the ascendancy of one idea. It preys upon him, embitters every moment of his painful life, and will shorten it."

She stopping, he said again: "Speak freely to me. Trust me."

253

"We have had five children before this darling, and they all lie in their little graves. He believes that they have withered away under a curse, and that it will blight this child like the rest."

"Under what curse?"

"Both I and he have it on our conscience that we tried you very heavily, and I do not know but that, if I were as ill as he, I might suffer in my mind as he does. This is the constant burden:--'I believe, Beatrice, I was the only friend that Mr. Jackson ever cared to make, though I was so much his junior. The more influence he acquired in the business, the higher he advanced me, and I was alone in his private confidence. I came between him and you, and I took you from him. We were both secret, and the blow fell when he was wholly unprepared. The anguish it caused a man so compressed must have been terrible; the wrath it awakened inappeasable. So, a curse came to be invoked on our poor, pretty little flowers, and they fall.'"

"And you, Beatrice," he asked, when she had ceased to speak, and there had been a silence afterwards, "how say you?"

"Until within these few weeks I was afraid of you, and I believed that you would never, never forgive."

"Until within these few weeks," he repeated. "Have you changed your opinion of me within these few weeks?"

"Yes."

"For what reason?"

"I was getting some pieces of music in a shop in this town, when, to my terror, you came in. As I veiled my face and stood in the dark end of the shop, I heard you explain that you wanted a musical instrument for a bedridden girl. Your voice and manner were so softened, you showed such interest in its selection, you took it away yourself with so much tenderness of care and pleasure, that I knew you were a man with a most gentle heart. Oh,

Mr. Jackson, Mr. Jackson, if you could have felt the refreshing rain of tears that followed for me!"

"I inquired in the shop where you lived, but could get no information. As I had heard you say that you were going back by the next train (but you did not say where), I resolved to visit the station at about that time of day, as often as I could, between my lessons, on the chance of seeing you again. I have been there very often, but saw you no more until to-day. You were meditating as you walked the street, but the calm expression of your face emboldened me to send my child to you. And when I saw you bend your head to speak tenderly to her, I prayed to GOD to forgive me for having ever brought a sorrow on it. I now pray to you to forgive me, and to forgive my husband. I was very young, he was young too, and, in the ignorant hardihood of such a time of life, we don't know what we do to those who have undergone more discipline. You generous man! You good man! So to raise me up and make nothing of my crime against you!"—for he would not see her on her knees, and soothed her as a kind father might have soothed an erring daughter--"thank you, bless you, thank you!"

When he next spoke, it was after having drawn aside the window curtain and looked out awhile. Then he only said: "Is Polly asleep?"

"Yes. As I came in, I met her going away upstairs, and put her to bed myself."

"Leave her with me for to-morrow, Beatrice, and write me your address on this leaf of my pocket-book. In the evening I will bring her home to you--and to her father."

* * *

"Hallo!" cried Polly, putting her saucy sunny face in at the door next morning when breakfast was ready: "I thought I was fetched last night?"

"So you were, Polly, but I asked leave to keep you here for the day, and to take you home in the evening."

"Upon my word!" said Polly. "You are very cool, ain't you?"

However, Polly seemed to think it a good idea, and added: "I suppose I must give you a kiss, though you are cool."

The kiss given and taken, they sat down to breakfast in a highly conversational tone.

"Of course, you are going to amuse me?" said Polly.

"Oh, of course!" said Barbox Brothers.

In the pleasurable height of her anticipations, Polly found it indispensable to put down her piece of toast, cross one of her little fat knees over the other, and bring her little fat right hand down into her left hand with a business-like slap. After this gathering of herself together, Polly, by that time a mere heap of dimples, asked in a wheedling manner:

"What are we going to do, you dear old thing?"

"Why, I was thinking," said Barbox Brothers, "--but are you fond of horses, Polly?"

"Ponies, I am," said Polly, "especially when their tails are long. But horses--n-no--too big, you know."

"Well," pursued Barbox Brothers, in a spirit of grave mysterious confidence adapted to the importance of the consultation, "I did see yesterday, Polly, on the walls, pictures of two long-tailed ponies, speckled all over--"

"No, no, NO!" cried Polly, in an ecstatic desire to linger on the charming details. "Not speckled all over!"

"Speckled all over. Which ponies jump through hoops--"

"No, no, NO!" cried Polly as before. "They never jump through hoops!"

"Yes, they do. Oh, I assure you they do! And eat pie in pinafores--"

"Ponies eating pie in pinafores!" said Polly. "What a story-teller you are, ain't you?"

"Upon my honour.--And fire off guns."

(Polly hardly seemed to see the force of the ponies resorting to fire-arms.)

"And I was thinking," pursued the exemplary Barbox, "that if you and I were to go to the Circus where these ponies are, it would do our constitutions good."

"Does that mean amuse us?" inquired Polly. "What long words you do use, don't you?"

Apologetic for having wandered out of his depth, he replied: "That means amuse us. That is exactly what it means. There are many other wonders besides the ponies, and we shall see them all. Ladies and gentlemen in spangled dresses, and elephants and lions and tigers."

Polly became observant of the teapot, with a curled-up nose indicating some uneasiness of mind.

"They never get out, of course," she remarked as a mere truism.

"The elephants and lions and tigers? Oh, dear no!"

"Oh, dear no!" said Polly. "And of course nobody's afraid of the ponies shooting anybody."

"Not the least in the world."

"No, no, not the least in the world," said Polly.

"I was also thinking," proceeded Barbox, "that if we were to look in at the toy-shop, to choose a doll--"

"Not dressed!" cried Polly with a clap of her hands. "No, no, NO, not dressed!"

"Full-dressed. Together with a house, and all things necessary for housekeeping--"

Polly gave a little scream, and seemed in danger of falling into a swoon of bliss.

"What a darling you are!" she languidly exclaimed, leaning back in her chair. "Come and be hugged, or I must come and hug you."

This resplendent programme was carried into execution with the utmost rigour of the law. It being essential to make the purchase of the doll its first feature--or that lady would have lost the ponies--the toy-shop expedition took precedence. Polly in the magic warehouse, with a doll as large as herself under each arm, and a neat assortment of some twenty more on view upon the counter, did indeed present a spectacle of indecision not quite compatible with unalloyed happiness, but the light cloud passed.

The lovely specimen oftenest chosen, oftenest rejected, and finally abided by, was of Circassian descent, possessing as much boldness of beauty as was reconcilable with extreme feebleness of mouth, and combining a sky-blue silk pelisse with rose-coloured satin trousers, and a black velvet hat: which this fair stranger to our northern shores would seem to have founded on the portraits of the late Duchess of Kent.

The name this distinguished foreigner brought with her from beneath the glowing skies of a sunny clime was (on Polly's authority) Miss Melluka, and the costly nature of her outfit as a housekeeper, from the Barbox coffers, may be inferred from the two facts that her silver tea-spoons were as large as her kitchen poker, and that the proportions of her watch exceeded those of her frying-pan. Miss Melluka was graciously pleased to express her entire approbation of the Circus, and so was Polly; for the ponies were speckled, and brought down nobody when they fired, and the savagery of the wild beasts appeared to be mere smoke--which article, in fact, they did produce in large quantities from their insides. The Barbox absorption in the general subject throughout the realisation of these delights was again a sight to see, nor was it less worthy to behold at dinner, when he drank to Miss Melluka, tied stiff in a chair opposite to Polly (the fair Circassian possessing an unbendable spine), and even induced the waiter to assist in carrying out with due decorum the prevailing glorious idea. To wind up, there came the agreeable fever of getting Miss Melluka and all her wardrobe and rich possessions into a fly with Polly, to be taken home. But, by that time, Polly had become unable to look upon such accumulated joys with waking eyes, and had withdrawn her consciousness into the wonderful Paradise of a child's sleep. "Sleep, Polly, sleep," said Barbox Brothers, as her head dropped on his shoulder; "you shall not fall out of this bed easily, at any rate!"

What rustling piece of paper he took from his pocket, and carefully folded into the bosom of Polly's frock, shall not be mentioned. He said nothing about it, and nothing shall be said about it. They drove to a modest suburb of the great ingenious town, and stopped at the fore-court of a small house. "Do not wake the child," said Barbox Brothers softly to the driver; "I will carry her in as she is."

Greeting the light at the opened door which was held by Polly's mother, Polly's bearer passed on with mother and child in to a ground-floor room. There, stretched on a sofa, lay a sick man, sorely wasted, who covered his eyes with his emaciated hand.

"Tresham," said Barbox in a kindly voice, "I have brought you back your Polly, fast asleep. Give me your hand, and tell me you are better."

The sick man reached forth his right hand, and bowed his head over the hand into which it was taken, and kissed it. "Thank you, thank you! I may say that I am well and happy."

"That's brave," said Barbox. "Tresham, I have a fancy--Can you make room for me beside you here?" He sat down on the sofa as he said the words, cherishing the plump peachey cheek that lay uppermost on his shoulder. "I have a fancy, Tresham (I am getting quite an old fellow now, you know, and old fellows may take fancies into their heads sometimes), to give up Polly, having found her, to no one but you. Will you take her from me?"

As the father held out his arms for the child, each of the two men looked steadily at the other.

"She is very dear to you, Tresham?"

"Unutterably dear."

"God bless her! It is not much, Polly," he continued, turning his eyes upon her peaceful face as he apostrophized her, "it is not much, Polly, for a blind and sinful man to invoke a blessing on something so far better than himself as a little child is; but it would be much--much upon his cruel head, and much upon his guilty soul--if he could be so wicked as to invoke a curse. He had better have a millstone round his neck, and be cast into the deepest sea. Live and thrive, my pretty baby!" Here he kissed her. "Live and prosper, and become in time the mother of other little children, like the Angels who behold The Father's face!"

He kissed her again, gave her up gently to both her parents, and went out. But he went not to Wales. No, he never went to Wales. He went straightway for another stroll about the town, and he looked in upon the people at their work, and at their play, here, there, every-there, and where not. For he was Barbox Brothers and Co. now, and had taken thousands of partners into the solitary firm.

He had at length got back to his hotel room, and was standing before his fire refreshing himself with a glass of hot drink which he had stood upon the chimney-piece, when he heard the town clocks striking, and, referring to his watch, found the evening to have so slipped away, that they were striking twelve. As he put up his watch again, his eyes met those of his reflection in the chimney-glass.

"Why, it's your birthday already," he said, smiling. "You are looking very well. I wish you many happy returns of the day."

An Unpremeditated Ceremony

Lucy Maud Montgomery Short Stories, 1904

L.M. Montgomery [1874-1942]

Selwyn Grant sauntered in upon the assembled family at the homestead as if he were returning from an hour's absence instead of a western sojourn of ten years. Guided by the sound of voices on the still, pungent autumnal air, he went around to the door of the dining room which opened directly on the poppy walk in the garden.

Nobody noticed him for a moment and he stood in the doorway looking at them with a smile, wondering what was the reason of the festal air that hung about them all as visibly as a garment. His mother sat by the table, industriously polishing the best silver spoons, which, as he remembered, were only brought forth upon some great occasion. Her eyes were as bright, her form as erect, her nose—the Carston nose—as pronounced and aristocratic as of yore.

Selwyn saw little change in her. But was it possible that the tall, handsome young lady with the sleek brown pompadour and a nose unmistakably and plebeianly Grant, who sat by the window doing something to a heap of lace and organdy in her lap, was the little curly-headed, sunburned sister of thirteen whom he remembered? The young man leaning against the sideboard must be Leo, of course; a fine-looking, broad-shouldered young fellow who made Selwyn think suddenly that he must be growing old. And there was the little, thin, grey father in the corner, peering at his newspaper with nearsighted eyes. Selwyn's heart gave a bound at the sight of him which not even his mother had caused. Dear old Dad! The years had been kind to him.

Mrs. Grant held up a glistening spoon and surveyed it complacently. "There, I think that is bright enough even to suit Margaret Graham. I shall take over the whole two dozen teas and one dozen desserts. I wish, Bertha, that you would tie a red cord around each of the handles for me. The Carmody spoons are the same pattern and I shall always be convinced that Mrs. Carmody carried off two of ours the time that Jenny Graham was married. I don't mean to take any more risks. And, Father——"

Something made the mother look around, and she saw her first-born!

When the commotion was over Selwyn asked why the family spoons were being rubbed up.

"For the wedding, of course," said Mrs. Grant, polishing her gold-bowed spectacles and deciding that there was no more time for tears and sentiment just then. "And there, they're not half done—and we'll have to dress in another hour. Bertha is no earthly use— she is so taken up with her bridesmaid finery."

"Wedding? Whose wedding?" demanded Selwyn, in bewilderment.

"Why, Leo's, of course. Leo is to be married tonight. Didn't you get your invitation? Wasn't that what brought you home?"

"Hand me a chair, quick," implored Selwyn. "Leo, are you going to commit matrimony in this headlong fashion? Are you sure you're grown up?"

"Six feet is a pretty good imitation of it, isn't it?" grinned Leo. "Brace up, old fellow. It's not so bad as it might be. She's quite a respectable girl. We wrote you all about it three weeks ago and broke the news as gently as possible."

"I left for the East a month ago and have been wandering around preying on old college chums ever since. Haven't seen a letter. There, I'm better now. No, you needn't fan me, Sis. Well, no family can get through the world without its seasons of tribulations. Who is the party of the second part, little brother?"

"Alice Graham," replied Mrs. Grant, who had a habit of speaking for her children, none of whom had the Carston nose.

"Alice Graham! That child!" exclaimed Selwyn in astonishment.

Leo roared. "Come, come, Sel, perhaps we're not very progressive here in Croyden, but we don't actually stand still. Girls are apt to stretch out some between ten and twenty, you know. You old bachelors think nobody ever grows up. Why, Sel, you're grey around your temples."

"Too well I know it, but a man's own brother shouldn't be the first to cast such things up to him. I'll admit, since I come to think of it, that Alice has probably grown bigger. Is she any better-looking than she used to be?"

"Alice is a charming girl," said Mrs. Grant impressively. "She is a beauty and she is also sweet and sensible, which beauties are not always. We are all very much pleased with Leo's choice. But we have really no more time to spare just now. The wedding is at seven o'clock and it is four already."

"Is there anybody you can send to the station for my luggage?" asked Selwyn. "Luckily I have a new suit, otherwise I shouldn't have the face to go."

"Well, I must be off," said Mrs. Grant. "Father, take Selwyn away so that I shan't be tempted to waste time talking to him."

In the library father and son looked at each other affectionately.

"Dad, it's a blessing to see you just the same. I'm a little dizzy with all these changes. Bertha grown up and Leo within an inch of being married! To Alice Graham at that, whom I can't think of yet as anything else than the long-legged, black-eyed imp of mischief she was when a kiddy. To tell you the truth, Dad, I don't feel in a mood for going to a wedding at Wish-ton-wish tonight. I'm sure you don't either. You've always hated fusses. Can't we shirk it?"

They smiled at each other with chummy remembrance of many a family festival they had "shirked" together in the old days. But Mr. Grant shook his head. "Not this time, sonny. There are some things a decent man can't shirk and one of them is his own boy's wedding. It's a nuisance, but I must go through with it. You'll understand how it is when you're a family man yourself. By the way, why aren't you a family man by this time? Why haven't I been put to the bother and inconvenience of attending your wedding before now, son?"

Selwyn laughed, with a little vibrant note of bitterness in the laughter, which the father's quick ears detected. "I've been too busy with law books, Dad, to find me a wife."

Mr. Grant shook his bushy grey head. "That's not the real reason, son. The world has a wife for every man; if he hasn't found her by the time he's thirty-five, there's some real reason for it. Well, I don't want to pry into yours, but I hope it's a sound one and not a mean, sneaking, selfish sort of reason. Perhaps you'll choose a Madam Selwyn some day yet. In case you should I'm going to give you a small bit of good advice. Your mother—now, she's a splendid woman, Selwyn, a splendid woman. She can't be matched as a housekeeper and she has improved my finances until I don't know them when I meet them. She's been a good wife and a good mother. If I were a young man I'd court her and marry her over again, that I would. But, son, when you pick a wife pick one with a nice little commonplace nose, not a family nose. Never marry a woman with a family nose, son."

A woman with a family nose came into the library at this juncture and beamed maternally upon them both. "There's a bite for you in the dining room. After you've eaten it you must dress. Mind you brush your hair well down, Father. The green room is ready for you, Selwyn. Tomorrow I'll have a good talk with you, but tonight I'll be too busy to remember you're around. How are we all going to get over to Wish-ton-wish? Leo and Bertha are going in the pony carriage. It won't hold a third passenger. You'll have to squeeze in with Father and me in the buggy, Selwyn."

"By no means," replied Selwyn briskly. "I'll walk over to Wish-ton-wish. Ifs only half a mile across lots. I suppose the old way is still open?"

"It ought to be," answered Mr. Grant drily; "Leo has kept it well trodden. If you've forgotten how it runs he can tell you."

"I haven't forgotten," said Selwyn, a little brusquely. He had his own reasons for remembering the wood path. Leo had not been the first Grant to go courting to Wish-ton-wish.

When he started, the moon was rising round and red and hazy in an eastern hill-gap. The autumn air was mild and spicy. Long shadows stretched across the fields on his right and silvery mosaics patterned the floor of the old beechwood lane. Selwyn walked slowly. He was thinking of Esme Graham or, rather, of the girl who had been Esme Graham, and wondering if he would see her at the wedding. It was probable, and he did not want to see her. In spite of ten years' effort, he did not think he could yet look upon Tom St. Clair's wife with the proper calm indifference. At the best, it would taint his own memory of her; he would never again be able to think of her as Esme Graham but only as Esme St. Clair.

The Grahams had come to Wish-ton-wish eleven years before. There was a big family of girls of whom the tall, brown-haired Esme was the oldest. There was one summer during which Selwyn Grant had haunted Wish-ton-wish, the merry comrade of the younger girls, the boyishly, silently devoted lover of Esme. Tom St. Clair had always been there too, in his right as second cousin, Selwyn had supposed. One day he found out that Tom and Esme had been engaged ever since she was sixteen; one of her sisters told him. That had been all. He had gone away soon after, and some time later a letter from home made casual mention of Tom St. Clair's marriage.

He narrowly missed being late for the wedding ceremony. The bridal party entered the parlour at Wish-ton-wish at the same moment as he slipped in by another door. Selwyn almost whistled with amazement at sight of the bride. That Alice Graham, that tall, stately, blushing young woman, with her masses of dead-black hair, frosted over by the film of wedding veil! Could that be the scrawny little tomboy of ten years ago? She looked not unlike Esme, with that subtle family resemblance that is quite independent of feature and colouring.

Where was Esme? Selwyn cast his eyes furtively over the assembled guests while the minister read the marriage ceremony. He recognized several of the Graham girls but he did not see Esme, although Tom St. Clair, stout and florid and prosperous-looking, was standing on a chair in a faraway corner, peering over the heads of the women.

After the turmoil of handshakings and congratulations, Selwyn fled to the cool, still outdoors, where the rosy glow of Chinese lanterns mingled with the waves of moonshine to make fairyland. And there he met her, as she came out of the house by a side door, a tall, slender woman in some glistening, clinging garment, with white flowers shining like stars in the coils of her brown hair. In the soft glow she looked even more beautiful than in the days of her girlhood, and Selwyn's heart throbbed dangerously at sight of her.

"Esme!" he said involuntarily.

She started, and he had an idea that she changed colour, although it was too dim to be sure. "Selwyn!" she exclaimed, putting out her hands. "Why, Selwyn Grant! Is it really you? Or are you such stuff as dreams are made of? I did not know you were here. I did not know you were home."

He caught her hands and held them tightly, drawing her a little closer to him, forgetting that she was Tom St. Clair's wife, remembering only that she was the woman to whom he had given all his love and life's devotion, to the entire beggaring of his heart.

"I reached home only four hours ago, and was haled straightway here to Leo's wedding. I'm dizzy, Esme. I can't adjust my old conceptions to this new state of affairs all at once. It seems ridiculous to think that Leo and Alice are married. I'm sure they can't be really grown up."

Esme laughed as she drew away her hands. "We are all ten years older," she said lightly.

"Not you. You are more beautiful than ever, Esme. That sunflower compliment is permissible in an old friend, isn't it?"

"This mellow glow is kinder to me than sunlight now. I am thirty, you know, Selwyn."

"And I have some grey hairs," he confessed. "I knew I had them but I had a sneaking hope that other folks didn't until Leo destroyed it today. These young brothers and sisters who won't stay children are nuisances. You'll be telling me next thing that 'Baby' is grown up."

"'Baby' is eighteen and has a beau," laughed Esme. "And I give you fair warning that she insists on being called Laura now. Do you want to come for a walk with me—down under the beeches to the old lane gate? I came out to see if the fresh air would do my bit of a headache good. I shall have to help with the supper later on."

They went slowly across the lawn and turned into a dim, moonlight lane beyond, their old favourite ramble. Selwyn felt like a man in a dream, a pleasant dream from which he dreads to awaken. The voices and laughter echoing out from the house died away behind them and the great silence of the night fell about them as they came to the old gate, beyond which was a range of shining, moonlight-misted fields.

For a little while neither of them spoke. The woman looked out across the white spaces and the man watched the glimmering curve of her neck and the soft darkness of her rich hair. How virginal, how sacred, she looked! The thought of Tom St. Clair was a sacrilege.

"It's nice to see you again, Selwyn," said Esme frankly at last. "There are so few of our old set left, and so many of the babies grown up. Sometimes I don't know my own world, it has changed so. It's an uncomfortable feeling. You give me a pleasant sensation of really belonging here. I'd be lonesome tonight if I dared. I'm going to miss Alice so much. There will be only Mother and Baby and I left now. Our family circle has dwindled woefully."

"Mother and Baby and you!" Selwyn felt his head whirling again. "Why, where is Tom?"

He felt that it was an idiotic question, but it slipped from his tongue before he could catch it. Esme turned her head and looked at him wonderingly. He knew that in the sunlight her eyes were as mistily blue as early meadow violets, but here they looked dark and unfathomably tender.

"Tom?" she said perplexedly. "Do you mean Tom St. Clair? He is here, of course, he and his wife. Didn't you see her? That pretty woman in pale pink, Lil Meredith. Why, you used to know Lil, didn't you? One of the Uxbridge Merediths?"

To the day of his death Selwyn Grant will firmly believe that if he had not clutched fast hold of the top bar of the gate he would have tumbled down on the moss under the beeches in speechless astonishment. All the surprises of that surprising evening were as nothing to this. He had a swift conviction that there were no words in the English language that could fully express his feelings and that it would be a waste of time to try to find any. Therefore he laid hold of the first baldly commonplace ones that came handy and said tamely, "I thought you were married to Tom."

"You—thought—I—was—married—to—Tom!" repeated Esme slowly. "And have you thought that all these years, Selwyn Grant?"

"Yes, I have. Is it any wonder? You were engaged to Tom when I went away, Jenny told me you were. And a year later Bertha wrote me a letter in which she made some reference to Tom's marriage. She didn't say to whom, but hadn't I the right to suppose it was to you?"

"Oh!" The word was partly a sigh and partly a little cry of long-concealed, long-denied pain. "It's been all a funny misunderstanding. Tom and I were engaged once—a boy-and-girl affair in the beginning. Then we both found out that we had made a mistake—that what we had thought was love was merely the affection of good comrades. We broke our engagement shortly before you went away. All the older girls knew it was broken but I suppose nobody mentioned the matter to Jen. She was such a child, we never thought about her. And you've thought I was Tom's wife all this time? It's—funny."

"Funny. You mean tragic! Look here, Esme, I'm not going to risk any more misunderstanding. There's nothing for it but plain talk when matters get to such a state as this. I love you—and I've loved you ever since I met you. I went away because I could not stay here and see you married to another man. I've stayed away for the same reason. Esme, is it too late? Did you ever care anything for me?"

268

"Yes, I did," she said slowly.

"Do you care still?" he asked.

She hid her face against his shoulder. "Yes," she whispered.

"Then we'll go back to the house and be married," he said joyfully.

Esme broke away and stared at him. "Married!"

"Yes, married. We've wasted ten years and we're not going to waste another minute. We're not, I say."

"Selwyn! It's impossible."

"I have expurgated that word from my dictionary. It's the very simplest thing when you look at it in an unprejudiced way. Here is a ready-made wedding and decorations and assembled guests, a minister on the spot and a state where no licence is required. You have a very pretty new dress on and you love me. I have a plain gold ring on my little finger that will fit you. Aren't all the conditions fulfilled? Where is the sense of waiting and having another family upheaval in a few weeks' time?"

"I understand why you have made such a success of the law," said Esme, "but—"

"There are no buts. Come with me, Esme. I'm going to hunt up your mother and mine and talk to them."

Half an hour later an astonishing whisper went circulating among the guests. Before they could grasp its significance Tom St. Clair and Jen's husband, broadly smiling, were hustling scattered folk into the parlour again and making clear a passage in the hall. The minister came in with his blue book, and then Selwyn Grant and Esme Graham walked in hand in hand.

When the second ceremony was over, Mr. Grant shook his son's hand vigorously. "There's no need to wish you happiness, son; you've got it. And you've made one fuss and bother do for both weddings, that's what I call genius. And"—this in a careful whisper, while

Esme was temporarily obliterated in Mrs. Grant's capacious embrace—"she's got the right sort of a nose. But your mother is a grand woman, son, a grand woman."

The Celestial Railroad

Nathaniel Hawthorne [1804-1864]

Not a great while ago, passing through the gate of dreams, I visited that region of the earth in which lies the famous City of Destruction. It interested me much to learn that by the public spirit of some of the inhabitants a railroad has recently been established between this populous and flourishing town and the Celestial City. Having a little time upon my hands, I resolved to gratify a liberal curiosity by making a trip thither. Accordingly, one fine morning after paying my bill at the hotel, and directing the porter to stow my luggage behind a coach, I took my seat in the vehicle and set out for the station-house. It was my good fortune to enjoy the company of a gentleman—one Mr. Smooth-it-away—who, though he had never actually visited the Celestial City, yet seemed as well acquainted with its laws, customs, policy, and statistics, as with those of the City of Destruction, of which he was a native townsman. Being, moreover, a director of the railroad corporation and one of its largest stockholders, he had it in his power to give me all desirable information respecting that praiseworthy enterprise.

Our coach rattled out of the city, and at a short distance from its outskirts passed over a bridge of elegant construction, but somewhat too slight, as I imagined, to sustain any considerable weight. On both sides lay an extensive quagmire, which could not have been more disagreeable either to sight or smell, had all the kennels of the earth emptied their pollution there.

"This," remarked Mr. Smooth-it-away, "is the famous Slough of Despond—a disgrace to all the neighborhood; and the greater that it might so easily be converted into firm ground."

"I have understood," said I, "that efforts have been made for that purpose from time immemorial. Bunyan mentions that above twenty thousand cartloads of wholesome instructions had been thrown in here without effect."

"Very probably! And what effect could be anticipated from such unsubstantial stuff?" cried Mr. Smooth-it-away. "You observe this convenient bridge. We obtained a sufficient foundation for it by throwing into the slough some editions of books of morality, volumes of French philosophy and German rationalism; tracts, sermons, and essays of modern clergymen; extracts from Plato, Confucius, and various Hindoo sages together with a few ingenious commentaries upon texts of Scripture,—all of which by some scientific process, have been converted into a mass like granite. The whole bog might be filled up with similar matter."

It really seemed to me, however, that the bridge vibrated and heaved up and down in a very formidable manner; and, in spite of Mr. Smooth-it-away's testimony to the solidity of its foundation, I should be loath to cross it in a crowded omnibus, especially if each passenger were encumbered with as heavy luggage as that gentleman and myself. Nevertheless we got over without accident, and soon found ourselves at the stationhouse. This very neat and spacious edifice is erected on the site of the little wicket gate, which formerly, as all old pilgrims will recollect, stood directly across the highway, and, by its inconvenient narrowness, was a great obstruction to the traveller of liberal mind and expansive stomach. The reader of John Bunyan will be glad to know that Christian's old friend Evangelist, who was accustomed to supply each pilgrim with a mystic roll, now presides at the ticket office. Some malicious persons it is true deny the identity of this reputable character with the Evangelist of old times, and even pretend to bring competent evidence of an imposture. Without involving myself in a dispute I shall merely observe that, so far as my experience goes, the square pieces of pasteboard now delivered to passengers are much more convenient and useful along the road than the antique roll of parchment. Whether they will be as readily received at the gate of the Celestial City I decline giving an opinion.

A large number of passengers were already at the station-house awaiting the departure of the cars. By the aspect and demeanor of these persons it was easy to judge that the feelings of the community had undergone a very favorable change in reference to the celestial pilgrimage. It would have done Bunyan's heart good to see it. Instead of a lonely and ragged man with a huge burden on his back, plodding along sorrowfully on foot while the whole city hooted after him, here were parties of the first gentry and most respectable people in the neighborhood setting forth towards the Celestial City as cheerfully as if the pilgrimage were merely a summer tour. Among the gentlemen were characters of deserved eminence—magistrates, politicians, and men of wealth, by whose example religion could not but be greatly recommended to their meaner brethren. In the ladies' apartment, too, I rejoiced to distinguish some of those flowers of fashionable society who are so well fitted to adorn the most elevated circles of the Celestial City. There was much pleasant conversation about the news of the day, topics of business and politics, or the lighter matters of amusement; while religion, though indubitably the main thing at heart, was thrown tastefully into the background. Even an infidel would have heard little or nothing to shock his sensibility.

One great convenience of the new method of going on pilgrimage I must not forget to mention. Our enormous burdens, instead of being carried on our shoulders as had been the custom of old, were all snugly deposited in the baggage car, and, as I was assured, would be delivered to their respective owners at the journey's end. Another thing, likewise, the benevolent reader will be delighted to understand. It may be remembered that there was an ancient feud between Prince Beelzebub and the keeper of the wicket gate, and that the adherents of the former distinguished personage were accustomed to shoot deadly arrows at honest pilgrims while knocking at the door. This dispute, much to the credit as well of the illustrious potentate above mentioned as of the worthy and enlightened directors of the railroad, has been pacifically arranged on the principle of mutual compromise. The prince's subjects are now pretty numerously employed about the station-house, some in taking care of the baggage, others in collecting fuel, feeding the engines, and such congenial occupations; and I can conscientiously affirm that persons more attentive to their business, more willing to accommodate, or more generally agreeable to the passengers, are not to be found on any railroad. Every good heart must surely exult at so satisfactory an arrangement of an immemorial difficulty.

"Where is Mr. Greatheart?" inquired I. "Beyond a doubt the directors have engaged that famous old champion to be chief conductor on the railroad?"

"Why, no," said Mr. Smooth-it-away, with a dry cough. "He was offered the situation of brakeman; but, to tell you the truth, our friend Greatheart has grown preposterously stiff and narrow in his old age. He has so often guided pilgrims over the road on foot that he considers it a sin to travel in any other fashion. Besides, the old fellow had entered so heartily into the ancient feud with Prince Beelzebub that he would have been perpetually at blows or ill language with some of the prince's subjects, and thus have embroiled us anew. So, on the whole, we were not sorry when honest Greatheart went off to the Celestial City in a huff and left us at liberty to choose a more suitable and accommodating man. Yonder comes the engineer of the train. You will probably recognize him at once."

The engine at this moment took its station in advance of the cars, looking, I must confess, much more like a sort of mechanical demon that would hurry us to the infernal regions than a laudable contrivance for smoothing our way to the Celestial City. On its top sat a personage almost enveloped in smoke and flame, which, not to startle the reader, appeared to gush from his own mouth and stomach as well as from the engine's brazen abdomen.

"Do my eyes deceive me?" cried I. "What on earth is this! A living creature? If so, he is own brother to the engine he rides upon!"

"Poh, poh, you are obtuse!" said Mr. Smooth-it-away, with a hearty laugh. "Don't you know Apollyon, Christian's old enemy, with whom he fought so fierce a battle in the Valley of Humiliation? He was the very fellow to manage the engine; and so we have reconciled him to the custom of going on pilgrimage, and engaged him as chief engineer."

"Bravo, bravo!" exclaimed I, with irrepressible enthusiasm; "this shows the liberality of the age; this proves, if anything can, that all musty prejudices are in a fair way to be obliterated. And how will Christian rejoice to hear of this happy transformation of his old antagonist! I promise myself great pleasure in informing him of it when we reach the Celestial City."

The passengers being all comfortably seated, we now rattled away merrily, accomplishing a greater distance in ten minutes than Christian probably trudged over in a day. It was laughable, while we glanced along, as it were, at the tail of a thunderbolt, to observe two dusty foot travellers in the old pilgrim guise, with cockle shell and staff, their mystic rolls of parchment in their hands and their intolerable burdens on their backs. The preposterous obstinacy of these honest people in persisting to groan and stumble along the difficult pathway rather than take advantage of modern improvements, excited great mirth among our wiser brotherhood. We greeted the two pilgrims with many pleasant gibes and a roar of laughter; whereupon they gazed at us with such woful and absurdly compassionate visages that our merriment grew tenfold more obstreperous. Apollyon also entered heartily into the fun, and contrived to flirt the smoke and flame of the engine, or of his own breath, into their faces, and envelop them in an atmosphere of scalding steam. These little practical jokes amused us mightily, and doubtless afforded the pilgrims the gratification of considering themselves martyrs.

At some distance from the railroad Mr. Smooth-it-away pointed to a large, antique edifice, which, he observed, was a tavern of long standing, and had formerly been a noted stopping-place for pilgrims. In Bunyan's road-book it is mentioned as the Interpreter's House.

"I have long had a curiosity to visit that old mansion," remarked I.

"It is not one of our stations, as you perceive," said my companion "The keeper was violently opposed to the railroad; and well he might be, as the track left his house of entertainment on one side, and thus was pretty certain to deprive him of all his reputable customers. But the footpath still passes his door, and the old gentleman now and then receives a call from some simple traveller, and entertains him with fare as old-fashioned as himself."

Before our talk on this subject came to a conclusion we were rushing by the place where Christian's burden fell from his shoulders at the sight of the Cross. This served as a theme for Mr. Smooth-it-away, Mr. Live-for-the-world, Mr. Hide-sin-in-the-heart, Mr. Scaly-conscience, and a knot of gentlemen from the town of Shun-repentance, to descant upon the inestimable advantages resulting from the safety of our baggage. Myself, and all the passengers indeed, joined with great unanimity in this view of the matter; for our burdens were rich in many things esteemed precious throughout the world; and, especially, we each of us possessed a great variety of favorite Habits, which we trusted would not be out of fashion even in the polite circles of the Celestial City. It would have been a sad spectacle to see such an assortment of valuable articles tumbling into the sepulchre. Thus pleasantly conversing on the favorable circumstances of our position as compared with those of past pilgrims and of narrow-minded ones at the present day, we soon found ourselves at the foot of the Hill Difficulty. Through the very heart of this rocky mountain a tunnel has been constructed of most admirable architecture, with a lofty arch and a spacious double track; so that, unless the earth and rocks should chance to crumble down, it will remain an eternal monument of the builder's skill and enterprise. It is a great though incidental advantage that the materials from the heart of the Hill Difficulty have been employed in filling up the Valley of Humiliation, thus obviating the necessity of descending into that disagreeable and unwholesome hollow.

"This is a wonderful improvement, indeed," said I. "Yet I should have been glad of an opportunity to visit the Palace Beautiful and be introduced to the charming young ladies—Miss Prudence, Miss Piety, Miss Charity, and the rest—who have the kindness to entertain pilgrims there."

"Young ladies!" cried Mr. Smooth-it-away, as soon as he could speak for laughing. "And charming young ladies! Why, my dear fellow, they are old maids, every soul of them—prim, starched, dry, and angular; and not one of them, I will venture to say, has altered so much as the fashion of her gown since the days of Christian's pilgrimage."

"Ah, well," said I, much comforted, "then I can very readily dispense with their acquaintance."

The respectable Apollyon was now putting on the steam at a prodigious rate, anxious, perhaps, to get rid of the unpleasant reminiscences connected with the spot where he had so disastrously encountered Christian. Consulting Mr. Bunyan's road-book, I perceived that we must now be within a few miles of the Valley of the Shadow of Death, into which doleful region, at our present speed, we should plunge much sooner than seemed at all desirable. In truth, I expected nothing better than to find myself in the ditch on one side or the Quag on the other; but on communicating my apprehensions to Mr. Smooth-it-away, he assured me that the difficulties of this passage, even in its worst condition, had been vastly exaggerated, and that, in its present state of improvement, I might consider myself as safe as on any railroad in Christendom.

Even while we were speaking the train shot into the entrance of this dreaded Valley. Though I plead guilty to some foolish palpitations of the heart during our headlong rush over the causeway here constructed, yet it were unjust to withhold the highest encomiums on the boldness of its original conception and the ingenuity of those who executed it. It was gratifying, likewise, to observe how much care had been taken to dispel the everlasting gloom and supply the defect of cheerful sunshine, not a ray of which has ever penetrated among these awful shadows. For this purpose, the inflammable gas which exudes plentifully from the soil is collected by means of pipes, and thence communicated to a quadruple row of lamps along the whole extent of the passage. Thus a radiance has been created even out of the fiery and sulphurous curse that rests forever upon the valley—a radiance hurtful, however, to the eyes, and somewhat bewildering, as I discovered by the changes which it wrought in the visages of my companions. In this respect, as compared with natural daylight, there is the same difference as between truth and falsehood, but if the reader have ever traveled through the dark Valley, he will have learned to be thankful for any light that he could get—if not from the sky above, then from the blasted soil beneath. Such was the red brilliancy of these lamps that they appeared to build walls of fire on both sides of the track, between which we held our course at lightning speed, while a reverberating thunder filled the Valley with its echoes. Had the engine run off the track,—a catastrophe, it is whispered, by no means unprecedented,—the bottomless pit, if there be any such place, would undoubtedly have received us. Just as some dismal fooleries of this nature had made my heart quake there came a tremendous shriek, careering along the valley as if a thousand devils had burst their lungs to utter it, but which proved to be merely the whistle of the engine on arriving at a stopping-place.

The spot where we had now paused is the same that our friend Bunyan—a truthful man, but infected with many fantastic notions—has designated, in terms plainer than I like to repeat, as the mouth of the infernal region. This, however, must be a mistake, inasmuch as Mr. Smooth-it-away, while we remained in the smoky and lurid cavern, took occasion to prove that Tophet has not even a metaphorical existence. The place, he assured us, is no other than the crater of a half-extinct volcano, in which the directors had caused forges to be set up for the manufacture of railroad iron. Hence, also, is obtained a plentiful supply of fuel for the use of the engines. Whoever had gazed into the dismal obscurity of the broad cavern mouth, whence ever and anon darted huge tongues of dusky flame, and had seen the strange, half-shaped monsters, and visions of faces horribly grotesque, into which the smoke seemed to wreathe itself, and had heard the awful murmurs, and shrieks, and deep, shuddering whispers of the blast, sometimes forming themselves into words almost articulate, would have seized upon Mr. Smooth-it-away's comfortable explanation as greedily as we did. The inhabitants of the cavern, moreover, were unlovely personages, dark, smoke-begrimed, generally deformed, with misshapen feet, and a glow of dusky redness in their eyes as if their hearts had caught fire and were blazing out of the upper windows. It struck me as a peculiarity that the laborers at the forge and those who brought fuel to the engine, when they began to draw short breath, positively emitted smoke from their mouth and nostrils.

Among the idlers about the train, most of whom were puffing cigars which they had lighted at the flame of the crater, I was perplexed to notice several who, to my certain knowledge, had heretofore set forth by railroad for the Celestial City. They looked dark, wild, and smoky, with a singular resemblance, indeed, to the native inhabitants, like whom, also, they had a disagreeable propensity to ill-natured gibes and sneers, the habit of which had wrought a settled contortion of their visages. Having been on speaking terms with one of these persons,—an indolent, good-for-nothing fellow, who went by the name of Take-it-easy,—I called him, and inquired what was his business there.

"Did you not start," said I, "for the Celestial City?"

"That's a fact," said Mr. Take-it-easy, carelessly puffing some smoke into my eyes. "But I heard such bad accounts that I never took pains to climb the hill on which the city stands. No business doing, no fun going on, nothing to drink, and no smoking allowed, and a thrumming of church music from morning till night. I would not stay in such a place if they offered me house room and living free."

"But, my good Mr. Take-it-easy," cried I, "why take up your residence here, of all places in the world?"

"Oh," said the loafer, with a grin, "it is very warm hereabouts, and I meet with plenty of old acquaintances, and altogether the place suits me. I hope to see you back again some day soon. A pleasant journey to you."

While he was speaking the bell of the engine rang, and we dashed away after dropping a few passengers, but receiving no new ones. Rattling onward through the Valley, we were dazzled with the fiercely gleaming gas lamps, as before. But sometimes, in the dark of intense brightness, grim faces, that bore the aspect and expression of individual sins, or evil passions, seemed to thrust themselves through the veil of light, glaring upon us, and stretching forth a great, dusky hand, as if to impede our progress. I almost thought that they were my own sins that appalled me there. These were freaks of imagination—nothing more, certainly-mere delusions, which I ought to be heartily ashamed of; but all through the Dark Valley I was tormented, and pestered, and dolefully bewildered with the same kind of waking dreams. The mephitic gases of that region intoxicate the brain. As the light of natural day, however, began to struggle with the glow of the lanterns, these vain imaginations lost their vividness, and finally vanished from the first ray of sunshine that greeted our escape from the Valley of the Shadow of Death. Ere we had gone a mile beyond it I could well-nigh have taken my oath that this whole gloomy passage was a dream.

At the end of the valley, as John Bunyan mentions, is a cavern, where, in his days, dwelt two cruel giants, Pope and Pagan, who had strown the ground about their residence with the bones of slaughtered pilgrims. These vile old troglodytes are no longer there; but into their deserted cave another terrible giant has thrust himself, and makes it his business to seize upon honest travellers and fatten them for his table with plentiful meals of smoke, mist, moonshine, raw potatoes, and sawdust. He is a German by birth, and is called Giant Transcendentalist; but as to his form, his features, his substance, and his nature generally, it is the chief peculiarity of this huge miscreant that neither he for himself, nor anybody for him, has ever been able to describe them. As we rushed by the cavern's mouth we caught a hasty glimpse of him, looking somewhat like an ill-proportioned figure, but considerably more like a heap of fog and duskiness. He shouted after us, but in so strange a phraseology that we knew not what he meant, nor whether to be encouraged or affrighted.

It was late in the day when the train thundered into the ancient city of Vanity, where Vanity Fair is still at the height of prosperity, and exhibits an epitome of whatever is brilliant, gay, and fascinating beneath the sun. As I purposed to make a considerable stay here, it gratified me to learn that there is no longer the want of harmony between the town's-people and pilgrims, which impelled the former to such lamentably mistaken measures as the persecution of Christian and the fiery martyrdom of Faithful. On the contrary, as the new railroad brings with it great trade and a constant influx of strangers, the lord of Vanity Fair is its chief patron, and the capitalists of the city are among the largest stockholders. Many passengers stop to take their pleasure or make their profit in the Fair, instead of going onward to the Celestial City. Indeed, such are the charms of the place that people often affirm it to be the true and only heaven; stoutly contending that there is no other, that those who seek further are mere dreamers, and that, if the fabled brightness of the Celestial City lay but a bare mile beyond the gates of Vanity, they would not be fools enough to go thither. Without subscribing to these perhaps exaggerated encomiums, I can truly say that my abode in the city was mainly agreeable, and my intercourse with the inhabitants productive of much amusement and instruction.

Being naturally of a serious turn, my attention was directed to the solid advantages derivable from a residence here, rather than to the effervescent pleasures which are the grand object with too many visitants. The Christian reader, if he have had no accounts of the city later than Bunyan's time, will be surprised to hear that almost every street has its church, and that the reverend clergy are nowhere held in higher respect than at Vanity Fair. And well do they deserve such honorable estimation; for the maxims of wisdom and virtue which fall from their lips come from as deep a spiritual source, and tend to as lofty a religious aim, as those of the sagest philosophers of old. In justification of this high praise I need only mention the names of the Rev. Mr. Shallow-deep, the Rev. Mr. Stumble-at-truth, that fine old clerical character the Rev. Mr. This-today, who expects shortly to resign his pulpit to the Rev. Mr. That-tomorrow; together with the Rev. Mr. Bewilderment, the Rev. Mr. Clog-the-spirit, and, last and greatest, the Rev. Dr. Wind-of-doctrine. The labors of these eminent divines are aided by those of innumerable lecturers, who diffuse such a various profundity, in all subjects of human or celestial science, that any man may acquire an omnigenous erudition without the trouble of even learning to read. Thus literature is etherealized by assuming for its medium the human voice; and knowledge, depositing all its heavier particles, except, doubtless, its gold becomes exhaled into a sound, which forthwith steals into the ever-open ear of the community. These ingenious methods constitute a sort of machinery, by which thought and study are done to every person's hand without his putting himself to the slightest inconvenience in the matter. There is another species of machine for the wholesale manufacture of individual morality. This excellent result is effected by societies for all manner of virtuous purposes, with which a man has merely to connect himself, throwing, as it were, his quota of virtue into the common stock, and the president and directors will take care that the aggregate amount be well applied. All these, and other wonderful improvements in ethics, religion, and literature, being made plain to my comprehension by the ingenious Mr. Smooth-it-away, inspired me with a vast admiration of Vanity Fair.

It would fill a volume, in an age of pamphlets, were I to record all my observations in this great capital of human business and pleasure. There was an unlimited range of society—the powerful, the wise, the witty, and the famous in every walk of life; princes, presidents, poets, generals, artists, actors, and philanthropists,—all making their own market at the fair, and deeming no price too exorbitant for such commodities as hit their fancy. It was well worth one's while, even if he had no idea of buying or selling, to loiter through the bazaars and observe the various sorts of traffic that were going forward.

Some of the purchasers, I thought, made very foolish bargains. For instance, a young man having inherited a splendid fortune, laid out a considerable portion of it in the purchase of diseases, and finally spent all the rest for a heavy lot of repentance and a suit of rags. A very pretty girl bartered a heart as clear as crystal, and which seemed her most valuable possession, for another jewel of the same kind, but so worn and defaced as to be utterly worthless. In one shop there were a great many crowns of laurel and myrtle, which soldiers, authors, statesmen, and various other people pressed eagerly to buy; some purchased these paltry wreaths with their lives, others by a toilsome servitude of years, and many sacrificed whatever was most valuable, yet finally slunk away without the crown.

There was a sort of stock or scrip, called Conscience, which seemed to be in great demand, and would purchase almost anything. Indeed, few rich commodities were to be obtained without paying a heavy sum in this particular stock, and a man's business was seldom very lucrative unless he knew precisely when and how to throw his hoard of conscience into the market. Yet as this stock was the only thing of permanent value, whoever parted with it was sure to find himself a loser in the long run. Several of the speculations were of a questionable character. Occasionally a member of Congress recruited his pocket by the sale of his constituents; and I was assured that public officers have often sold their country at very moderate prices. Thousands sold their happiness for a whim. Gilded chains were in great demand, and purchased with almost any sacrifice. In truth, those who desired, according to the old adage, to sell anything valuable for a song, might find customers all over the Fair; and there were innumerable messes of pottage, piping hot, for such as chose to buy them with their birthrights. A few articles, however, could not be found genuine at Vanity Fair. If a customer wished to renew his stock of youth the dealers offered him a set of false teeth and an auburn wig; if he demanded peace of mind, they recommended opium or a brandy bottle.

Tracts of land and golden mansions, situate in the Celestial City, were often exchanged, at very disadvantageous rates, for a few years' lease of small, dismal, inconvenient tenements in Vanity Fair. Prince Beelzebub himself took great interest in this sort of traffic, and sometimes condescended to meddle with smaller matters. I once had the pleasure to see him bargaining with a miser for his soul, which, after much ingenious skirmishing on both sides, his highness succeeded in obtaining at about the value of sixpence. The prince remarked with a smile, that he was a loser by the transaction.

Day after day, as I walked the streets of Vanity, my manners and deportment became more and more like those of the inhabitants. The place began to seem like home; the idea of pursuing my travels to the Celestial City was almost obliterated from my mind. I was reminded of it, however, by the sight of the same pair of simple pilgrims at whom we had laughed so heartily when Apollyon puffed smoke and steam into their faces at the commencement of our journey. There they stood amidst the densest bustle of Vanity; the dealers offering them their purple and fine linen and jewels, the men of wit and humor gibing at them, a pair of buxom ladies ogling them askance, while the benevolent Mr. Smooth-it-away whispered some of his wisdom at their elbows, and pointed to a newly-erected temple; but there were these worthy simpletons, making the scene look wild and monstrous, merely by their sturdy repudiation of all part in its business or pleasures.

One of them—his name was Stick-to-the-right—perceived in my face, I suppose, a species of sympathy and almost admiration, which, to my own great surprise, I could not help feeling for this pragmatic couple. It prompted him to address me.

"Sir," inquired he, with a sad, yet mild and kindly voice, "do you call yourself a pilgrim?"

"Yes," I replied, "my right to that appellation is indubitable. I am merely a sojourner here in Vanity Fair, being bound to the Celestial City by the new railroad."

"Alas, friend," rejoined Mr. Stick-to-the-truth, "I do assure you, and beseech you to receive the truth of my words, that that whole concern is a bubble. You may travel on it all your lifetime, were you to live thousands of years, and yet never get beyond the limits of Vanity Fair. Yea, though you should deem yourself entering the gates of the blessed city, it will be nothing but a miserable delusion."

"The Lord of the Celestial City," began the other pilgrim, whose name was Mr. Foot-it-to-heaven, "has refused, and will ever refuse, to grant an act of incorporation for this railroad; and unless that be obtained, no passenger can ever hope to enter his dominions. Wherefore every man who buys a ticket must lay his account with losing the purchase money, which is the value of his own soul."

"Poh, nonsense!" said Mr. Smooth it-away, taking my arm and leading me off, "these fellows ought to be indicted for a libel. If the law stood as it once did in Vanity Fair we should see them grinning through the iron bars of the prison window."

This incident made a considerable impression on my mind, and contributed with other circumstances to indispose me to a permanent residence in the city of Vanity; although, of course, I was not simple enough to give up my original plan of gliding along easily and commodiously by railroad. Still, I grew anxious to be gone. There was one strange thing that troubled me. Amid the occupations or amusements of the Fair, nothing was more common than for a person—whether at feast, theatre, or church, or trafficking for wealth and honors, or whatever he might be doing, to vanish like a soap bubble, and be never more seen of his fellows; and so accustomed were the latter to such little accidents that they went on with their business as quietly as if nothing had happened. But it was otherwise with me.

Finally, after a pretty long residence at the Fair, I resumed my journey towards the Celestial City, still with Mr. Smooth-it-away at my side. At a short distance beyond the suburbs of Vanity we passed the ancient silver mine, of which Demas was the first discoverer, and which is now wrought to great advantage, supplying nearly all the coined currency of the world. A little further onward was the spot where Lot's wife had stood forever under the semblance of a pillar of salt. Curious travellers have long since carried it away piecemeal. Had all regrets been punished as rigorously as this poor dame's were, my yearning for the relinquished delights of Vanity Fair might have produced a similar change in my own corporeal substance, and left me a warning to future pilgrims.

The next remarkable object was a large edifice, constructed of moss-grown stone, but in a modern and airy style of architecture. The engine came to a pause in its vicinity, with the usual tremendous shriek.

"This was formerly the castle of the redoubted giant Despair," observed Mr. Smooth-it-away; "but since his death Mr. Flimsy-faith has repaired it, and keeps an excellent house of entertainment here. It is one of our stopping-places."

"It seems but slightly put together," remarked I, looking at the frail yet ponderous walls. "I do not envy Mr. Flimsy-faith his habitation. Some day it will thunder down upon the heads of the occupants."

"We shall escape at all events," said Mr. Smooth-it-away, "for Apollyon is putting on the steam again."

The road now plunged into a gorge of the Delectable Mountains, and traversed the field where in former ages the blind men wandered and stumbled among the tombs. One of these ancient tombstones had been thrust across the track by some malicious person, and gave the train of cars a terrible jolt. Far up the rugged side of a mountain I perceived a rusty iron door, half overgrown with bushes and creeping plants, but with smoke issuing from its crevices.

"Is that," inquired I, "the very door in the hill-side which the shepherds assured Christian was a by-way to hell?"

"That was a joke on the part of the shepherds," said Mr. Smooth-it-away, with a smile. "It is neither more nor less than the door of a cavern which they use as a smoke-house for the preparation of mutton hams."

My recollections of the journey are now, for a little space, dim and confused, inasmuch as a singular drowsiness here overcame me, owing to the fact that we were passing over the enchanted ground, the air of which encourages a disposition to sleep. I awoke, however, as soon as we crossed the borders of the pleasant land of Beulah. All the passengers were rubbing their eyes, comparing watches, and congratulating one another on the prospect of arriving so seasonably at the journey's end. The sweet breezes of this happy clime came refreshingly to our nostrils; we beheld the glimmering gush of silver fountains, overhung by trees of beautiful foliage and delicious fruit, which were propagated by grafts from the celestial gardens. Once, as we dashed onward like a hurricane, there was a flutter of wings and the bright appearance of an angel in the air, speeding forth on some heavenly mission. The engine now announced the close vicinity of the final station-house by one last and horrible scream, in which there seemed to be distinguishable every kind of wailing and woe, and bitter fierceness of wrath, all mixed up with the wild laughter of a devil or a madman. Throughout our journey, at every stopping-place, Apollyon had exercised his ingenuity in screwing the most abominable sounds out of the whistle of the steam-engine; but in this closing effort he outdid himself and created an infernal uproar, which, besides disturbing the peaceful inhabitants of Beulah, must have sent its discord even through the celestial gates.

While the horrid clamor was still ringing in our ears we heard an exulting strain, as if a thousand instruments of music, with height and depth and sweetness in their tones, at once tender and triumphant, were struck in unison, to greet the approach of some illustrious hero, who had fought the good fight and won a glorious victory, and was come to lay aside his battered arms forever. Looking to ascertain what might be the occasion of this glad harmony, I perceived, on alighting from the cars, that a multitude of shining ones had assembled on the other side of the river, to welcome two poor pilgrims, who were just emerging from its depths. They were the same whom Apollyon and ourselves had persecuted with taunts, and gibes, and scalding steam, at the commencement of our journey—the same whose unworldly aspect and impressive words had stirred my conscience amid the wild revellers of Vanity Fair.

"How amazingly well those men have got on," cried I to Mr. Smooth-it-away. "I wish we were secure of as good a reception."

"Never fear, never fear!" answered my friend. "Come, make haste; the ferry boat will be off directly, and in three minutes you will be on the other side of the river. No doubt you will find coaches to carry you up to the city gates."

A steam ferry boat, the last improvement on this important route, lay at the river side, puffing, snorting, and emitting all those other disagreeable utterances which betoken the departure to be immediate. I hurried on board with the rest of the passengers, most of whom were in great perturbation: some bawling out for their baggage; some tearing their hair and exclaiming that the boat would explode or sink; some already pale with the heaving of the stream; some gazing affrighted at the ugly aspect of the steersman; and some still dizzy with the slumberous influences of the Enchanted Ground. Looking back to the shore, I was amazed to discern Mr. Smooth-it-away waving his hand in token of farewell.

"Don't you go over to the Celestial City?" exclaimed I.

"Oh, no!" answered he with a queer smile, and that same disagreeable contortion of visage which I had remarked in the inhabitants of the Dark Valley. "Oh, no! I have come thus far only for the sake of your pleasant company. Good-by! We shall meet again."

And then did my excellent friend Mr. Smooth-it-away laugh outright, in the midst of which cachinnation a smoke-wreath issued from his mouth and nostrils, while a twinkle of lurid flame darted out of either eye, proving indubitably that his heart was all of a red blaze. The impudent fiend! To deny the existence of Tophet, when he felt its fiery tortures raging within his breast. I rushed to the side of the boat, intending to fling myself on shore; but the wheels, as they began their revolutions, threw a dash of spray over me so cold—so deadly cold, with the chill that will never leave those waters until Death be drowned in his own river—that with a shiver and a heartquake I awoke. Thank Heaven it was a Dream!

Fiction

The Elephant's Child

Rudyard Kipling [1865-1936]

IN the High and Far-Off Times the Elephant, O Best Beloved, had no trunk. He had only a blackish, bulgy nose, as big as a boot, that he could wriggle about from side to side; but he couldn't pick up things with it. But there was one Elephant—a new Elephant—an Elephant's Child—who was full of 'satiable curtiosity, and that means he asked ever so many questions. And he lived in Africa, and he filled all Africa with his 'satiable curtiosities. He asked his tall aunt, the Ostrich, why her tail-feathers grew just so, and his tall aunt the Ostrich spanked him with her hard, hard claw. He asked his tall uncle, the Giraffe, what made his skin spotty, and his tall uncle, the Giraffe, spanked him with his hard, hard hoof. And still he was full of 'satiable curtiosity! He asked his broad aunt, the Hippopotamus, why her eyes were red, and his broad aunt, the Hippopotamus, spanked him with her broad, broad hoof; and he asked his hairy uncle, the Baboon, why melons tasted just so, and his hairy uncle, the Baboon, spanked him with his hairy, hairy paw. And still he was full of 'satiable curtiosity! He asked questions about everything that he saw, or heard, or felt, or smelt, or touched, and all his uncles and his aunts spanked him. And still he was full of 'satiable curtiosity!

One fine morning in the middle of the Precession of the Equinoxes this 'satiable Elephant's Child asked a new fine question that he had never asked before. He asked, 'What does the Crocodile have for dinner?' Then everybody said, 'Hush!' in a loud and dretful tone, and they spanked him immediately and directly, without stopping, for a long time.

By and by, when that was finished, he came upon Kolokolo Bird sitting in the middle of a wait-a-bit thorn-bush, and he said, 'My father has spanked me, and my mother has spanked me; all my aunts and uncles have spanked me for my 'satiable curtiosity; and still I want to know what the Crocodile has for dinner!'

Then Kolokolo Bird said, with a mournful cry, 'Go to the banks of the great grey-green, greasy Limpopo River, all set about with fever-trees, and find out.'

That very next morning, when there was nothing left of the Equinoxes, because the Precession had preceded according to precedent, this 'satiable Elephant's Child took a hundred pounds of bananas (the little short red kind), and a hundred pounds of sugar-cane (the long purple kind), and seventeen melons (the greeny-crackly kind), and said to all his dear families, 'Goodbye. I am going to the great grey-green, greasy Limpopo River, all set about with fever-trees, to find out what the Crocodile has for dinner.' And they all spanked him once more for luck, though he asked them most politely to stop.

Then he went away, a little warm, but not at all astonished, eating melons, and throwing the rind about, because he could not pick it up.

He went from Graham's Town to Kimberley, and from Kimberley to Khama's Country, and from Khama's Country he went east by north, eating melons all the time, till at last he came to the banks of the great grey-green, greasy Limpopo River, all set about with fever-trees, precisely as Kolokolo Bird had said.

Now you must know and understand, O Best Beloved, that till that very week, and day, and hour, and minute, this 'satiable Elephant's Child had never seen a Crocodile, and did not know what one was like. It was all his 'satiable curtiosity.

The first thing that he found was a Bi-Coloured-Python-Rock-Snake curled round a rock.

''Scuse me,' said the Elephant's Child most politely, 'but have you seen such a thing as a Crocodile in these promiscuous parts?'

'Have I seen a Crocodile?' said the Bi-Coloured-Python-Rock-Snake, in a voice of dretful scorn. 'What will you ask me next?'

''Scuse me,' said the Elephant's Child, 'but could you kindly tell me what he has for dinner?'

Then the Bi-Coloured-Python-Rock-Snake uncoiled himself very quickly from the rock, and spanked the Elephant's Child with his scalesome, flailsome tail.

'That is odd,' said the Elephant's Child, 'because my father and my mother, and my uncle and my aunt, not to mention my other aunt, the Hippopotamus, and my other uncle, the Baboon, have all spanked me for my 'satiable curtiosity—and I suppose this is the same thing.

So he said good-bye very politely to the Bi-Coloured-Python-Rock-Snake, and helped to coil him up on the rock again, and went on, a little warm, but not at all astonished, eating melons, and throwing the rind about, because he could not pick it up, till he trod on what he thought was a log of wood at the very edge of the great grey-green, greasy Limpopo River, all set about with fever-trees.

But it was really the Crocodile, O Best Beloved, and the Crocodile winked one eye— like this!

''Scuse me,' said the Elephant's Child most politely, 'but do you happen to have seen a Crocodile in these promiscuous parts?'

Then the Crocodile winked the other eye, and lifted half his tail out of the mud; and the Elephant's Child stepped back most politely, because he did not wish to be spanked again.

'Come hither, Little One,' said the Crocodile. 'Why do you ask such things?'

''Scuse me,' said the Elephant's Child most politely, 'but my father has spanked me, my mother has spanked me, not to mention my tall aunt, the Ostrich, and my tall uncle, the Giraffe, who can kick ever so hard, as well as my broad aunt, the Hippopotamus, and my hairy uncle, the Baboon, and including the Bi-Coloured-Python-Rock-Snake, with the scalesome, flailsome tail, just up the bank, who spanks harder than any of them; and so, if it's quite all the same to you, I don't want to be spanked any more.'

'Come hither, Little One,' said the Crocodile, 'for I am the Crocodile,' and he wept crocodile-tears to show it was quite true.

Then the Elephant's Child grew all breathless, and panted, and kneeled down on the bank and said, 'You are the very person I have been looking for all these long days. Will you please tell me what you have for dinner?'

'Come hither, Little One,' said the Crocodile, 'and I'll whisper.'

Then the Elephant's Child put his head down close to the Crocodile's musky, tusky mouth, and the Crocodile caught him by his little nose, which up to that very week, day, hour, and minute, had been no bigger than a boot, though much more useful.

'I think, said the Crocodile—and he said it between his teeth, like this—'I think to-day I will begin with Elephant's Child!'

At this, O Best Beloved, the Elephant's Child was much annoyed, and he said, speaking through his nose, like this, 'Led go! You are hurtig be!'

Then the Bi-Coloured-Python-Rock-Snake scuffled down from the bank and said, 'My young friend, if you do not now, immediately and instantly, pull as hard as ever you can, it is my opinion that your acquaintance in the large-pattern leather ulster' (and by this he meant the Crocodile) 'will jerk you into yonder limpid stream before you can say Jack Robinson.'

This is the way Bi-Coloured-Python-Rock-Snakes always talk.

Then the Elephant's Child sat back on his little haunches, and pulled, and pulled, and pulled, and his nose began to stretch. And the Crocodile floundered into the water, making it all creamy with great sweeps of his tail, and he pulled, and pulled, and pulled.

And the Elephant's Child's nose kept on stretching; and the Elephant's Child spread all his little four legs and pulled, and pulled, and pulled, and his nose kept on stretching; and the Crocodile threshed his tail like an oar, and he pulled, and pulled, and pulled, and at each pull the Elephant's Child's nose grew longer and longer—and it hurt him hijjus!

Then the Elephant's Child felt his legs slipping, and he said through his nose, which was now nearly five feet long, 'This is too butch for be!'

Then the Bi-Coloured-Python-Rock-Snake came down from the bank, and knotted himself in a double-clove-hitch round the Elephant's Child's hind legs, and said, 'Rash and inexperienced traveller, we will now seriously devote ourselves to a little high tension, because if we do not, it is my impression that yonder self-propelling man-of-war with the armour-plated upper deck' (and by this, O Best Beloved, he meant the Crocodile), 'will permanently vitiate your future career.

That is the way all Bi-Coloured-Python-Rock-Snakes always talk.

So he pulled, and the Elephant's Child pulled, and the Crocodile pulled; but the Elephant's Child and the Bi-Coloured-Python-Rock-Snake pulled hardest; and at last the Crocodile let go of the Elephant's Child's nose with a plop that you could hear all up and down the Limpopo.

Then the Elephant's Child sat down most hard and sudden; but first he was careful to say 'Thank you' to the Bi-Coloured-Python-Rock-Snake; and next he was kind to his poor pulled nose, and wrapped it all up in cool banana leaves, and hung it in the great grey-green, greasy Limpopo to cool.

'What are you doing that for?' said the Bi-Coloured-Python-Rock-Snake.

''Scuse me,' said the Elephant's Child, 'but my nose is badly out of shape, and I am waiting for it to shrink.

'Then you will have to wait a long time, said the Bi-Coloured-Python-Rock-Snake. 'Some people do not know what is good for them.'

The Elephant's Child sat there for three days waiting for his nose to shrink. But it never grew any shorter, and, besides, it made him squint. For, O Best Beloved, you will see and understand that the Crocodile had pulled it out into a really truly trunk same as all Elephants have to-day.

At the end of the third day a fly came and stung him on the shoulder, and before he knew what he was doing he lifted up his trunk and hit that fly dead with the end of it.

"Vantage number one!' said the Bi-Coloured-Python-Rock-Snake. 'You couldn't have done that with a mere-smear nose. Try and eat a little now.'

Before he thought what he was doing the Elephant's Child put out his trunk and plucked a large bundle of grass, dusted it clean against his fore-legs, and stuffed it into his own mouth.

'Vantage number two!' said the Bi-Coloured-Python-Rock-Snake. 'You couldn't have done that with a mear-smear nose. Don't you think the sun is very hot here?'

'It is,' said the Elephant's Child, and before he thought what he was doing he schlooped up a schloop of mud from the banks of the great grey-green, greasy Limpopo, and slapped it on his head, where it made a cool schloopy-sloshy mud-cap all trickly behind his ears.

'Vantage number three!' said the Bi-Coloured-Python-Rock-Snake. 'You couldn't have done that with a mere-smear nose. Now how do you feel about being spanked again?'

"Scuse me,' said the Elephant's Child, 'but I should not like it at all.'

'How would you like to spank somebody?' said the Bi-Coloured-Python-Rock-Snake.

'I should like it very much indeed,' said the Elephant's Child.

'Well,' said the Bi-Coloured-Python-Rock-Snake, 'you will find that new nose of yours very useful to spank people with.'

'Thank you,' said the Elephant's Child, 'I'll remember that; and now I think I'll go home to all my dear families and try.'

So the Elephant's Child went home across Africa frisking and whisking his trunk. When he wanted fruit to eat he pulled fruit down from a tree, instead of waiting for it to fall as he used to do. When he wanted grass he plucked grass up from the ground, instead of

293

going on his knees as he used to do. When the flies bit him he broke off the branch of a tree and used it as fly-whisk; and he made himself a new, cool, slushy-squshy mud-cap whenever the sun was hot. When he felt lonely walking through Africa he sang to himself down his trunk, and the noise was louder than several brass bands.

He went especially out of his way to find a broad Hippopotamus (she was no relation of his), and he spanked her very hard, to make sure that the Bi-Coloured-Python-Rock-Snake had spoken the truth about his new trunk. The rest of the time he picked up the melon rinds that he had dropped on his way to the Limpopo—for he was a Tidy Pachyderm.

One dark evening he came back to all his dear families, and he coiled up his trunk and said, 'How do you do?' They were very glad to see him, and immediately said, 'Come here and be spanked for your 'satiable curtiosity.'

'Pooh,' said the Elephant's Child. 'I don't think you peoples know anything about spanking; but I do, and I'll show you.' Then he uncurled his trunk and knocked two of his dear brothers head over heels.

'O Bananas!' said they, 'where did you learn that trick, and what have you done to your nose?'

'I got a new one from the Crocodile on the banks of the great grey-green, greasy Limpopo River,' said the Elephant's Child. 'I asked him what he had for dinner, and he gave me this to keep.'

'It looks very ugly,' said his hairy uncle, the Baboon.

'It does,' said the Elephant's Child. 'But it's very useful,' and he picked up his hairy uncle, the Baboon, by one hairy leg, and hove him into a hornet's nest.

Then that bad Elephant's Child spanked all his dear families for a long time, till they were very warm and greatly astonished. He pulled out his tall Ostrich aunt's tail-feathers; and he caught his tall uncle, the Giraffe, by the hind-leg, and dragged him through a thorn-bush; and he shouted at his broad aunt, the Hippopotamus, and blew bubbles into her ear when she was sleeping in the water after meals; but he never let any one touch Kolokolo Bird.

At last things grew so exciting that his dear families went off one by one in a hurry to the banks of the great grey-green, greasy Limpopo River, all set about with fever-trees, to borrow new noses from the Crocodile. When they came back nobody spanked anybody any more; and ever since that day, O Best Beloved, all the Elephants you will ever see, besides all those that you won't, have trunks precisely like the trunk of the 'satiable Elephant's Child.

I Keep six honest serving-men:

(They taught me all I knew)

Their names are What and Where and When

And How and Why and Who.

I send them over land and sea,

I send them east and west;

But after they have worked for me,

I give them all a rest.

I let them rest from nine till five.

For I am busy then,

As well as breakfast, lunch, and tea,

For they are hungry men:

But different folk have different views:

I know a person small—

Fiction

She keeps ten million serving-men,

Who get no rest at all!

She sends 'em abroad on her own affairs,

From the second she opens her eyes—

One million Hows, two million Wheres,

And seven million Whys!

Section D: Exercises in Fiction

CREATIVITY EXERCISE: Fifteen minute free-write. Set a timer for fifteen minutes; then go and take a seat. Pick up a pen, and write about something, anything, until the timer chimes. Don't stop. Begin with the writing prompt, and if you get stumped, insert a flashback scene, "Three days earlier…" Have fun! (C3 Scale)

Prompt: The clouds parted just before sunset; the night was still and crisp, and the stars were bright…

Exercise 1: Think of one event you've recently witnessed. Outline the narrative (what might have come before and what might come after the event). If you were to write a story based on this narrative, where would you begin it? (C1 Scale)

Exercise 2: In Exercise 1 of Unit III, you wrote a narrative about a personal experience. In the style of either realistic or fairy-tale fiction, embellish the details of your previous narrative. Add relevant dialog and description. (C2 Scale)

Exercise 3: In Exercise 4 of Unit III, you wrote with the intention of imparting a lesson. With that same life lesson in mind, write an allegory this time. (C1 Scale)

Exercise 4: Write a short story (narrative, description, and dialog) involving the two characters you sketched in Unit II. (C2 Scale)

Exercise 5: **Final Assignment:** Write the story of Joseph's life again. Add scenes, but stay true to character. Weave narrative, description, and dialog. Avoid anachronism. (C2 Scale)

Grading Scales

C1 Scale

Twenty possible points for each

Rank each from 1-20

1) _____shows understanding of the assignment

2) _____good sentence structure, or structure of ideas

3) _____interesting; creative

4) _____shows thought; not rushed

5) _____neat appearance

C2 Scale

Ten possible points for each

1) _____shows understanding of the assignment

2) _____good sentence structure, or structure of ideas

3) _____reader interest

4) _____shows thought; not rushed

5) _____neat appearance

6) _____intro and conclusion paragraphs (where applicable)

7) _____punctuation

8) _____ overall grammar (except spelling)

9) _____ spelling

10) _____ creativity and originality

C3 Scale

Graded on completion

Either a 100 or a zero!

Made in the USA
Columbia, SC
18 January 2018